Pimpin' Ain't Easy

WITHDRAWN

Pimpin' Ain't Easy

Selling Black Entertainment Television

BERETTA E. SMITH-SHOMADE

Routledge
Taylor & Francis Group
New York   London

Routledge
Taylor & Francis Group
270 Madison Avenue
New York, NY 10016

Routledge
Taylor & Francis Group
2 Park Square
Milton Park, Abingdon
Oxon OX14 4RN

Printed in the United States of America on acid-free paper
10 9 8 7 6 5 4 3 2 1

International Standard Book Number-13: 978-0-415-97679-4 (Softcover) 978-0-415-97678-7 (Hardcover)

Library of Congress Cataloging-in-Publication Data

Smith-Shomade, Beretta E., 1965-
    Pimpin' ain't easy : selling Black Entertainment Television / Beretta E. Smith-Shomade.
      p. cm.
    Includes bibliographical references and index.
    ISBN 978-0-415-97678-7 (hardback : alk. paper) -- ISBN 978-0-415-97679-4 (pbk. : alk. paper) 1. Black Entertainment Television. 2. African Americans on television. I. Title.

PN1992.92.B53S65 2007
384.55'0657308996073--dc22   2007005615

Visit the Taylor & Francis Web site at
http://www.taylorandfrancis.com

and the Routledge Web site at
http://www.routledge.com

Contents

Dedication

vii

Acknowledgments

ix

Introduction

xiii

Chapter 1

**Eyes Wide Shut:
Capitalism, Class, and the Promise of Black Media**

1

Chapter 2

Now That's Black! BET Business

31

Chapter 3

I'm Rick James, BitchHHHH! BET Programming

71

Chapter 4

The Impossibility of Us: BET Impact

115

Chapter 5

It's Your Turn: Black to the Future

149

Endnotes

181

Bibliography

189

Index

199

Dedication

This book is dedicated to the one who gave me life
Evelyn Inell Cain-Smith
(September 14, 1934–September 5, 2003)
and
the one who saved it
Salmoncain Leopaul Smith-Shomade
(March 3, 2004–)

Acknowledgments

Over the past few years that I've been grappling with this manuscript, many have contributed to its development. In terms of institutional support, I am grateful to the University of Houston's African-American Studies program for selecting me as its 2002–2003 visiting scholar, especially the selection committee of Alexander Brown and Janice Hutchinson. This award gave me the time and opportunity to launch this project. While there, Angie Williams-Phillips, Phyllis Bearden-Strawder, James Conyers Jr., and J.R. Wilson were kind and supportive. Once contracted, I was awarded a University of Arizona Provost's Author Support grant. This funding enabled me to purchase rights for photos, lyrics, and *The Boondocks* cartoon strips spread throughout the text. I thank especially Dean Juan Garcia in this regard and for overall support.

Janet Staiger, John Downing, and Craig Watkins at the University of Texas offered early support of this project as well as Karen Riggs of Ohio University, and for all three I am very appreciative. I thank Ayanna Whitworth-Barner, Deborah Barnes, and Kristin Baranack who served as graduate assistants at different stages as well as Shannon E. Franklin, Josefina Cain, Crystal Quintero, Carmen Noriega, Anay Bickham, and DeAndra Devoe—young sistahs—for their assistance (both intellectual and anecdotal). Plus, they kept me current! I acknowledge my cousin Melford McCormick who really made me consider this project as a conundrum worth pondering—thank you.

In addition, I am especially indebted to groups of students around the country who really helped me understand young folks' (and young at hearts') contemporary negotiations with BET. All of the insights gleaned from the focus groups proved invaluable in helping me think through not only BET historically but also its contemporary relevance for audiences. I thank each for their time, candor, fun, and knowledge. At the University of Houston, Fredrick Walker, Desmond Jackson, Kurt Richardson, and Alysia Minor-Ferrell each in their own way tremendously influenced this work. The fellas especially provided me with a thorough grounding in Generation X's intersections with BET. I thank you.

At Texas Southern University in Houston, appreciation goes to Josie Cain, Daidrik Cooper, Derrick C. LaBrie, Corey H. Markey, Charles Porch, Joesette Simeon, and Nefertari Williams for opening up the complexities of the topic. With the Tucson Urban League, I appreciate Alice Begay, Christopher Bliss, Annaleigh Chico, Nathan Horton, Monique Leal, Kyle Lewis, Janay Lissade, Irma Miranda, Rey Rey Monteño, Kevin Moore, Anthony Muñoz, Brenda Nario, Stephanie Paco, Roberto Padilla, Will Sparks, Alex Witherspoon, and Michael Woods for their youthful energy and southwest flavor. To the Clair Memorial United Methodist Church youth group in Omaha, Nebraska, I thank Chris Bradford, Kenny Bradford, Jeannee Bradley, Courtney Brooks, Antonio Duncan, Cianna Franklin, Jennifer Jackson, Troy Johnson, Ashley Minnifield, Ramone Mosley, Todd Richardson, Jamie Stewart, and LeNeir Whitemon.

The young women of Spelman College provided great insight and awareness of BET's programming. Thanks go to Bridgette Aaron, Moya Bailey, Monique Brantly, Cindy Evans, Felicia Freeman, Susanna Hutton, Constance Jackson, Leslie Josephs, Amber Kingsley, Lauren N. Stokes, Regina Strong, Rykiel Weekes, Alexis Wells, Belinda Williams, and Ashli Wilson.

The huge group of freshmen honors program students at my alma mater Clark Atlanta University helped me immensely. I'm grateful to: Stephen Adkins, Rosa Burdulis, Ryan C. Butler, Michael Chambers, Ashley Cochria, Stacia Comrie, Erica Davis, Lezé de Klerk, Carrie Dean, Carolee Estelle, Destiny Fitzpatrick, Mandilyn Green, Christyna Harris, Jeremy Headed, Rhonda Hogan,

Mario Howell, Mika Hynson, Brichelle Jackson, Isaiah Jones, Ashley Kennedy, Gwannettia King, Whitney Lankford, Laceriza London, Lionel J. London, Keriki N. Purkiss, David Richardson, Shayla Riddick, Essence Rome, Jasmine Taylor, Stephanie E. Tellis, Chris Thomas, Chiara White, and Sherese Williams.

Finally, I thank the young people at the University of Arizona who provided a multiracial insight that was crucial for the development of my understanding BET's mission and its success. They include Christina Del Rio, Christina Fassett, Vanessa Kramer, Kathleen Kuehn, David Rokeach, Jeffrey Sackheim, Allison Siegel, Hector Urias, Darah Wagner, Kristen Warner, and a few others who didn't want to be specifically named.

I send a special thank you to those Atlanta women-folks who laid BET out for me: Denise Davis-Maye, Zabrina Furlow, Maria Odum Hinmon, Lisa E. Lyons, Florence Randall, Ronnette V. Smith, and especially Kerri Burton-Danner who hosted us. You all are brilliant and passionate about your vision for black communities. Plus, numbers of unnamed BET workers gave me their thoughts sans their names. For these unnamed, I am truly grateful for your time and your insights.

I am especially obliged to those helping to facilitate the focus groups including: Obidike Kamau at TSU, Laurie Ocampo, Charles E. Monroe, and Ayanna Whitworth-Barner in Tucson, Tracii L. Hicks in Omaha, and Isabella Jenkins, Daniel P. Black, and Tarshia Stanley in Atlanta (for Clark Atlanta University and Spelman College).

I thank Raegan Carmona at Universal Press Syndicate for really working with me in licensing *The Boondocks* strips as well as both Laura Shively at BMG and Kenneth Higney at Regent Music for licensing "Who Are the Pimps?" Thank you Jermine Benton at *Black Enterprise* for facilitating the March 2003 cover for me. I give a special shout out to the wonderful folks at the UA Learning Technologies Center who always take care of my visual needs: Heather Lares, Tony Gallego, Gary Darnell, and especially on this project, Roxanna Porter.

My colleagues at the University of Arizona are a constant sounding board, especially Barbara Selznick, Kevin Sandler, Yuri

Makino, and Michael Mulcahy. I am grateful to my writing group, Deborah Elizabeth Whaley and Dana Mastro, who brought a richness and rigor to my writing and thinking, from very different perspectives. As well, I thank the readers of the book proposal, Krystal Brent Zook and Mark Anthony Neal, not only for their support and encouragement of this work but also for their specific insights into making it a better one. Plus, I thank you both for wrestling me away from—at least a little bit—my fixation on the demon of capitalism ;>). I am grateful also to those who have listened to me present some of this material at conferences and other speaking spaces and offered comments and suggestions.

I am blessed to have tremendous colleague–friends around the country who always read a chapter, lend an ear, and make me feel like I'm the best thing since sliced bread. They are all critical thinkers and compassionate human beings who make me a better scholar and person just because of who they are. They include Daniel L. Bernardi, Bambi L. Haggins, Lahn S. Kim, Kathy Powers, and Karla Rae Fuller. Several others took time to contribute to this work either through suggestions, articles, resources, or just talking with me about BET. They include William Broussard, Christopher T. Craddock, Ron deCastro, Leteshia Lowe, Mashadi Matabane, and Rachel Raimist. Finally, I thank John T. Caldwell just because I'm grateful to be a part of the club!

I treasure my great uncle, Harvey Lee McCormick, Esq. for his wonderful sense of history, intellect, and commitments to truth and family (I listen more than you know). I continue to acknowledge and revel in the spirit of my father, Leo Smith (August 22, 1934–July 5, 1986) for his entrepreneurial zeal and enthusiasm for me. Of course I'm constantly indebted to my brilliant and kind husband, Salmon A. Shomade and our fabulous son Salmoncain, (my everythangs), who make the world a place worth living in. I love you both with all of my heart. And finally, I honor my mother who continues to live in every part of my being. Thank you for your sacrifices for me and everything you made me. I miss you.

Introduction

I don't know why yaw'll want to watch that thing. There ain't nothin'
but white people on it.

> Fredonia Bell Jackson McCormick,
> 1950s, Smith County, Texas

In an ideal world, we can click on the television and see black,
brown, yellow, and red faces on every channel. Women cheer black
women's stories of tragedy and triumph on Lifetime—Television
for Women. Our neighbor learns about the world from Charlayne
Hunter-Gault anchoring the weekday national network news instead
of Carole Simpson and Connie Chung for years on the weekends.
Students laugh with animated black characters on *King of the Hill*
and *South Park* who find their voices in something beyond their
big black chocolate balls. New Yorkers feel empathy for a black or
Puerto Rican or Native American friend on *Friends*. And Generation X sees more than a bee-otch shaking her ta-tas in music videos on BET. In a democratic and multi-ethnic society, this desire
stands as the purported underpinning, goal, and gift of living in and
building an exemplary nation. But like many ideals—that visioning
exists in a world far, far away and beyond the realms of capitalism,
contemporary television, and cable.

For those who subscribe to cable, selecting Time Warner channel
63 in Los Angeles (South Bay), Cox 49 in Tucson, Arizona, Comcast

75 in Chicago, Cox 39 in Omaha, Cox 32 in Tyler, Texas, Comcast 72 in Atlanta, and Time Warner 42 in Manhattan brings you to Black Entertainment Television—the most widely distributed U.S. provider of black imagery. With access to BET, homes join more than eighty million other subscriber homes nationwide. Launched in January 1980 by former cable lobbyist Robert Louis Johnson, BET transformed U.S. conceptions of blackness and pushed it to profitability worldwide.

What I remember most about BET's arrival in Omaha was the amount of time I spent watching it. The other cable channels were okay, but BET provided a constant mirror moment. It offered singers and groups that I admired and music I bought—ones not necessarily validated by white pop radio of the 1980s and earlier. No longer watching across the grain or in opposition, as cultural theorist Stuart Hall calls it, I am validated as an African-American citizen—due in part to seeing and hearing a reflection of the culture I am intimately acquainted with on a daily basis. The problem is as I matured and changed, BET stayed the same. After twenty years in the cable business, in 2000, Johnson sold the company to the Viacom conglomerate for $2.33 billion. In making BET a part of its monolith, Viacom president Mel Karmazin believed that his sales staff could effectively press BET advertisers for better rates and broaden BET's subscriber base. In other words, he promised to sell black America to a wider range of corporations and for more money.

Black Entertainment Television's success has relied on several factors that include the dearth of African-American televisual representation, the rise of cable, and the centrality of music in black culture (and other cultures as well). In its acquired programming (mostly music videos), BET visually excluded other African-American cultural practices in favor of the beat, bling, bodies, and burdens of Generation X. As a result of this programming focus, some consider BET a sellout—a vehicle for concretizing the hierarchy of whiteness in its invocation of black bodies and pursuit of white consumers. In other words, some maintain that BET used black folks as bait for white customers. At the same time, many within black communities connect BET with feelings of accomplishment and family. These competing notions about what people think BET is and what it could and should be ground the complex and paradoxical ways its significance resonates within black communities. Paradox also embodies the watershed impact of hip hop music and style on world culture and its relationship to BET. The tensions of invisibility and visibility, increased commerce, and black folks' limited mattering beyond representation coalesced to provide BET with 27 years of continued growth, prominence, and problematic visual constructions of a certain African-America.

Only a small number of texts interrogate the intersections of television and race beyond news, especially in the areas of blackness and the relatively new cable arena. Jannette Dates's *Split Image: African-Americans in the Media* (1990), J. Fred MacDonald's *Blacks and White TV: African Americans in Television Since 1948* (1992), Herman Gray's *Watching Race: Television and the Struggle for Blackness* (1995) and his *Cultural Moves: African Americans and the Politics of Representation* (2005), Donald Bogle's *Primetime Blues: African Americans on Network Television* (2004), and Darnell Hunt's *Channeling Blackness: Studies on Television and Race in America* (2005) contribute important perspectives on the various ways race and representation manifest in television. However, none of them focus on BET. Other more general texts on television and cable mention the network only as a parenthetical—even ones published in the 21st century. The company seems to have received a sacred cow status for being "the first" and the only network for black people—a holiness that clings to it less in 2007 but remains nonetheless. Alternatively, perhaps its existence fails to register as a viable scholarly consideration in part due to the marginalized status black representation garners in general.

While there has not been a great deal of research specifically on BET, several books relate to the work presented here that include: Kristal Brent Zook's *Color by Fox: The Fox Network and the Revolution in Black Television* (1999), Robin Means Coleman's *African American Viewers and the Black Situation Comedy* (2000), my own *Shaded Lives: African-American Women and Television* (2002), Sasha Torres's *Black White and In Color: Television and Black Civil Rights* (2003), Christine Acham's *Revolution Televised:*

Prime Time and the Struggle for Black Power (2004), and most
significantly, Brett Pulley's *The Billion Dollar BET: Robert Johnson
and the Inside Story of Black Entertainment Television* (2004).
These books examine the ways in which black folks are represented
on television through textual analysis, traverse the industrial landscape in which black characterizations and programs exist, discuss
the production processes within black programs, and theorize about
the larger meanings attached to black representation. Along with
a few academic articles, they provide the growing but still rather
limited engagement with black televisual representations. *Pimpin'
Ain't Easy* thus seeks to position the seemingly untouchable BET in
a scholarly world that has substantially ignored it.

Beyond academic circles, industrial conditions paved the path
for a BET. Specifically in the 1970s, Hollywood began to create
blockbuster films that failed to include African-Americans—except
in disguise as Darth Vader (James Earl Jones) to be vanquished. In
fact in the whole decade of the 1970s, less than ten blacks appeared
in speaking roles within the top ten grossing films. While films
directed at black audiences, (some derisively call blaxploitation
cinema), helped save Hollywood from bankruptcy, the production
of those films disappeared in a few short years. In this same time
frame, broadcast television created series targeted at black audiences with programs such as: *Julia* (1968–1971), *The Flip Wilson
Show* (1970–1974), *Sanford & Son* (1972–1977), *Good Times* (1974–
1979), and *The Jeffersons* (1975–1985). Yet for the most part, these
television series met the same fate as their film counterparts.

From the late 1960s, discourses surrounding a new television possibility emerged. Proponents claimed cable television to
be "pregnant with the promise of a broadband, interactive communication network that could help bind communities, deliver a
wealth of human services from education to health care, and create
a public forum for universal debate on the important issues of the
day. It would displace the oligopoly held by the three major television networks and usher in a new era in television" (Parsons: 45).
These cable discourses suggested the welcoming of new voices and
entrepreneurial spirits. While African-American entrepreneurs
understood media as both a business opportunity and a vehicle to

encourage civil and social rights, before BET, few had made inroads into this area beyond individual radio and television stations. This dearth left black folks hungry for representational consistency—a visual savior. BET appeared like "the one."

In *Pimpin' Ain't Easy: Selling Black Entertainment Television*, I interrogate what this network provides to the larger U.S. and to its target demographic through its business practices, programming, and subsequent impact. This book examines whether the company fulfills its stated goals and implied obligation to the African-American community. Does BET change the way African-Americans see themselves and the way that others see them? I question what BET means to African-Americans and the larger African diasporic world. Has BET's success help solidify the viability of market capitalism for African-Americans? In addressing these questions, the book positions the network in a larger historical, industrial, and cultural context that exposes the under-examined links between capitalism, African-American representation, the television industry, and notions of black progress. In other words, this book attempts to show why and how BET exemplifies both the proof of capitalism's success and the justification for its failings for African-Americans.

Pursuing traditional secondary scholarly research along with some first person ethnographic sampling (focus groups) and interviews, *Pimpin' Ain't Easy* gives a consumerist assessment of the network's achievements and failures. I use the information gleaned from the focus groups and interviews as both support for and anecdotal evidence of my arguments.[1] With this research, I hope targeted demographic populations will begin to truly reevaluate what representation means against the rhetoric of capitalist progress and find ways to undermine a system that makes images the most fertile ground for people to challenge. Second, I want this work to open up more spaces to examine and make central the possibility and criticality of black television. In other words, what African-Americans watch on television matters inasmuch as those black folks "seeing" and "being seen"—those represented—get more than just representation from these portrayals. The images fulfill a crucial need for visioning and supplementing feelings of self-worth and self-actualization. However, this understanding of and interrogation into black television is only limitedly addressed in academic discourses.

Chapter 1, "Eyes Wide Shut: Capitalism, Class, and the Promise of Black Media," frames BET within the larger parameters of U.S. society: that of capitalism and the mantras for black business that permeate African-American communities. The necessity for beginning here is twofold. First, the pursuit of the capitalist American dream privileges individual effort and material attainment above all else which in many ways runs counter to the communal history and ways of being of African peoples. While capitalism is positioned by the U.S. as the de facto operating system for the world, it functions by keeping most of its participants in debt, incarcerated, enamored with things, and ostensibly enslaved. In the United States, people of color and specifically African-Americans find themselves a large part of the building blocks for the wealthy of the system.

Second in terms of black business development, most of the businesses that African-Americans pursue—what some call the "shadow economy"—bring a ready-made market and a seemingly endless supply of consumers. Whether service based or retail, the black business economy relies on the uplift discourses of black progress to encourage and guilt black folks to purchase. These ideas suggest that the surest way for African-Americans to move ahead is through creating and supporting black businesses. In the film *Barbershop* (2002), for example, the emphasis on family legacy, black history, and sacred spaces for black talk and understanding becomes a metaphor for black ownership. BET draws on these mantras—these cultural understandings—to garner African-American support for the creation and building of the network.

"Now That's Black: BET Business"—chapter 2—lays out the twenty-first century media landscape and African-American insertion into this realm. Specifically, I examine the development of the cable business and the historic media precursors to BET. Branding, BET advertisers, niche marketing, and the black consumer form a platform for BET to develop, grow, and prosper. Johnson's entrepreneurship (not to mention his vision) develops with an assumption of capitalism's value for and within black communities. Many of the changes in the television industry, as precipitated by media mergers and the rise of cable, make BET (and other similar networks) possible. This chapter traces the key business maneuvers of the network and the development of this business. I question how BET defines blackness. What does "Black Star Power" mean in terms of forwarding the careers of entertainers and the aspirations of its consumers? How is BET able to negotiate issues of age, gender, and class? Moreover, I link BET's growth to that of the hip hop cultural explosion.

Over the latter part of the twentieth century, hip hop becomes popular culture. Due to its relationship to the primary people who create the sound and to the music itself, BET is uniquely positioned to capitalize on this explosion—which is exactly what it does. A part of the masculinist' ethos of hip hop is the pimp. Within hip hop, the pimp returns as a metaphor for the African-American man thinking about business and women. In titling this book *Pimpin' Ain't Easy*, I invoke this pimping aesthetic and business practice. *Pimpin'* resembles BET because of its duplicitous nature—offering customers and audiences both the love and the slap at the same time. The title also addresses many popular rap artists of the 21st century and makes a surprisingly important link to Robert L. Johnson's approach to building Black Entertainment Television.

Chapter 3 delves into the area of greatest contest for BET—its programming. In "I'm Rick James, Bitchhhhh!" I examine BET's programming choices, practices, and the degree to which its move to Viacom changes it. The response in black communities to BET's sale was a kind of incredulity. It invoked discussions of image control, "the Man," and African-American progress in the U.S. In addition to textual analysis of specific programs, I look at larger internal BET issues that impact its programming such as the firing of Tavis Smiley and Johnson's on-air response, the continued manifestation of religious programming, and the perception that the programming somehow changed after Viacom's acquisition. This chapter also looks at the aesthetic and ideological choices BET engages in order to deliver the black audience to its advertisers.

In chapter 4, I scrutinize the peculiar practice of making black folks synonymous with consumer products as situated within larger discussions of wealth building, welcoming Jesus, and widespread

globalization. The "Impossibility of Us: BET Impact" explores
BET's significance to black communities and to the larger world that
receives these images of black Americans. When talking about BET
and what it means to African-American communities, conflicts of
loyalty, pride, performance, and capitalism take center stage. While
BET began with the financial and operational support of Telecommunications, Inc., it banked on the allegiance of African-Americans to support black representation. It promised that through its
existence, a more diverse media universe would surface.

In chapter 5, I attempt to bring all of the pieces of the BET puz-
zle together. In the 2005 opening session of the National Association
of Television Program Executives (NATPE) in Las Vegas, President
Rick Feldman asserted proudly: "We are a mirror of our business."
Yet surveying those listening to him, the business continued to be
very, very white and male—unlike the people, the consumers—it
serves. Understanding the seeming disconnection between those
that make television and those that watch it, "It's Your Turn: Black
to the Future" suggests ways to navigate the visually white representational and business spaces of television that operate within
an increasingly colorized U.S. population. For all who can find no
"safety in ambiguity" (Noguera 2003); where in fact, ambiguity is
not an option, BET offered up a notion of blackness that dominates
twenty-first century popular culture. However, it is a representation that exists only in product form, making reconsiderations of
its value crucial to differently visioning African-American images,
commercial media, and class within a capitalist system.

Wanting and needing enhanced representation and voice due to
their historic absence on television, marginalized audience members suffer vision fatigue. The demands for these portrayals are both
paradoxical and paralyzing. Nonetheless in this chapter, I present
critical insights on making a difference and offer new ways of seeing for those who endure and delight in BET's representations.

Black Entertainment Television exemplifies some of the most
confounding and critical questions facing black America, especially
for those who have an investment in African-American cultures
and notions of black progress. I came to this project through a
series of unrelated conversations. One of these was with my mom's

first cousin, attorney Melford McCormick, who in his own didactic way went on a rant about how bad BET had become over the last few years (since the "take over"). While I listened and limitedly interjected, I thought, "What is he talking about? In my estimation, BET appeared very much the same as always. While this book is expressly about Black Entertainment Television, its macro interrogations of BET's constructions of blackness, black wealth, black entrepreneurship, black aesthetics, and black progress make my great grandmother's quandary in the 1950s all the more viable and necessary to engage contemporarily. *Pimpin' Ain't Easy* marshals the circulating discourses about Black Entertainment Television in order to highlight and make sense of the paradoxes that shape and forward the network and African-Americans' continuing desire for black representation.

Chapter 1

Eyes Wide Shut

Capitalism, Class, and the Promise of Black Media

Capitalism—the system of pimps and hoes
I'm sorry that's the way it goes
In this particular system everyone's a slave
Racist is how they want us to behave
White Johnny be fighting black Michael
Both are blind to the system's sick cycle
In a circle psychotically they slay each other
With a grin because of color of a skin
Pick up that money hoe!

—"Who Are the Pimps?" Boogie Down Productions (1992)

Why talk about capitalism in a book ostensibly about Black Enter-tainment Television? One of the foundational conundrums raised in this book is the work and understanding of capitalism by and

1

for African-Americans. The capitalist system undergirds all media, image making, and ideas of prosperity in the U.S., and BET, in many ways, represents the quintessential example of black television success. Yet for African-Americans, both the implementation and articulation of capitalism has posed the greatest divisions and hardships. Thus, it is necessary to begin with a discussion of capitalism as an increasingly global system and one in which the commodification of African-American blackness makes it available to all.

The intellectual father of capitalism, economist Adam Smith, theorized the nature of capital and its variant uses in his 1776 tome *An Inquiry into the Nature and Causes of the Wealth of Nations.* The modern textbook *The Capitalist System* gives flesh to his theoretical framework. In this work, economic scholars Richard C. Edwards, Michael Reich, and Thomas E. Weisskopf defined capitalism and its operation this way:

> Capitalist relations of production are characterized by the complete separation of the producers (wage-workers) from the means of production. Capitalists as a class have a monopoly on the means of production while workers have only their labor-power, which they must sell to the capitalists for a wage if they are to subsist ... *In respect to control of the work process and ownership of the means of production, capitalism resembles slavery* and differs from feudalism and petty commodity production. The objective of the capitalists is to expand their initial capital by combining labor and means of production and selling the resultant commodities, which are their property, for a profit. *Hence, capitalist production is for exchange, not for use* (Edwards et al.: 41).[1]

Phrased in a more contemporary vernacular, sociologist James Fulcher wrote that capitalism "involves the investment of money to make more money ... [It] depends on the exploitation of wage labour, which also fuels the consumption of the goods and services produced by capitalist enterprises" (Fulcher: 18). Beyond strict definitions, different types of capitalism enjoy ideological currency and influence the way citizens process the system.

For example, the pro-capitalist writings of philosopher Ayn Rand linked capitalism to free markets, individual rights, and most especially, liberty. Her work claimed capitalism as a progressive, ethical, and objective ideal because it allows "men" the freedom to pursue their own happiness and be moral. Natural capitalism is a system based on strategies that help "enable countries, companies, and communities to operate by behaving as if all forms of capital were valuable" (www.smartcommunities.ncat.org). The offshoot crony capitalism poses the idea of business success as heavily dependent on friendships and family rather than on market forces and open competition. When asking my focus groups of young people (junior high schoolers through collegiate) for their definition of capitalism, responses ranged from "trying to get money as profit" to "supply and demand" to "I dunno." It seems their definitions, when they could articulate them, hinged strictly on the ability to acquire capital—and spend it excessively at will.

All of these definitions—academic and everyday—treat profit, exploitation, and satisfaction as mutually exclusive entities, thereby ignoring the invisible hand of economics that links them together. Thinking through these viable, (though certainly not all-inclusive), definitions of capitalism and applying them to daily living experiences in the U.S. allows for a fuller appreciation of Boogie Down's employment of the pimps-and-hoes metaphor in this chapter's epigraph, especially insofar as it concerns American capitalism and its adherents. The lyrics are an especially apt observation with regard to African-Americans and their introduction to the capitalistic means of production. Most African-Americans' preamble to America's capital system is as manual laborers and as property. While definitions of capitalism are extensive and continually expanding, this book uses the definition that situates capitalism as a system that privileges and demands accumulation of capital (money) for the sake of the individual. For the media industry, it rewards producers, creates and requires consumers, and mandates the existence of poor folks in order to operate successfully. As this chapter will show, this definition works well in connecting the bling, banter, and Black Star Power of BET. However, it is first necessary to work through the ways capitalism has evolved with and resonated in the lives of African-Americans.

Capitalism Manifest

From approximately 1550 to 1850, the Atlantic slave trade existed as one of the most lucrative and successful business ventures in world history. Many scholars who study the founding of the U.S. agree that the presence and work of enslaved Africans "made the flowering of capitalism possible ..." (Frazier: 15). One of the earliest ways that capitalism circulated was through the missionary impulse. England, Spain, and Portugal (later the Dutch, Arabs, and French) all sent traders and Christian and Islamic missionaries to the African continent—to do business and to proselytize about the wonders of Jesus and Muhammad. Thus alongside their admonition of these deities they introduced the practices of monopoly capitalism—first looking at the continent as a treasure of raw materials, later as a market.[2] Slavery and later the mantra of Manifest Destiny allowed the U.S. to establish a solid economic foundation by exploiting free labor, usurping occupied lands, and murdering its prior inhabitants, aka the natives who didn't work out as laborers. Furthermore, as business scholar Juliet E.K. Walker so persuasively argued, the U.S. government partnered with business to create success—in direct contradiction to the principles of laissez-faire (Walker 1998: xix).

The slave trade's commercial imperatives made the Negro an "article of commerce" or an "animate tool."[3] Enslaved Africans, who later became Americans, were actively involved in the slave trade. However, for the most part, they failed to benefit from its profits or have any say in the direction of slavery as a business. The enterprise operated alongside the developing mythology that defined the American Dream as democracy, freedom, and capitalism. The flourishing practice of enslaving Africans and ideologies of the American Dream shaped capitalism's growth and dictated how African-Americans interpreted their place and participation in this system—an interpretation that called for blacks to engage in said system wholeheartedly, despite the seeming contradiction of this move given their history with capitalism.

As president of the Freedmen's Savings Bank (1874), Frederick Douglass suggested:

[t]he history of civilization shows that no people can well rise to a high degree of mental or even moral excellence without wealth. A people uniformly poor and compelled to struggle for barely a physical existence will be dependent and despised by their neighbors and will finally despise themselves. While it is impossible that every individual of any race shall be rich—and no man may be despised for merely being poor—yet no people can be respected which does not produce a wealthy class.[4]

Ideas such as these circulated through nineteenth century America. Thus, the mantra to "toil and save" flowed through the teachings to newly emancipated slaves.

Freed black folks were focused on respectability. This idea of respectability, grounded in the economics of individual thrift, enterprise, and savings, existed in the surrounding dominant community. Prior to emancipation, it already manifested itself in the life of the free Negro, as in that of the white working class. And as has been asserted by scholars, "white philanthropists sought to indoctrinate the freedmen with this ideal through the missionary schools and the Freedmen's Bank" (Harris: 46). Making way for progress, the capitalist system transformed African-Americans from the consumed to consumers, at least at that point in history. For many, engaging capitalism appeared to be the only way up and out of poverty.

Resultantly, in the short history of the U.S., the racist system of capitalism has triumphed. This triumph seems clear with the continued perpetuation and inundation of global capitalism—touted by the U.S. across the globe—and implemented by trade agreements, the IMF, the World Bank, and waged war. Conflated with the mythology of the American Dream, capitalists exploit the economic systems' underpinnings to keep power confined to certain racialized (and gendered) groups. Philosopher Karl Marx critiqued this system in his *Capital: A Critique of Political Economy*, (more commonly known as *Das Kapital*), with a theory of exploitation of the proletariat, an exposition of the labor theory. He criticized Adam Smith (and others) for not realizing that their economic concepts reflected capitalist institutions, not innate natural properties of mankind. And while black (mostly male) leaders and scholars such as W.E.B. Du Bois, Marcus Garvey, Elijah Muhammad, Angela Davis, and the Black Panthers have offered ways to append capitalism, no serious attempt has ever been made to undermine capitalism's flawed foundation by any U.S. marginalized or mainstream group. However, the value of capitalism for black folks has not proceeded completely uncontested either.

Debate of this system came from many black activists and scholars who considered (and still talk about) themselves as either socialist or communist—in some ways, fighting the evils of capitalism by denying it. Revolutionary psychiatrist Frantz Fanon, economist Abram L. Harris, political theorist Manning Marable, and cultural scholar bell hooks, all provided powerful critiques of capitalism and the need for African-Americans to consider alternative means of progress. The socialism piece in particular reverberated quite acutely in black discourses due to the communal legacy of African ways of being—still manifested in most African-American communities. In other words, capitalism calls for an individualist state of being—a state that has traditionally been foreign to communities of color. These communities are organized around the family—with everything else, economics and politics, flowing from that foundation.[5] However, agreeing with hooks, desegregation has altered the way African-Americans think about community. She argued:

> Desegregation was the way to weaken the collective radicalization of black people that had been generated by militant civil rights and black power movement ... After years of collective struggle ... liberal individualism [has become] more the norm for black folks, particularly the black bourgeoisie, more so than the previous politics of communalism, which emphasized racial uplift and sharing resources. (hooks 2000: 92)

Moreover, cultural critic Paul Gilroy argued that even beyond critical cynicism, in the past people like Toni Cade Bambara and Amiri Baraka possessed a righteous anger "about the violence of [capitalism] and the way it delimits people's choices" (Gilroy, interviewed by hooks April 1996). Many of these same scholars and others acknowledge that even the minimal serious critiques of capitalism that once existed have virtually disappeared in favor of the global economy, especially in the United States. From the World Bank and the war on Iraq to the functioning of the Internet and Coca-Cola, capitalism reigns as the virtually uncontested authority of the new world order.

Capitalism does not value extended family support, collective engagement, or community gardens. Psychologist Na'im Akbar argued that at least a part of African-American attitudes toward capital comes from a slave mentality. Specifically, he maintained "… material objects or dregs of property became equated in the African-Americans' thinking with the full power of freedom and self-determination which the master enjoyed" (Akbar 1984: 13). Thinking about the impact of a slave mindset alone makes clear that a more crucial conflict emerges at the very outset of African-Americans relationship with capitalism. And whether or not one agrees with the assessment, one must concede that for whatever reason, African-Americans and capitalism make awkward dance partners. Beyond this observation, some scholars have suggested that the debate of blacks and capitalism is the wrong one anyway.

In his seminal text, *How Capitalism Underdeveloped Black America*, political theorist Manning Marable argued that people forget (or choose to ignore) the racist nature of capitalism. As I maintain, whether talking about capitalism for the masses or black capitalism, the structure retains a hierarchy and fixity that allows only a few to accumulate capital or "make it"—not altering in the least its built-in inequalities. In revisiting his work some years later, Marable remained firm in saying that the "U.S. capitalist state, in the final analysis, will never be cajoled or persuaded to reform itself through appeals of moral suasion. Fundamental change will require a massive democratic resistance movement largely from below and anchored in the working class and among oppressed minority groups" (Marable 2000: xxxviii)—what he called "non-reformist reform."

Historian John Henrik Clarke suggested that investment in any economic or political system was not as crucial as survival and progression of African people. While espousing socialism himself, Clarke believed in black ownership of black communities as an "economic means to effect social change in our favor"

(Clarke 1991: 10). Activist Malcolm X concurred with Clarke's position stating: "Our economic philosophy is that we should gain economic control over the economy of our own community, the businesses and the other things which create employment so that we can provide jobs for our own people instead of having to picket and boycott and beg someone else for a job" (X 1964: 272–273). Mantras such as these continue to encourage and hold sway over black entrepreneurial efforts.

Yet others such as historian Chancellor Williams suggest that blacks need not "wholly accept [capitalism], but they should reject 'black capitalism' as a solution of the economic bondage problems of the masses ... [instead, they should focus] on a system that *directly* benefits the people lower down, the great common people, and not just the further enrichment of Blacks who are already well-off and far ahead" (Williams 1971: 332). He argued further that both capitalism and communism were here to stay despite groups shouting 'destroy the system.' Economist Julianne Malveaux constantly indicts the U.S. government for its misuse of capitalists' tools. And lest we forget, capitalism is intimately linked to most other ridiculous operating isms—sexism, racism, and classism—isms that are taken to task regularly in academic communities, even if the capitalist elephant in the room often gets a pass. Regardless of the stance, in many areas of African-American scholarship, one can find a critique of capitalism. All of these scholarly observations are particularly implicated in a business like BET through its appeal to black consumers.

And beyond academia, discussions about capitalism within African-American communities yield insights into the psychic platform of BET's foundation and launch. Some argue that blacks are capitalists in the surest sense of the system; what's the problem? Others say that blacks are oppressed by capitalism and should relinquish its trappings. While still others believe that it's all about the money, and things will be bought and sold regardless of the seller's race. So, it might as well be a black man (or woman) who makes the dollars—C.R.E.A.M., "get the money, dollar, dollar bill yaw'll."[6]

Journalist/writer Cora Daniels argued that the post-Civil Rights generation sees capitalism as a movement. She wrote: "The post-civil rights generation has known no other kind of Black power but that of the business world" (Daniels 2004: 145). In the same vein, focus group participant and college student Fred Walker concluded, "I had to make a realization, a strong realization ... that I am a capitalist. I like making money. I want to make money. And I'm not talking about this gross materialism either" (U of Houston focus group February 2003). One of the central flaws with both of these notions is that they either ignore or pervert the meaning and function of capitalism. Capitalism is not—cannot be—a power movement nor is having the desire to make money capitalism. Moreover, their ideas belie capitalism's central tenet of individualism—an individualism that receives limited manifestation in terms of African-Americans as they endure constant group identification.[7] Or, as cultural critic Greg Tate eloquently mused, " ... maybe in a virtual America like the one we inhabit today, the only Black culture that matters is the one that can be downloaded and perhaps needs only business leaders at that. Certainly it's easier to speak of hip hop hoop dreams than of structural racism and poverty, because for hip hop America to not just desire wealth but demand power with a capital P would require thinking way outside the idiot box" (Tate 2005). Being trapped within or catering to a specific "idiot box"— in the case of BET television—is exemplified quite well in Spike Lee's *Bamboozled* (2000). As television executive Pierre Delacroix (Damon Wayans) agonized over what to feed the television (the idiot box) in order to continue working, he led audiences to circulating judgments about capitalism in popular media culture.

In the media realm, critiques of capital abound beside often hypocritical examples of its benefits. The black music industry offers ample and sustained review of capitalism, (although most lyrics hoist up getting money as a really, really good thing). In the 1970s, for example, The O'Jays sang about the evil people perpetuate "For the Love of Money" (1974); later, Tina Turner bemoaned what many women do as "Private Dancer[s]" to get money (1984); Tracy Chapman was "Talkin About a Revolution" against the system (1988); and of course, Boogie Down Production's "Who Are the Pimps," cited at the beginning of the chapter, all overtly attack the system of capital.

Figure 1.1   *Barbershop.*

Yet, the lyrics and images within music videos, the staple of BET no less, serve up near naked women draped over Bentleys in front of mansions as examples of music business success (see any past Jay-Z, 50 cent, Big Tymers, or even Lil' Kim video for proof). Having or acquiring money serves as the primary motivation in many black film narratives as well. For example, films ranging from *Let's Do It Again* (Sidney Poitier, 1975) to *Barbershop* (Tim Story, 2002) illustrate the need and schemes necessary to possess capital—whether or not it is in service to a larger black community.

The Hughes brothers' *Dead Presidents* (Allen and Albert Hughes, 1995) foregrounds the psychological detriments of having no money; and hip hop gangsta films like *New Jack City* (Mario Van Peebles, 1991), *Clockers* (Spike Lee, 1995), *Set It Off* (F. Gary Gray, 1996), *Sugar Hill* (Leon Ichaso, 1999), and *Paid in Full* (Charles Stone III, 2002), all revolve around the acquisition of capital.[8] Assertions of capitalist dreams and deferrals abound. And it cannot be overlooked that an obvious link exists between capitalism and sexism—owning capital is seen as congruent with owning women in almost all visual and aural media formats.[9]

Furthermore, regardless of whatever common evaluations surface about the viability and legitimacy of capitalism, alternate ways of acquiring capital are also sanctioned in most U.S. communities. Both legal and under-the-table means of acquiring capital receive

Figure 1.2   *In Living Color.*

validation, as long as money is made. The same person who condemns the drug trade will participate in insider trading or buy, download, or somehow acquire a bootleg copy of music or a film still playing in the theater. Both *Barbershop* and the Wayans brothers' "Homeboy Shopping Network" from *In Living Color* (**FOX** 1990–1994) illustrate this underground capitalism well with the slogan, "mo' money, mo' money, mo' money!"

But for all the decrying of and debate over illegality and legality, the centrality of capital operating in a way antithetical to humanity—especially black humanity—receives rare attention. Plus, living in the U.S. prevents anyone from escaping the machinations of capitalism altogether. It also virtually precludes any serious consideration of any other type of economic order. Yet, the arguments for and against capitalism advanced by black economists of the early twentieth century reverberate still. These debates are articulated in writings by members of the National Editorial Board of the News & Letters Committees, a Marxists/Humanists organization committed to the abolition of capitalism. Using the 1992 Los Angeles Riots/Rebellion as a foundation, they argued:

> Black masses today continue to be engaged in both a struggle against capitalism and an internal struggle against their own Black middle class, which is ideologically and economically integrated into the

crevices of capitalism ... while Black masses in practice do challenge
and show that the bourgeois theory of the state is a mere mask that
hides the class rule of capitalism, the Black leader will follow capitalism and say it's only through the bourgeois state that African Americans can be emancipated (National Editorial Board October 2003).

Can we give a shout out to black mega-church leaders, hip hop
moguls, and Jesse 'nem? Furthermore, the observations of an essay
on millennium capitalism resonate here: "The return on capital has
suddenly become more spiritually compelling and imminent ... than
the return of Christ" (Eric Kramer quoted in Comaroff 2001: 24).
This framework of raging internal paradox provides an opportunity
to move from a discussion of capitalism and its impact in the U.S.
to one about class construction and the development of black media
businesses—thus, moving more closely to the emergence of BET.

The Wages of Class

"No Class" –the Cosby Kids, *Fat Albert and the Cosby Kids*
(1972–1984)

Class divisions are a long-standing reality of black life—in all of
American life, truth be told. Beyond master's romp through the
slave house (as Me'Shell NdegéOcello penned), the separation of
folks via income, education, status, ability, and shading harkens
back to the African continent and other continents and peoples.
However, the articulation of class in African-American communities has taken a less well-paved route. Class is not talked about, at
least not directly, in everyday discourses. Assumptions of class are
coded in words, looks, behaviors, dress. Community members on
all sides of the class prism know how "no home training," "bougie,"
"keeping it real," "ghetto," and "siddity" translate. They are covert
ways to separate and distinguish folks, one from another; rich (or at
least having a white collar or entertainment job) versus poor; educated (from college) versus street cred; haute couture versus ghetto
fabulous; Lenox versus Greenbriar. Cultural critic bell hooks called
the contemporary iteration of class distinction among youth the
wrath of the "me-me" class, the young and the ruthless.

So what does the term class mean? Like capitalism, class is an idea that employs multiple and varied definitions. Clearly philosophers Karl Marx and Friedrich Engels played an influential role in bringing the ideas and value of class study and struggle to the forefront of scholarly and political consciousness. Others such as historian E. P. Thompson made the lives of the working class worthy of study. In a summary of some of the central ways class analysis has developed, political scientist R.J. Rummel wrote:

> Classes have been defined by property ownership (Marx), position or role (Mosca 1939; Pareto 1963), status rank (Warner 1960; Lenski 1966), prestige (Barber 1957); or by intermarriage (Schumpeter 1951) … class membership is not biologically determined, but is a form of social stratification based on laws, esteem, wealth, or power. …In all cases … class is a vertical division into superior-inferior …. Class is a division in privileges … [C]lass is a dividing line between different kinds of behavior. What these behaviors are depends on the actual definition, but nonetheless all definitions assume that different classes can be separated empirically according to different patterns of behavior, such as intermarriages, social mixing, organizational memberships, travel, etiquette, and mannerisms (Rummel, 1976).

As should be evident by Rummel's assessment of class definitions, the term is not only wide-ranging but also contested among scholars. But why is it important to talk about class along with capitalism, race, media, and BET? Look no further than the devastation of the 2005 Hurricane Katrina in New Orleans and Gulf Port, Mississippi where the preponderance of the residents are poor and black. U.S. President George W. Bush stepped in four days after the disaster and flaunted his ineffectualness and complete disconnection from those unlike himself—wealthy and white. As the bodies continued to be gathered and the stench swelled, fingers point dexterously at one another. But I assert, along with many others, that as the smoke has cleared, the displaced "evacuees," (aka looters or refugees depending on what you watched and read), found themselves in the same, impoverished position—in other cities with their own ignored and impoverished populations. So when producer and rapper Kanye West stated matter-of-factly that among other things, "George Bush doesn't care about Black people," he's talking as much about racist animosity as class divisions.[10]

The relevance of class distinctions for African-Americans is a relatively new development given black folks' historic positioning. Internally, African-American-class differences are so emotionally raw that it is often painful to even address underlying and systematic shared concerns. Yet business scholar Juliet E.K. Walker believed that class fails to play any role in the development of black enterprises. She surmised that between slavery, debt peonage, and the "deliberate, systematic, and institutionalized actions of whites to exclude blacks from free access to and participation in the American business community during the age of slavery—almost 250 years," racism has been the primary barrier to black business success (Walker 1998: xviii).

African-Americans know race and recognize racist thoughts, behaviors, and most manifestations. Racism is confronted daily on jobs, on the street, watching television, in classrooms, and at the grocery store. Racism is so much a part of the fabric of the U.S. that it doesn't surprise and rarely excites (O.J., Rodney King, Amadou Diallo, Jasper, Texas, Michael Jackson, Columbine, and Kanye's comments notwithstanding). So while I do not disagree with Walker's assessment of the severity of racist affects on African-Americans and black business, I believe that a strong connection exists between race, class, black entrepreneurship, and media. Class is significant in understanding how the demands of capitalism have shaped African-American consciousness and enterprises—especially in the business of image-making.

Let me offer an example from my own biography to emphasize the African-American class conundrum. My mother's family grew up dirt poor in Smith County, Texas, just outside of Tyler—eleven children, a farmer and laborer father and a home-making and early-deceased mother, poor.[11] The family's saving grace beyond a hard-work mandate was education and extended familial support. Not unlike many black families in the early part of the twentieth century, education (or the military)[12] was touted in my family as a way out of no way. This foundation accorded a certain status upon the family—poor but respectable and respected in the community. Buoyed by several family teachers, entrepreneurs, and one lawyer, my mother and most of her siblings found ways to move economically beyond their upbringing. In this case, the manifestation of class allowed the promise and fallacy of boot straps and efforts to distinguish folks—one from another—hard workers from the so-called lazy. Black success was thus used to deny systematic forms of racism that keep the masses of black folks subordinate.

In my generation, the class dilemma becomes evident as an adult with a Ph.D. People assume a certain class status and mindset for me—for both my past and my present—based on those three letters after my name. Far from the poverty of my parents upbringing, I grew up and flourished in a predominately black working class North Omaha community. Housing projects were as much a part of the community landscape as single-family homes. In a *Christian Science Monitor* story about blacks returning to their roots, a high school classmate, Kenny Cowan, remembered being inspired by living next door to doctors and lawyers in our neighborhoods. He said these were "the kind of people you dreamed of growing up to be" (Axtman 29 April 2004).

Unlike Kenny, I remember older, retired black folks who looked out for me. I have no idea how they earned a living. I remember friends' mothers who worked as teachers and some sorts of administrative personnel and who exposed their children to classes of dance, music, 4-H, softball, and of course, church. I remember the less well-off and the okay (us) engaging one another on our school bus (part of Omaha's desegregation plan), on the softball field, and in the cafeteria, (both with those who had government subsidized meal tickets and those who paid cash—me having both at different points of my schooling). Folks were always proud when you achieved and encouraged you to do so. They held you accountable to certain classist standards. "Liberal individualism" failed to play in my household—in my family and larger family and friend circles. Fortunately for my friends and me, communalism was a way of life. These "old school" class-less communities and ways of thinking were what BET counted on, reaffirmed with subscribers, and sold to advertisers. The usage of class is also one of the reasons why what transpired with the development of BET serves as an oxymoron—community capitalism. Recognizing this, the interplay of class, race, and media cannot be negated or ignored.

Ironically, however, complex narratives like mine, and of other class disparities, rarely appear in visual culture—not in film, not on radio, (except in a very problematic way on the *Tom Joyner Morning Show*)[13], and certainly not on mainstream television. When class conflict appears, it is generally in a television episode—a snippet of its actual existence—that quickly disappears and is almost always shown as humor. Several examples illustrate this point. In a filmic example, Sidney Poitier's *Uptown Saturday Night* (1974) provides a scene where the protagonists Wardell Franklin (Bill Cosby) and Steve Jackson (Sidney Poitier) enter Madame Zenobia's (Lee Chamberlin) world of black elegance and exclusivity—a place where black people possess wealth, privilege, and correct behavior and consumption habits (or at least appear to)—very unlike the manual labor status for Franklin and Jackson (Figure 1.3).

In the extremely popular and profitable mainstream series *Sex and the City* (Darren Star, creator, HBO, 1998–2004), class emerges as a side thought. The episode "The Caste System" brings visual attention to the lack of class dialogue (or even consciousness) to the four white female protagonists as they chat with one another during their spa pedicures. Literally sitting at their feet we see the backs of presumably, four Asian women. The women can only nod

Figure 1.3   *Uptown Saturday Night.*

sheepishly when Charlotte (Kristin Davis) points out the fact that class disparities live as evidenced by their pedicurists. And in a second, this moment of consciousness is gone as they quickly move on to talk about class and wealth through one of their paramour's servants. Yet in George C. Wolfe's *Colored Museum* (as presented on PBS, 1991), he revealed the life of black models as reflective of any black folks on display. During "The Photo Session" exhibit, Female Model (Suzzanne Douglass) and Male Model (Victor Love) pose their way into the consciousness of black America proclaiming:

Female: The world was becoming too much for us.

Male: We couldn't resolve the contradictions of our existence.

Female: And we couldn't resolve yesterday's pain (pain).

Male: So we gave our lives, and now we live inside *Ebony* magazine. (We're fabulous.)

Female: Yes, we live inside a world where everyone is beautiful and wears fabulous clothes.

Male: And no one says anything profound.

Female: Or meaningful.

Male: Or contradictory.

Female: We just smile and show off our cheekbones.

Perhaps it is as communications scholar Jennie L. Phillips argues: "[S]ocial class, particularly any semblance of the upper-middle class, is so firmly entrenched in television programming that its complete normalization masks its presence. It is not that class is absent from television, but rather that it appears as virtually transparent" (Phillips 2004: 1–2).

In the black version of *Sex and the City*, *Girlfriends* (Mara Brock Akil, creator, 2000), class surprisingly enters the narrative as a fairly central issue with the four female black protagonists but here, as the butt of humor and through a racialized subtext (Figure 1.4). For example, one of the early running gags in the program is Lynn's (Persia White) bi-racial status and how that makes her a quasi-outsider of these four girlfriends. Bi-racialness confirms a particular form of class consciousness for African-Americans—derived straight from the house nigger/field nigger foundation of early American

Figure 1.4   *Girlfriends* cast.

history. Lynn's white half accords her a privilege, mindset, and pass for inadequacies that "full-blood" black women are not accorded. Meaning, Lynn's constant joblessness, lack of responsibility, and relish in promiscuity are attributes associated with white girls in black communities—rightly or wrongly. Ironically, the actor Tracee Ellis Ross who serves as the main character Joan, is biologically bi-racial but positioned as having or living 100% black blood lines and culture—making her more authentic, more black. Her class status, along with their friend Toni's (Jill Marie Jones), gets a pass.[14]

In a different example from the same series, the episode "New York Bound" finds Maya (Golden Brooks)—the community college attending, remarried to the same man, teenaged mother of one—selling her book, *Oh, Hell Yes*, from the trunk of her car on Crenshaw Boulevard. This action initiates a whole lot of class confrontation in the episode.

In one way her efforts highlight the black entrepreneurial spirit that hip hop advocates, (a point of which I discuss in chapter 2). In another way, however, *Oh, Hell Yes* and Maya's approach to book distribution reek with black recognition of lack as she is already positioned as lower class throughout the series as shown through her dress, job, friends, and speech.[15] Furthermore, as boss and secretary for the better part of the series, Joan and Maya must negotiate a difficult and awkward friendship. Class tensions pervade all of these women's relationships—albeit in humorous and quickly resolved ways.[16]

The significance of class in this book about BET lies in its invisibility and its normalization of wretched inequalities and disparities.

Sociologist William Julius Wilson's first major book, *The Declining Significance of Race: Blacks and Changing American Institutions* (1978), caused a stir in academic communities because of its assertion that class divisions are more damaging than racial ones. Historian Robin D.G. Kelley waxed eloquently about the ways in which folks deemed "underclass" negotiate their identity and real-lived positioning as working class in *Race Rebels: Culture, Politics, and the Black Working Class* (1994). Others write about the ways in which class shapes our desires and goals. In *Pimpin Ain't Easy*, economic and social class function as significant tools in constructing consumers. By the twenty-first century, possessing the ability to consume (or at least the access to credit) translated into having equitability and power. When people look to Puffy's white party and who attends as a measure of influence, it is clear that the myth of classlessness conversion is complete—the twistedness of the dress color code making this myth all the more striking. Yet recognizing and calling class out in a class conscious-less, image-making society is necessary to fully digest the paradox of Black Entertainment Television and to begin visioning and thinking through the worth and measure of African-American representation. The circulating understanding of and relationship African-Americans have to class both perpetuate and resist racist underpinnings. These underpinnings traverse both capitalism and class to inform and shape the ideas and goals of black business development.

Black Business

Look at those Korean motherfuckers across the street. I betcha they haven't been a year off da motherfucking boat before they opened up their own place ... A motherfucking year off the motherfucking boat and got a good business in our neighborhood occupying a building that had been boarded up for longer than I care to remember, and I've been here a long time ... Now for the life of me, I haven't been able to figure this out. Either dem Koreans are geniuses or we Blacks are dumb.

—ML **(Paul Benjamin)**, *Do the Right Thing* **(Spike Lee 1989)**
(Figure 1.5)

Figure 1.5 Three community griots in *Do the Right Thing*.

According to many, the confluence of blacks and business is oxymoronic. Whether it comes from in-house critiques by academics like Thomas Sowell who believed: "Race does not change the fundamental principles of economics" (Sowell 1994: 81), E. Franklin Frazier who called "Negro Business: A Social Myth" (Frazier 1957: 129) or outside assessments by people like Gunnar Myrdal who labeled black businesses marginal (1944), a continuing mindset suggests that African-Americans' biological and cultural make-up make them ill-equipped to do business. Yet quiet as it's kept, black businesses existed even in Colonial America—service businesses such as restaurants, hairdressers, and trading posts. Business scholar Juliet E.K. Walker's books on the history of African-American businesses lay out the ways in which blacks have always been interested and successful business people. Economist Abram L. Harris maintained: "Like the white working men of the eighteenth century, the free Negroes were 'men on the make' hoping to escape the wage-earning class through business enterprise and by accumulating wealth" (Harris 1936: 3). Most black enterprises developed post-emancipation and included endeavors like lumbering, life insurance companies, real estate, catering, and tailoring. The largest number of successful black business ventures were in the field of personal services. In these businesses, racial discrimination became more general. Thus, they wetre often described as "defensive enterprises,"—businesses that somewhat shielded the owner against overt, more specified racism —"the product of racial segregation" (Harris 1936: 54).

From the 1880s, the so-called Negro lumpenproletariat, urged by black leaders, placed increasing faith in business and property as a way of escaping poverty and achieving economic independence. "Although ostensibly sponsored as the means of self-help or racial cooperation …. Negro business enterprise was motivated primarily by the desire for private profit and looked toward the establishment of a Negro capitalist employer class" (Harris 1936: 49–50). Yet, Madam C.J. Walker, the nation's first self-made female millionaire, not only adhered to the dogma of money-making but also to community needs and expectations with her beauty business. The dichotomous assertions by Harris and illustrated through Walker can be supported by looking at the writings and speeches of the culture-defining men of the times, Booker T. Washington and William Edward Burghardt Du Bois.

Booker T. Washington encouraged the colored man to proceed with conciliation, to start at the bottom, work hard, and earn the trust of the white man. While his speech at the 1895 Atlanta Cotton States' International Exposition propelled him to leading spokesman for his people, (at least in the minds of whites), it also yielded castigation from black scholars like W.E.B. Du Bois. Distilled, Washington suggested: "No race that has anything to contribute to markets of the world is long in any degree ostracized. It is important and right that all privileges of the law be ours, but it is vastly more important that we be prepared for the exercise of these privileges. The opportunity to earn a dollar in a factory just now is worth infinitely more than the opportunity to spend a dollar in an opera house" (Washington 1895). In a nutshell, Washington believed in both working your way up and in black entrepreneurship. His problematic stance regarding civil rights notwithstanding, Washington's economic plan presented a viable blueprint for black progress (even if propelled in large measure by white politicians and businessmen). Political theorist Manning Marable evaluated Washington's stance when he wrote, "Washington devoutly believed that corporate capitalism would usher in a wave of prosperity to the black peasantry and working class … [His] program was the origin of what we call today 'black capitalism'" (Marable, "History", 1998). It is indeed Washington's admonition that African-American entrepreneurs followed despite sustained criticism of this philosophy.

W.E.B. Du Bois, on the other hand, was a twentieth century privileged scholar and activist. He believed in an ideology and group of people that he dubbed the Talented Tenth—the top ten percent of all blacks who will lead the masses of uneducated and uncultured Negroes to prosperity and better standards of living via the tenth's acquisition of professional occupations and business development. In direct rebuke to the industrial proposals of Washington, Du Bois founded the unsuccessful but significant Niagara Movement in 1905 to demand civil rights for blacks and later, initiated conferences at Atlanta University on the progress of black businesses. With Du Bois at its helm, several resolutions pertaining to the development of black businesses were adopted at the 1898 Fourth Atlanta University Conference. Two of those resolutions are salient to this work: 1) business men should be congratulated and patronized, and 2) agitation for the necessity of business careers for young people should continue in churches, schools, newspapers, and by all other avenues (Harris 1936: 52–53). The different approaches that these men offered for black folks' progress resonate contemporarily. In fact, their works' relevance to BET makes understanding their assertions crucial. Through the codes of contemporary understanding, Robert L. Johnson usurped salient aspects of both Washington and Du Bois's trajectories to make the case for the necessity of his BET.

Much later in his life, Du Bois repudiated the viability of capitalism for American Negroes in favor of socialism writing: "I myself long stressed Negro private business enterprise but I soon saw a 'group economy' was necessary for protection" (1957). He also modified his position on the viability of the Talented Tenth saying: "Willingness to work and make personal sacrifice for solving these problems was, of course, the first prerequisite and sine qua non. I did not stress this, I assumed it … I assumed that with knowledge, sacrifice would automatically follow. In my youth and idealism, I did not realize that selfishness is even more natural than sacrifice"

(1948). But Du Bois's original notion of the Talented Tenth and both he and Washington's advocacy for black business development stuck and became a part of the perceived best path for African-American progress. Their mantras give insight into the veneration Robert L. Johnson received during his reign at BET (or most of it) and the role of the black press in making BET prominent.

Proliferating alongside the efforts of men such as Frederick Douglass, Washington, and Du Bois's encouragement of black business are a number of critics who published work questioning these philosophies. E. Franklin Frazier believed that Du Bois's black elite fostered a "myth" about the significance of black ownership. He suggested that the rise of industrial schools under the encouragement of Washington (business included), trained students to not only become a part of the capitalist operating system but also to predict and forward its perpetuation. This very idea made the 1933 monumental work, *The Mis-Education of the Negro*, that much more powerful. In this text, educator Carter G. Woodson made assertions that remain valid, some seventy plus years later. He observed: " ... Negroes are trained exclusively in the psychology and economics of Wall Street and are, therefore, made to despise the opportunities to run ice wagons, push banana carts, and sell peanuts among their own people. Foreigners, who have not studied economics but have studied Negroes, take up this business and grow rich" (Woodson 1933: 5). Woodson's observation gives credence to both the phenomenon and incredulity of M.L.'s comments within the narrative of *Do the Right Thing* cited earlier.

Furthermore, in a contemporary example of these philosophies, management scholar Salmon A. Shomade reflected upon his transformation from a black college radical to a corporate suit. Pursuing an MBA degree in part because it sounded professional, he became quickly disappointed in his black (and white) classmates as issues of race in the business world were deemed unimportant. At the beginning he said, "I could care less about what white folks did." However over the course of his two-year tenure, his interest in radicalism subsided. This transformation was fueled by a defining classroom discussion on the 1987 stock market crash. While everyone gushed about the craziness of the market, Shomade wanted to discuss all the people who lost their jobs. His classmates looked at him as if he were crazy. He concluded: "In corporate America, you are more worried about what people put on your desk. I was muted because there was no fuel to keep the fire [of radicalism] burning .... My arguments shifted from black versus white to rich versus poor" (Shomade).

Shomade's observations fall in line with an earlier assessment of Frazier. In it, he maintained "business education is given professional status and is glorified because of the myth of Negro business as a way to economic salvation for the Negro in American society" (Frazier 1957: 137). In the past, he argued, poor students believed that accessing business education would put them squarely in the middle class. "For they have been taught that money will bring them justice and equality in American life, and they propose to get money" (Frazier 1957: 76). Contemporary MBA degree pursuers seek a more advanced goal—riches.

In partial response to both Du Bois and the 1944 study conducted by Gunnar Myrdal, *An American Dilemma*—a report that called the situation of the Negroes in America "pathological," Frazier wrote:

> One of the most striking indications of the unreality of the social world which the black bourgeoisie created is its faith in the importance of 'Negro business,' i.e., the business enterprises owned by Negroes and catering to Negro customers. Although these enterprises have little significance either from the standpoint of the American economy or the economic life of the Negro, a social myth has been created that they provide a solution to the Negro's economic problems. Faith in this social myth and others is perpetuated by the Negro newspapers ... (Frazier 1957: 27)

His last statement finds concrete support when looking at the most popular twenty-first century publications targeting African-American audiences. The top five magazines, *Essence, Ebony, Jet, Black Enterprise*, and *Vibe*, highlight professional lifestyles (business, entertainment, sports), monetary acquisition, professional firsts, and the status conferred with these elements. Beyond pride, these magazines suggest that the lives of those featured in their pages are the exemplar of black success and the new millennial

Moses—they illustrate what can be if you play the game correctly. As has been shown in countless studies, black-owned businesses succeed by catering primarily to African-American consumers. In fact, most ethnically-defined businesses work this way. Economist Andrew F. Brimmer maintained: "Segregation served as a kind of protective tariff to black-owned businesses ... That was harsh for black consumers, but it provided a shield for black businesses" (quoted in Hoffer 1987). Thus, black business was born out of the necessity for goods and services as well as the capitalist impulse.

BET capitalized (literally) on several circulating ideas about and beliefs in black business as a source of racial uplift and pride: the lack of black television presence; the racialized realization of President Ronald Reagan's policies, and the belief in "black capitalism" (as found in the 1960s with SNCC and Stokely Carmichael's "communal economic effort," the SCLC's "Operation Breadbasket," and the Nation of Islam and Elijah Muhammad's "Economic Blueprint"). Many of these programs merged the tenets of capitalism with social or communal tendencies of African-Americans as both a progressive stance and a legacy of Washington, Garvey, and Du Bois. Like most businesses that rely on perceived and actual lack as an appeal, black businesses harp on these tendencies of African-Americans. Thus, I turn finally to an examination of the businesses most closely allied with Black Entertainment Television—communications businesses— in order to bring full circle this introduction to BET's foundation.

And the Promise...

From early on, African-Americans understood the potential and sought to harness the power of mass communications. Many believed that through this vehicle, equality, connection, and progress could be advanced and measured. It could serve also as a potentially lucrative, black business venture. So beyond the businesses and approaches, the communications industry attracted a variety of black capitalists. With this impetus, Marable suggested that ties to black business development made the "Black press ... the chief vehicle to control and to exploit the Black consumer market, as well as to promote the ideology of Black Capitalism to the masses" (Marable 2000: 146).

In the nineteenth century, black newspapers, magazines, and other printed media flourished and were noted for their crusading tenor. These publications "shined a bright spotlight on the ugly legacy of America's racially segregated past" (Walker 1999: 1). The U.S.'s first black newspaper, *Freedom's Journal*, began in 1827 with Samuel E. Cornish and John B. Russwurm reporting on foreign and domestic news, missions to Africa, and memoirs—with the credo that for "too long others have spoken for us."

In the early twentieth century, publisher Robert Sengstacke Abbott's *Chicago Defender* grew to be one of the largest black-owned newspapers in the country and the first with mass circulation. He pioneered the idea of the paper existing on circulation rather than advertising dollars.[17] Within its pages, Abbott encouraged the migration of African-Americans from the south to Chicago for better-paying jobs. While he certainly had his detractors, the proof of his acumen lies in both the number of papers that subsequently flourished under his model and more importantly, the existence of the *Chicago Defender* still in 2007. In the same Windy City, publisher John H. Johnson achieved millionaire status with the publication of *Negro Digest* (1942), *Ebony* (1945–Present), and *Jet* beginning in 1951 (Walker 1998: 300). The company currently stands as a wholly-owned family conglomerate and the second largest black-owned business in the U.S. It achieved this status by Johnson's "steady insistence in his company's mission—delivering positive portrayals of African-Americans, and securing value from advertisers for the audience he delivered" (Smikle 2005). Scholar and journalist George Sylvie found that into the twentieth century, more than 300 black newspapers continue to serve black communities in the U.S. and the larger business community despite their lack of adequate technology and access to capital (Sylvie 2001).

Yet it seems that the crusading image that enticed blacks to the communications industry has shifted to concentrate on the ethos of money-making. For example, Walker noted that Motown developed into the nation's first black multimillion dollar, multimedia entertainment company. Berry Gordy founded the company in 1959 and was influenced by both John H. Johnson in terms of self discipline and individuality but also by the Ford Motor company's example of producing a consistent product. Yet its sale in 1988 seemed to "[represent] more than a business decision; it was a symbolic loss, a transfer of an institution important in the economic advancement of black America" (Walker 1998: 302). Furthermore, when *Essence* Magazine was sold to Time, Inc. in 2005, co-founder Edward Lewis remarked, " … we're looking forward to aggressively broadening the scope of the *Essence* brand and penetrating new markets around the world. It will give me great pride and comfort to know that *Essence* will be secure for generations to come and that its prospects for even greater success will be brighter now than ever" (*Jet*: 25 January 2005). The same thoughts seemed to flow behind the actions of owner and producer Quincy Jones as he sold *Vibe* magazine in July 2006. This new "forward" thinking of contemporary media moguls suggests (and seems to predict) the wave of the future. It is significant that while many prominent African-American communication and entertainment businesses are now being courted by and selling to large, multi-media corporations, others refuse to do so.[18] Yet both responses illustrate the continued belief in black entrepreneurship and capitalism.

Beyond the relationship between capitalism and business, communications-entertainment industries also offer the opportunity to transform black life and the way the larger society views African-Americans. In 1960, personal services and retailing accounted for more than half of all minority enterprises. Between 1960 and 1980, however, growth in minority enterprises occured outside of traditional lines of business. Communication was one those businesses (Jaynes and Williams 1989: 315). Initially, cinema stood as the ground by which transformation was thought to take place. Whether it was filmmaker Oscar Micheaux's prolific creative career as a filmmaker and novelist, early film production companies like the Lincoln Brothers, or later, the impulse of Melvin Van Peebles' film *Sweet Sweetback's Baadasssss Song* (1971), communications media have taken a leading role in its perceived ability to illuminate, subvert, and possibly overturn the devastating and lingering effects of slavery, racism, and exclusion from capitalistic progress.

Examples bear this idea out with Elijah Muhammad's 1963 Economic Blueprint plan. In it, technology and communication garnered its own line item—with the newspaper *Muhammad Speaks* at the top of the list. Since the early 1980s, educational consultant and entrepreneur Jawanza Kunjufu used his publication house, African American Images, as a platform for proselytizing on everything black—from the raising of black boys to business development for African-Americans. And broadcaster and scholar Tony Brown employs his long-running syndicated television program, *Tony Brown's Journal* and book publication as a platform for the value of black capitalism.

As should be evident, Robert L. Johnson's idea for BET followed in a long tradition of black business acumen and information dissemination. While the name Black Entertainment Television expressed its intention, the company's marketing relied on the legacy and impetuses of the black press for black communities' support. Johnson's entrepreneurship and vision developed with an assumption of capitalism's value for and within black communities and with knowledge of this population's craving for representation—as is alluded to in Aaron McGruder's strip (Figure 1.6). Moreover, as cultural critic bell hooks argued, Johnson (and others) make "selling blackness" their biggest commodity. "They make sure they mask their agenda so black capitalism looks like black self-determination" (hooks 2000: 94). Examining the confluence of capitalism, class, and black media provides needed background into both the ideological foundation and impulse of BET's business development and consumer-defining goals. As will become evident through the forthcoming chapters, BET benefits from and depends upon circulating black binaries of power and wealth, representation and invisibility. In its quest for existence and then prominence, BET has developed into the leading provider of U.S. black imagery.

Figure 1.6 The Boondocks. THE BOONDOCKS © (2003) Aaron McGruder. Dist. By Universal Press Syndicate. Reprinted with permission. All rights reserved.

Chapter 2

Now That's Black!

BET Business

Communications must be in the hands of Blacks for the purpose of developing a Black identity through which national liberation can be achieved. It must advance our respective religions, recapture and explain our true history, aid in the education and use of political, economic, social and community organizations ... Communications is the cornerstone in the struggle for our survival.

> —Tony Brown, Coordinator's Statement—
> First Modern Pan-African Congress 1972

The Black business class and their representatives in power don't know how to liberate anybody—they know how to get paid.

> —Bruce Dixon, Black Mecca: The Death of an Illusion—
> *The Black Commentator* 2005

As suggested in the introduction and chapter 1, the success of Black Entertainment Television can be attributed to a multiplicity of factors—factors that overlap and shift. They include the dearth of African-American television representation, belief in black capitalism, the rise of cable, the centrality of music in black culture, and the explosion of hip hop and hip hop's attendant shaping. Along with the waging of capitalism, class divisions, and black business mantras, these phenomena help make BET significant to black and world popular culture.

In the book *The Billion Dollar BET*, journalist Brett Pulley wrote a convincing historical account of the founding and development of Black Entertainment Television. Centering Robert Louis Johnson's narrative, Pulley employed interviews conducted over several years and new ones as grounding for his work. With this engaging text already circulating, the goal of this chapter is not to reiterate BET's history but rather, to trace key developments of BET as an image-making business and the methods by which it set and achieved its goals. Using the aforementioned factors as a framework, this chapter addresses BET as a capitalist enterprise—a paradoxical black business that melds blackness with profit.

The Cable Business

To understand BET's evolution, the U.S. television industrial, regulatory, and cultural landscape must be examined. I begin with the emergence of the cable industry that has actually had a fairly short history in the world of visual representation. However, as discussed in my article, "Narrowcasting on the Information Super-Highway," huge differences characterize the largely monopolistic cable industry of today and its predecessor of just fifty years ago. Cable's initial design to provide television reception to remote areas of the country in the 1950s morphed with the arrival of the satellite in the late 1960s. Satellite technology prepared cable to move from being just a conduit for broadcast signals to a producer of content. The idea of expanded cable capabilities fostered a "Blue Sky" discourse—one insisting that the world would become a different, better place with cable. The chorus of voices predicted cable linkages to banking, retail, entertainment, and news, all through the little wire and all for consumers' benefit (Streeter 1997). These benefits seemingly made the case for governmental deregulation. Not unlike most U.S. avenues of work, the cable industry was reportedly then very white and slow to change in terms of employment, rank, responsibility, and programming (Gupta 1981: 94). Yet for people of color and those concerned with their representation, cable was marketed as the cure all for a very white television world.[1]

In 1975, Home Box Office (HBO) aired the Muhammad Ali versus Joe Frazier fight via satellite. The "Thrilla in Manilla" bout launched that network to profitability and set cable on its course. Cable scholars Patrick R. Parsons and Robert M. Frieden maintained: "As HBO began signing up systems and customers for a regular schedule of uncut, uninterrupted films and sport events, it was raising the curtain on a new era in national telecommunications technology and business" (Parsons and Frieden 1998: 54). Cable for consumer entertainment exploded the formerly closed world of network television.

Over the span of broadcast and cable's histories, the Federal Communications Commission (FCC) implemented policies to regulate and control these expanding industries. Many of these regulations directly impacted African-American and larger minority access and entry into this business arena. In 1978, for example, the FCC issued a "Statement of Policy on Minority Ownership of Broadcast Facilities" to address what it perceived as a lack of minority broadcast ownership in the U.S. At that time, minorities controlled less than one percent of all existing television stations. Believing that minority participation in the nation's broadcast industry would result in more diverse programming, the FCC pledged to issue tax credits to broadcasters that agreed to sell their stations to parties "where minority ownership is in excess of 50 percent or controlling" (Center for Digital Democracy 16 December 2002).

Ironically the program was canceled, in some measure, because of an African-American businessman's application and the ensuing litigation that followed. The Mitgo Corporation, a company owned by black entrepreneur Frank Washington, became the poster child for the abuse of the program. Washington was part of a 2.3 billion dollar deal put together by himself and two white-owned companies with Viacom, Inc. The deal disintegrated when critics successfully argued that Washington served only as a front man for the white-owned operations due to his minimal capital contribution to the project. Following this 1995 fiasco, Congress repealed the minority tax certificate program.

The 1996 Telecommunications Act—an act that brought the most sweeping changes in communications policy since the creation of the FCC in 1934—further crippled minorities' ability to participate in ownership by lifting several legal and regulatory restrictions to open competition between the telephone, cable, satellite, broadcast, and utility companies. Ostensibly, these changes made way for an escalated building of multimedia empires—conglomerates that subsume but were not themselves owned by minority concerns. So when subsequent legislation was introduced to give companies who sold to minorities, small businesses, and new industry entrants a deferment of capital gains taxes in 1997, Robert L. Johnson called it a token gesture—claiming that doing so might force cable systems to make different choices—elimination choices—about certain network carriage. Johnson queried: "Why should we take BET off, take Discovery off, the History channel? So incumbent [broadcasters] can continue their dominance?" (McConnell 1999: 19). Self-serving as his protest was, it illustrated the short-sightedness (or perhaps tokenness) of federal efforts to shape the industry. In this new media world, the focus of all parties turned almost exclusively to profit—thereby making black-owned (and other minority-owned concerns) less advantageous as they target smaller markets.

Thus in a different context but with the same impetus post-BET's sale, Johnson sang differently in an article appearing in the *Financial Times* London: "You can't [reach the top of the media industry] as a black-owned business; there isn't that much capital. You have to do it as a white-owned business with black management" (quoted in Adetunji, 1 October 2002). In June 2003, the FCC voted to allow for even more media to be controlled by a few large corporations with the idea that the market would address issues of programming diversity and access. The trend of deregulation (aside from issues of indecency) and market fixes predominated the thinking of the Kevin Martin chaired FCC. Furthermore, the FCC continued to revisit the idea of "ala carte"—a scenario that would allow consumers to choose and only pay for the networks that they want to see as well as ones that serve in their best interest.[2]

This best-interest notion impacted BET as it was founded with the understanding and value of the "public good" and "public interest" looming large in the minds of black folks and well-intentioned policy makers. Some argue that the public's interest actually defines the public trust (Brenner 210)—as opposed to possessing objective criteria of its own. This mindset was clear as illustrated in a 1969 Presidential Task Force on Communication Policy recommendation that stated: "by allowing minorities and disaffected groups an outlet to express themselves and to communicate with the nation, [cable television] might reduce their feelings of alienation from American society." And thus, said cable scholar Thomas Streeter, "help to target the problems that had brought social unrest" (Streeter quoted in Wible 2004: 38). However in *Viewers Like You?*, media scholar Laurie Ouellette disputed this altruistic underpinning.

She asserted that in early policy formation, "the term *minority* was used in broadcast reform discourse primarily as a euphemism for educated white people with uncommonly sophisticated cultural tastes (146) ... race and class [were] for 'other people'" (Ouellette 2002: 174). If this plausible interpretation is to be accepted, the emergence of BET made perfect sense for early eighties U.S. culture. Ja'net DuBois had been singing about "Moving on Up" for five years by 1980.[3] African-Americans were being ushered into middle management and away from marching in the streets but rarely saw themselves reflected on television. The initial vision Johnson possessed for BET embraced a middle-class taste sensibility—one valued by educated white folks and aspiring black folks alike.

Yet in some ways conceding Johnson's earlier point, scholar Mara Einstein argued that the governmental and popular focus of ownership was ill-conceived. In *Media Diversity: Economics, Ownership, and the FCC* she maintained:

What we really want when we say diversity is quality programming, whether it is public affairs programs, children's programming, or yes, even entertainment programming. Instead, what regulation has done

is support broadcasters over new media options, forced programmers to come up with new economic models to compete in an overly
crowded media environment, and perpetuated an economic system
of 24-hour-per-day program service based on advertising support,
which perforce creates redundancy and inexpensive programming
(Einstein 2004: 38).[4]

Einstein made valid points especially in terms of audiences'
actual desires and exorbitant programming costs. But it seems she
overlooked the larger picture—one where people trying to play in
this arena were already priced out. These people included almost
all people of color. So it really didn't matter whether diversity was
voiced as bodies, visual representation, or content. While marketers positioned cable as the surest and most innovative way to make
television more profitable and to address issues of diversity—diversity still mostly defined by race and gender—Streeter argued that
the "discourse's predictions of abundant, diverse programming for
all have not been fully realized" (Streeter 1997: 237).

In 2007, blacks controlled only 20 of the 1,762 U.S. broadcast
television stations or about 1%. And with the enormous costs in
acquiring and maintaining technology, the propensity to consoli-
date, and continued federal deregulation, the twenty are likely to
decrease. In cable, systems grew from approximately 2,490 in 1970
to over 11,000 in 1995, dwindling to 7,090 by 2006. According to
the National Cable & Telecommunications Association, the number of basic subscribers escalated from 29 million in 1982 to over
65 million in 2006—a 58% penetration of all television households.[5]
For premium cable subscribers, (i.e., HBO, Showtime, Cinemax),
the subscriber estimate was over fifty million. In fact according to
the Cable Television Advertising Bureau, in 2006–2007, 54% of
all TV viewing is of cable networks. African-American ownership
of cable systems is zero. As of May 2007, the ownership (or partial
ownership) of national (or semi-national) cable networks stood at
TV One.

Although regulatory and economic constraints plagued it, cable
helped propel a transformation in the entertainment and information industry. Literally hundreds of cable networks, subnetworks,

and micronetworks exist—with hundreds more in development, despite the bleak outlook for start-ups. Beyond the expansion of satellite and the hype, the growth of cable networks and cable viewing has been predicated on corporations and audiences embracing the idea of narrowcasting. Narrowcasting, the targeting of niche audiences, became the 1980s buzzword. Since then, narrowcasting has not only been the sole way that cable exists, (with more general cable networks redefining—or branding—themselves), but also the lens by which broadcast networks have tried to figure out how to make themselves more distinctive in this continually growing, yet narrowing mediascape. BET is known in the industry as a theme network. Its content (at least up to mid-2007) has been rather narrow (with claims of broadness) with a purported narrow (black folks) target audience.

In their 1991 cable channel diversity study, communication scholars Allard S. De Jong and Benjamin J. Bates concluded that although growth in diversity had occurred in absolute terms, relative (content) diversity remained substantially less than its potential. In trying to reach large audiences, cable's claim for targeting specific interests was undermined. " ... [L]ess than one-third of the potential diversity is available to basic subscribers ... [It could be] like the basic notion of cable itself, additional diversity is available to those who are willing to pay extra for it" (De Jong and Bates 1991: 163–164). According to a 1995 study, television diversity existed primarily because of niche programming. The study maintained if " ... it were not for channels such as Black Entertainment Television and two independent Spanish language channels, the overall proportions of Blacks and Hispanics appearing on TV in this study would have been substantially lower than their proportion in the actual population as measured by the 1990 census. So across non-niche channels, television remains disproportionately White" (Kubey 1995: 467). While this study is more than a decade old, the television world has not changed substantially. As communication scholars Daniel G. McDonald and Shu-Fang Lin argued in their analysis of television diversity from 1986 to 2000: "Although overall diversity has increased, the traditional television networks have remained fairly constant in their level of diversity. The new cable and other nontraditional channels rose quickly to levels comparable to those of the traditional broadcast networks and, within a few years, surpassed the traditional networks' program diversity" (McDonald and Lin 2004: 117). Looking at the limited scope that existed prior, this is simultaneously both encouraging and discouraging. Furthermore, the Center for Digital Democracy contended that the cable industry has outright lied about programming diversity on many issues. It claimed, for example, that Viacom refused to allow BET to expand its news and programming services (Center for Digital Democracy 16 December 2002). True or not, BET's news offerings have continually dwindled.

Nonetheless in 2006, some organizations—organizations that simultaneously advocate for rights and representation such as the NAACP and GLAAD—insisted that cable serves their constituents better than broadcast. When economists examine the cable industry, they assess whether people (consumers) are willing to pay more than the service is worth.[6] According to the Cable Television Advertising Bureau and others including BET, advertisers still routinely undervalue African-American audiences. They fail to distinguish them across age, education, income levels, and lifestyles. And most still do not get the race thing—the disparities in the ways African-Americans and whites view the actualities of the present. Thus, for black-owned media providers (radio, television, cable), just getting equitable advertising rates for its audience continues to be a challenge. Despite these conundrums, the opportunities presented by cable and the lack of black representation made the media environment ripe for the entrance of a BET.

Number One—Robert L. Johnson and BET

Americans love firsts—the first to the moon, the first to hit a baseball milestone (with stats created perpetually to illuminate more firsts), the first this and the first that. In the fight for equality, fairness, and recognition, African-Americans in particular seem to cling to "firsts" as symbols of progress. Robert Louis Johnson garnered a surfeit of firsts in the twenty-seven years since he launched BET. He provided the first cable television network featuring African-Americans and dedicated to African-American audiences. He was the first to have a black-owned company on the New York Stock Exchange. He became the country's first black billionaire when he sold that network for $3 billion.[7] And despite its 80% black-player base, Johnson turned out to be the first black owner of a major sports team, (the NBA Charlotte Bobcats), in 2003 (Figure 2.1).

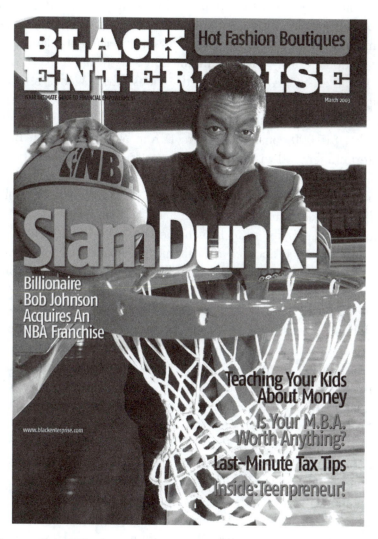

Figure 2.1 *Black Enterprise* magazine, March 2003.

When Johnson's story is told, it follows in the path of American iconography. Born poor in Hickory, Mississippi in 1946, the ninth child of a blue-collar family of ten, Johnson was determined to be the first in his family to finish college.[8] He was. One thing his parents instilled in him and his siblings was to be self-sufficient. To that end after earning a bachelor's degree from the University of Illinois and a Princeton master's degree in public administration, Johnson worked for the Corporation for Public Broadcasting as the public affairs director, the Washington Urban League as director of communications, and as vice president for government relations for the National Cable & Telecommunications Association (NCTA).

While at NCTA, he cultivated various advantageous relationships to help him toward his dream of starting a black television station. So while the story of his acquiring a $15,000 bank loan and another $15,000 consulting contract from NCTA to launch Black Entertainment Television in 1979 seems true, Johnson also began with $500K in support from media mogul John Malone of Telecommunications Inc. (TCI) along with a slot on the UA-Columbia Cablevision satellite. These additional variables played a critical role in Johnson's ability to launch the network. A couple of years later, he obtained another 20% financial partner, Taft Broadcasting Company, in exchange for $1 million in order to enhance BET beyond its two-hour block of programs on Friday nights (Pulley 2004: 52).

Johnson's relationship with TCI's Malone has been especially interesting in that they remained business partners for the duration of Johnson's ownership of BET but neither characterized their affiliation as friendship. Said Johnson, "My relationship with John Malone is strictly business. I've known him for 21 years. I've been in his house all of four times. Yet I've made more money with him than anybody" (quoted in Pulley 2004: 42). This confined business relationship to non-social interaction summons Booker T. Washington's hand philosophy. The connecting aspect of Washington's thoughts to Johnson were: "In all things that are purely social we can be as separate as the fingers, yet one as the hand in all things essential to mutual progress" (Washington 1895: 4). However the previous larger context of Washington's comments lends insight here as well when he stated:

> As we have proved our loyalty to you in the past, in nursing your children, watching by the sick bed of your mothers and fathers, and often following them with tear dimmed eyes to their graves, so in the future in our humble way, we shall stand by you with a devotion that no foreigner can approach, ready to lay down our lives, if need be, in defense of yours, interlacing our industrial, commercial, civil, and religious life with yours in a way that shall make the interests of both races one (Washington 1895: 4).

Figure 2.2 Robert L. Johnson.

Figure 2.3 John Malone.

African-Americans and white Americans share an historic, tortured relationship. That the way of business is all about the Benjamins contradicts all the scientific, scholarly, and anecdotal evidence to the contrary. While the partnership of integration and commerce defies the foundation of capitalism and belies the history of the U.S., social interaction always matters—especially in business.[9] Thus many of the accusations of Mitgo's puppetdom dogged Johnson regarding Malone. Furthermore, BET emerged just ahead of Ronald Reagan's presidency. Reagan rode in on the ideas of U.S. sovereignty, a Christian God reigning, and the reclamation of the nation by the right and white. Conservatism has always been a part of the capitalist ideology to maintain order and structure—something BET offered in the beginning.

Before BET, the closest thing to national television programming targeted at blacks was Sunday morning community program slots (or the one PBS turned commercially syndicated program *Tony Brown's Journal* 1978–Present), periodic nods to black sitcoms, and *Soul Train* (1970–Present). Robert L. Johnson's 1980 promotional tape alerted cable operators and advertisers to this dearth and promoted BET as a much-needed alternative *and* an ignored business opportunity. To these groups, he insisted that BET would provide a marketing tool to attract the black consumer, "the youngest, fastest growing in the country and most concentrated." Johnson asserted that BET would provide a quality black programming package with the widest and highest audience appeal (movies, specials, and sports); BET had the ability to reach black consumers with distinct consumption patterns and who spent more than $70 billion each year; and BET offered you, (cable provider or advertiser), the opportunity to be one of the first to capture the attention of this key market and build loyalty in it (Johnson 1980) (Figure 2.4).

Six national companies became the network's charter sponsors: Anheuser-Busch (BET's exclusive beer advertiser beginning in 1982), *Time*, Champale, Pepsi-Cola, Sears, and Kellogg. BET began with two hours of weekly programming to over 4.5 million homes. The first program to air at 11:00 pm on that January 25, 1980 night was the African-American film, *A Visit to a Chief's Son* (Lamont

Johnson 1974). Mid–1980, the company announced plans to spend $1 million to produce black college sports and special events. BET began airing 24 hours per day in 1983. And by the end of the decade in April 1989, BET moved into a new 10 million dol-lar studio in Washington, D.C.—

Figure 2.4   BET Logo.

later expanding the site into a corporate campus with an office tower. Like in the film *Boomerang* (Reginald Hudlin, 1992), Vice President of Entertainment Programming Curtis Gadson affirmed this auspicious facility and its inhabitants (Figure 2.5). "When I first walked into BET, I saw a sea of black people doing the same jobs that I had always seen only whites doing elsewhere. … I was almost in tears. The playing field was all of a sudden equal" (quoted in Pulley 2001). BET turned a profit six years after its inception, seemingly, a successful capitalist rite-of-passage.

BET achieved profitability due to its low programming costs. From 1990 to 1998, BET added about four million subscribers per year. It outlined its three major business goals as 1) to become the dominant medium used by advertisers to target the black consumer marketplace, 2) to become the dominant medium engaged in the production and distribution of quality black-oriented entertainment

Figure 2.5   *Boomerang.*

and information to cable television households, and 3) to use the powers of the medium to contribute to the cultural and social enrichment of the network's viewing audience. It was the first black-owned company to issue stock on the New York Stock Exchange in November 1991, generating $72 million.[10] Johnson and Malone took BET back private at $63 per share or $380 million in 1998. By 2000, nearly 70% of its network programming was music videos, supplied free from record companies, or music-related product.

In Johnson's quest to position his company as the preeminent supplier of black Americans to advertisers, he targeted three areas for expansion: entertainment, leisure products, and information. To that end beyond the BET Network, he created other cable channels: BET on Jazz: The Cable Jazz Channel (now BETJ),[11] Action Pay-Per-View, BET Movies/Starz3, and BET International. In publishing, BET Holdings acquired *Emerge* Magazine (later renamed *Savoy* and refocused more on entertainment and less on political and socio-cultural insight). The company introduced *YSB* (a magazine targeted at teens) and *BET Weekend*, a monthly newspaper insert. *YSB, BET Weekend*, and *Savoy* are no longer published.[12] The company purchased Arabesque Books (black romance novels) in 1998 and began to turn them into BET feature films in 1999. In terms of leisure products, Johnson built the BET Sound Stage Restaurant in Largo, Maryland, to capitalize on the BET brand and expanded that venture to Disney World and Las Vegas. It launched a Visa credit card and a clothing line. And for the focus on information, in 1996 BET partnered with Microsoft to launch bet.com with Microsoft's Bill Gates saying in a company press release: "It's a great combination of BET's strong leadership and experience in this market and Microsoft's leading-edge technology." In 2007, the website ranked as the second most popular destination for African-Americans according to Alexa Internet Research.[13] Johnson entered all of these new arenas as joint ventures with other corporations—lessening the financial outlay but with BET retaining content control.

With the sale of BET to Viacom in 2000, the business maneuvers of Johnson regarding the network seemed complete. BET now answered to the Viacom Corporation. Yet Johnson's departure ended only one era of the network's presence. In the initial press statements of the purchase, Viacom president Mel Karmazin queried: "How can you [corporations] justify these lower rates [to BET] other than discrimination? And obviously, you don't want to discriminate. BET has been getting its prices up but we think we can accelerate the process" (*New York Times*, 4 November 2000). This pronouncement suggested that now any big white-man company could successfully walk softly by articulating the discourses of diversity and race that minority companies employ while carrying the big stick of a media empire—Johnson insinuating this assumption prior.

The business trajectory of BET has been ambitious, strategic, and clearly lucrative for its key personnel.[14] However on a scale never seen before, BET promoted and offered up African-Americans as a brand—"an iconic brand that has penetrated the mindset of society."[15] Like soda, detergent, and shoes, BET has always aimed to sell black folks like any other merchandise. Clearly the phenomenon of targeting a particular demographic is a well-worn marketing practice. But in this instance, black folks were both the customer consuming and the *product* to be consumed—a paradox that calls for mediation.

Branding Blackness

In the same way the military calls for discipline, skills acquisition, and mental manipulation, especially transparent in times of war, Americans undergo capitalistic indoctrination. Before a baby's birth, she is branded with the accoutrements of products from Disney, Baby Gap, and Sesame Street. This in-womb branding represents capitalism at its best. For the past two decades, the expanded idea of branding has swept businesses across the country and the world. The brand, (the trade name, distinguishing image, symbol, or slogan and consumer feelings about those), gives value and meaning to services offered or products sold. Management strategist Vincent Grimaldi asserted that "branding is the blend of art and science that manages associations between a brand and memories in the mind of the brand's audience. It involves focusing resources on selected tangible and intangible attributes to differentiate the brand in an attractive, meaningful and compelling way for the targeted audience" (2003). Brand executive Jeremy Sampson added that ultimately, a brand is "a relationship that secures future earnings by securing customer loyalty" (quoted in Melewar 2003: 157). Branding is an important aspect of a company's marketing plan and increasingly, an integral part of its overall business strategy.

In 1981, long-time marketing consultants Al Ries and Jack Trout suggested that businesses needed a more effective way to communicate with the public given the increasing over saturation of competing media. They called this way positioning and contended: "Positioning starts with a product. A piece of merchandise, a service, a company, an institution, or even a person ... But positioning is not what you do to a product. Positioning is what you do to the mind of the prospect. That is, you position the product in the mind of the prospect" (Ries and Trout: 1986). While many of their arguments were taken to task,[16] their ideas and comments are still widely regarded and implemented in corporations and marketing firms alike.

When BET began in 1980, African-Americans on television represented about six percent of all characters featured in television narrative (Greenberg and Collette 1999). In his aforementioned promotional video to lure advertisers, Johnson hawked that African-Americans were an untapped market, a group that had been ignored, and a blue-chip investment. In these descriptors, one finds that Johnson banked on and offered up a monolithic black—in no way dissimilar to the way that the Nielsen Ratings Company mostly measures black and brown consumer audiences sans generation, class, ethnicity, or gender—just black and brown.

Beyond the visual lack factor, Johnson connected with the surging mantra of some in the 1980s to "buy Black." As the Director of Communications for the Washington, D.C. chapter of the Urban League, he recognized and understood the call for African-Americans to start and patronize black-owned businesses as a form of acquiring and asserting civil rights. Writers noted BET's direct appeal to African-Americans to support this infant enterprise—as a show of unity and collective advancement. According to *Black Enterprise*, Johnson was confident that the BET brand name could become the company's greatest asset. Achieving sustained growth by 1997, BET's buying back of its stock allowed it to expand in many different directions including restaurants, cosmetics, event promotion, and book publishing. Journalist Tariq K. Muhammad confirmed: "'Extending the brand' is now the company's mantra, punctuating conversations with executive vice presidents and mid-level managers alike" (Muhammad June 1997). Johnson envisioned his company as the preeminent supplier of black Americans to advertisers *in everything*. In both *Watching Race* and *Cultural Moves*, sociologist Herman S. Gray situated ideas of blackness within the contexts of its competing deployments. Used as a "cultural trope and social category," blackness referred to the "constellation of productions, histories, images, representations, and meanings associated with black presence in the United States" (Gray 2005: 19; 1995: 12).

Over the years, BET has employed various marketing slogans to characterize the network and identify with its consumers. In the early part of the twenty-first century, it offered "Now, That's Black." In honor of its 25th anniversary, the 2005 logo became "It's My Thing"—billed as "more down to earth" and focused on the audience. But the one that had the most staying power thus far and the greatest implication to the ideas presented here, is "BET, Black Star Power."

Black Star Power

The branding strategy of BET suggests that everything within African-American culture falls under its purview. The BET brand has emerged as young, black, urban, and hip. Movement (bodies, cameras, and graphics), material signs of prosperity, and music serve as its calling card. Perpetuated in various visual and developing technologies (including the Internet, ring tones, and wireless BET Mobile), the branding of BET entailed coalescing the African diaspora around BET name recognition and entertainers (music and sports) and forwarding BET as a lifestyle. Johnson aimed for BET to be black America's brand of choice.

Yet for the first time in 1999, the BET Network hired an outside image consultant to help with its reach. BET's problem—while 95% of African-Americans recognized the BET brand—that brand connected in most consumers' minds to music videos. BET wanted audiences to believe that the network was more than that (Hogan 2003).[17] Veronica Hutchinson, former vice president of creative services, created the slogan "Black Star Power" for the network in 1999. In this slogan, the network implied that BET helped not only to create successful artists—making them available for spectator consumption—but also that the network's audience played a role as well by watching them. Another way to think about "Black Star Power" is that the people, the stars, important to African-Americans, received validation and thus, power on BET. One example of how this particular interpretation resonates in popular culture was found in the June 27, 2003, news brief on SOHH.com, a hip hop site. It read:

> As Jay-Z stated on his 1996 debut Reasonable Doubt, "you can't knock the way a ni99a eatin ... " You may not like the kicks, but please don't front on the way these rap powerhouses have come together to cross-promote like true capitalists. It almost makes you wanna weep seeing two young black men put aside ego, show respect for each other's craft and get that white man's green. Now that's "black star power" ... for real (The Penguin 27 June 2003).

Thus in this vein, entertainers making money provided the real black star power. Or perhaps another way to look at Black Star Power is that BET possesses power due to its ability to air bona fide black and up-and-coming stars. Since entertainers or stars clearly are considered a form of capital in the media industries, black star power resonates as a *ching, ching* in the pocket of BET—thus, these stars reflect tangible commodities to use and profit from and by BET.[18]

The phrase "Black Star Power" may even pose a mild threat because in many ways, it invokes the radicalness of the 1960s and 1970s black power movement. With that black power—minus the star—a call for self-determination, self-respect, and self-defense was made, at least as articulated by US advocates and others.[19] Thus with this reading, African-American entertainers appearing on BET possibly strengthen their collective bargaining position within the industry. Whichever reading dominates, the coinage of "Black Star Power" encouraged a certain black solidarity that belied its capitalistic and divisional underpinnings. It also ignored the fact that Black Entertainment Television used black bodies to sell to advertisers while at the same time these same entertainers and spectators were to consume themselves—a paradoxical situation at best—now being used by others wanting to target specific ethnic audiences.[20]

This begs the business question of whether BET is dissimilar to any targeted cable network. For example, Lifetime: Television for Women provides programming about women targeted to women. The programming makes assumptions about gendered emotions and behaviors. Yet what distinguishes its approach from BET's is that it takes into account, albeit limitedly, race, class, and generation. It offers women in different roles and within different genres. BET, on the other hand, targets and offers demographic black programming seemingly designed for any African-American of any region, age, gender, economic status, or educational background. In fact, it actually targets one demographic, black youth—but not according to its own stated business philosophies.

Beyond this consolidation of difference, on the surface BET has applied the seventeenth century definition of blackness—the one-drop rule. This rule considered anyone possessing an African ancestor in the U.S., African-American. So visually, the extremely light, multiracial Mariah Carey to the never-going-to-pass Missy Elliott, all find themselves a part of the racially "Black" part of the BET moniker. While this embracing of various visual signifiers of African-America appears to be progressive and inclusive, it actually validates the racist assumptions of the one-drop rule and smears it across generation, gender, and class.

Moreover, questioning what actually is black enough, if physical features are key, remains unconsidered. An observation by anthropologist Rita Laura Segato about the fake construction of ethnicities in the U.S. yielded her comments that "despite the apparent loyalty to the 'race' struggle on the part of African-Americans classified by descent, it is still possible to question the obvious and exemplary cosmetic 'bleaching' of the artists of Black Entertainment

Television" (Segato: 233). Ultimately, Lifetime's target demographic of women fails to generate debates about humanity in the way that BET's targeting of blackness does—it, however, raises serious questions about women's commodification.[21]

Furthermore, one unrelated reflection of sociologist E. Franklin Frazier suggested a different way of thinking about the relationship of cable network to entertainer to consumer. In *Black Bourgeoisie*, he wrote, artists' "prestige is [owed] partly to the glamour of their personalities, but more especially to their financial success, which is due to their support by the white world" (1957: 109). In other words, Black Star Power may have less to do with BET and more to do with the entertainer's own consumer bling. Media scholar Todd Boyd broadened this idea when he talked about the "come up" as representing social mobility in hip hop's narratives. He wrote: "The expression of this upward mobility by these lower-class individuals, flossin' on one's cars, homes, clothes, money, and lifestyle, has become commonplace. As Biggie often said, 'Money, clothes and hoes, all a nigga knows'" (Boyd 2003: 77). So actually, the Black Star Power that BET claimed may be just a refraction of the entertainers' aired luminance—itself a refraction of white wealth and frighteningly, a secondary association of its brand.

When cultural anthropologist Arlene Dávila wrote about the construction of a Hispanic U.S. market in her book *Latinos, Inc.*, she commented on the making of one big black consumer market as well. She asserted:

> We can never lose sight of the fact that consumers are not all conceived as equally rational and hence "empowered" within a politics that prioritizes consumption; just as their needs are not considered worthy of attention by the powers that be ... I am skeptically cautious about the abundance of reports and discussions about Latinas as a market. Yes, Latinas are undoubtedly gaining visibility through such discussions, but only as a market, never as a people, and "markets" are vulnerable; they must be docile; they cannot afford to scare capital away. (Dávila 2001: 238)

Dávila's ideas about visibility and docility undoubtedly apply to BET and make all the more disquieting this branding of blackness.

What BET tapped into early on was the contempt for and willful inability of mass marketers to distinguish black folks. While BET claimed to target specifically 18- to 34-year-old African-Americans in 2006—a very specific and narrow demographic, it has also had targeted programs for 12- to 17-year-olds (*Teen Summit*), 34+ year olds (*Our Voices with Bev Smith, Bobby Jones Gospel*), and those in between. When pushed about it, officials like CEO Debra L. Lee stated: "People think because we target African-Americans that we're narrowcasting, but the truth is, we can't narrowcast. We can't be MTV and only appeal to a particular age group, because we have all age groups. We have to be full service" (quoted in Leigh 2000). Yet this statement reflects the double speak that BET often employs as on other occasions, Lee said: "We've realized you can't be all things to all people. That makes you schizophrenic, and then people don't know what to expect. We try to service the [older] demographic through bet.com with news, plus the Sunday gospel and family movie programming. We reach both audiences with our annual Walk of Fame special, during which younger artists pay tribute to legends. That has worked well for us, so we'll continue to do specials that have broad audience appeal" (quoted in Mitchell 2005).

More broadly, many scholars bemoan the cultural transformation of citizens to consumers. Scholar and filmmaker Saul Landau wrote in *The Business of America*:

> The profit-making TV world conditions each viewer to think of himself or herself as the center of the universe, the person whose highly individual "tastes" make the mass market function. Given the illusion TV creates of such potential power, it is small wonder that TV advertising then inculcates the notion of personal insufficiency as the viewer's only measure of himself (Landau 2004: 74).

Once again, this idea brings to mind the "Blue Sky" discourses of cable and cablers' ability to transform our landscape—but in this case, to individuals' very own specification.

In an NPR interview, Johnson said of BET's sale to Viacom "the time is now where strong African-American brands with tremendous value should put themselves in league with strong general market brands that can add even greater value ... I see this as a positive development ... And I hope one day there will be other African-American companies that create the kind of value created at BET" (quoted in Prakash 2000).[22] Organizations such as the National Association of Black Owned Broadcasters applauded the sale as a very positive development stating in part "we would, of course, prefer to see BET remain an African American owned company, however, it appears that the parties have negotiated a very fair deal and one which allows BET to continue to be an important voice for the African American community" (NABOB 29 November 2000). Others called it an end of an era. However, it seems to me, that the move reflects business as usual.

In that last regard, some maintain that Robert L. Johnson had been consistent about his focus on building business rather than addressing social and cultural concerns or community uplift. Many others insist that he had been duplicitous at best. For example, in the pages of *The Black World Today*, social and political activist Ron Daniels seethed remembering: " ... in Youngstown, Ohio, some years ago, I distinctly remember being called by representatives of a start up venture called BET to mobilize Black people to demand that the local cable company carry the programming of this embryonic network. Out of a sense of racial pride and social commitment, we did just that, and I am certain that scores of communities across the country did likewise" (Daniels 2000).

Journalist Brett Pulley confirmed Daniels assumption when he wrote: "To sign up cable operators and undercut the perception that the new channel would appeal only to blacks, Johnson shed the original name—Black Entertainment Television—calling it simply BET. Still, to build audience loyalty Johnson emphasized that this was a channel for black people, operated by black people. BET's salespeople visited black civic and social organizations across the country urging community leaders to lobby for their cable operators to carry the channel" (Pulley 2001). This strategy continued to obviously resonate as the Black Family Channel advertisements at the National Black MBA Conference in September 2005 show (Figures 2.6a and b).

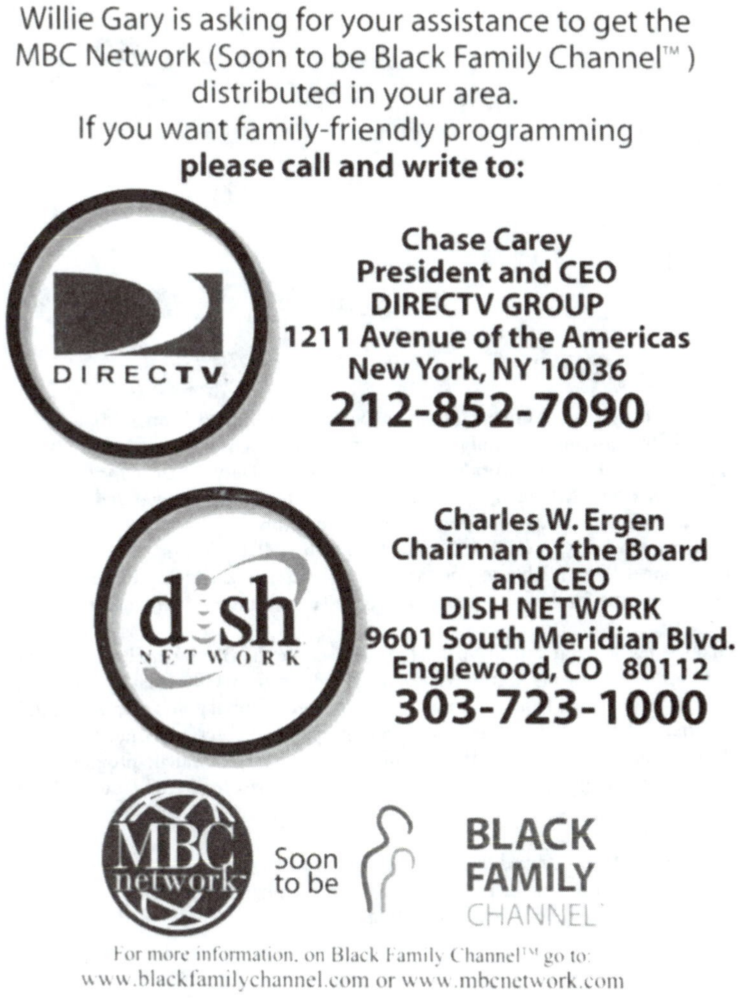
Willie Gary is asking for your assistance to get the
MBC Network (Soon to be Black Family Channel™)
distributed in your area.
If you want family-friendly programming
please call and write to:
DIRECTV
Chase Carey
President and CEO
DIRECTV GROUP
1211 Avenue of the Americas
New York, NY 10036
212-852-7090
dish NETWORK
Charles W. Ergen
Chairman of the Board
and CEO
DISH NETWORK
9601 South Meridian Blvd.
Englewood, CO 80112
303-723-1000
MBC network
Soon to be
BLACK
FAMILY
CHANNEL
For more information, on Black Family Channel™ go to:
www.blackfamilychannel.com or www.mbcnetwork.com

Figure 2.6a Advertisement for Black Family Channel.

Debra L. Lee was promoted from President to President and CEO in June 2005 as Johnson ended his five-year contract with Viacom. She asserted that BET's future would concentrate on original media development—television and film—rather than off-shoot endeavors. In doing so, BET attempted to solidify its position as *the* place to reach Black folks on cable. In fact, BET now claims to be the preeminent brand in African-American households.

SAMPLE LETTER

(Date)

[Name]
[Title]
[Company]
[Address]
[City, State, Zip]

SAMPLE LETTER

Dear [Name]:

I am aware that MBC Network (soon to be Black Family Channel ™) is a channel committed to providing family programming for African-Americans. It is my understanding that the network's executives, Willie Gary (*trial attorney*), Evander Holyfield (*boxing champion*), Cecil Fielder (*former major league baseball player*), Marlon Jackson (*member of the Jackson Five*) and Robert Townsend (*Hollywood actor director and producer*), are all dedicated to making MBC Network (soon to be Black Family Channel ™) available to your viewers. These men are highly respected amongst African-Americans for their accomplishments and contributions within our communities.

I am requesting that you launch MBC Network (soon to be Black Family Channel ™) on [DirecTV or Dish Network Here] to show your support for family-friendly programming. MBC (soon to be Black Family Channel ™) offers programming that empowers, informs, and entertains the entire family. As a parent and paying subscriber, I need to know that my dollars are earmarked for programming that I want to watch; programming that uplifts our communities – not tear them down. **I vote yes for MBC (soon to be Black Family Channel ™) on [DirecTV or Dish Network Here]!**

I thank you in advance for adding MBC (soon to be Black Family Channel ™) to your channel lineup. In a few days, I will follow up with a phone call to discuss the launch of MBC Network (soon to be Black Family Channel ™).

Sincerely,

(Your Name)

SAMPLE LETTER

Figure 2.6b   Sample letter for cable operators.

Yet in the name of making money, BET has led the way in several problematic business pursuits. For example, BET was the first network (cable or otherwise) to air liquor advertisements. Since 1936, the liquor industry had maintained a self-imposed ban on radio advertising and on television since 1948. While the broadcast networks continue the ban (in a similar effort as the liquor industry),

Crown Royal broke the liquor industry's self-imposed ban when it advertised on Black Entertainment Television in 1996. BET ran campaigns from both Joseph E. Seagram & Sons Inc. in 1996 and Hiram Walker & Sons in 1999. Since the late 1990s, a handful of other cable networks have aired some liquor ads as well (Pennock 2005).

When questioned about the judgment in running these ads, Johnson decried:

> Hypocrisy [!] ... You know, they were running liquor ads on Hispanic TV for five years, and nobody said a thing! But now when it's on regular TV, suddenly it's a health issue. Bullshit! I don't make money off liquor ads ... Maybe $60,000 ... That's out of $60 million in ad revenue. It's nothing. But ... it's the principle. Alcohol is alcohol. You don't see them rushing to take beer ads off the air, do you? (quoted in Mundy, 31 March 1997, *Mediaweek*).

He's correct in this. The hypocrisy of the media industry's stance regarding alcohol (and other stances like it) ground the mediascape and nation overall. Nonetheless, most cable programmers—from ESPN and Discovery Networks to Lifetime Television and the Turner networks—maintain that they have no plans to alter their stance against accepting liquor ads. And since by his own admission the money made was negligible, why contribute to the alcohol-related diseases that plague your target audience more than any other group if not for greed's sake?—principle, right.[23]

BET remains economically successful because it strictly follows the principle of profit. From airing free music videos to low pay, John Malone's advice to Johnson to "get your revenues up and keep your costs down" resonates within every aspect of the corporation (quoted in Pulley 2004: 41). The grumblings of low pay and poor treatment of employees are pervasive with former staffers of the network. For example after AFTRA (American Federation of Television and Radio Artists) published its grievances with BET in *Variety*, former *Comic View* host D.L. Hughley commented: "If a mainstream company were treating black people the way BET has and is, it would've been a big mess long before now ... Because it's black people mistreating black people, everyone's been hesitant to speak up. But wrong is wrong" (quoted in *Newsweek* 17 October 1999: online). I supply further illumination of this particular conundrum in writing about *Comic View* in chapter 3.

Connectedly in 1998, Urbanworld Film Festival Executive Director Stacy Spikes expressed that it would be difficult to convince African-American talent to work for Johnson given BET's reputation for low wages and union busting. Johnson countered: "If what we do is so rich in story and rich in character, they will come to this studio" (quoted in Katz 1998). Given the quality of aesthetics and narratives shown in their ten original films, Johnson's prediction hasn't quite materialized. More derisively, some suggest that BET functions like the parasitic animal system—a world where the symbiotic relationship benefits the parasite and causes definite harm to the parasite's partner or host. In this case, the African-American consumer and performer both serve as host with BET as the parasite—sucking the host silly. While this may be a harsh analogy, the relationship must be considered given its resonance in characterizing BET. Many of BET's business decisions may be attributed to having virtually no competition. It is indeed this lack that forces me to address where BET has faced contest—its competitors.

Competition

If capitalism prides itself on the viability of competition, BET has operated under a different system or at least, with a different set of

Figure 2.7a　The Boondocks. (The Boondocks) (2005) Aaron McGruder. Distributed by Universal Press Syndicate. Reprinted with permission. All rights reserved.

capitalist rules. For the existence of its life span, BET has run with virtually no competition. Like the cable industry at large that is, in the twenty-first century, just beginning to feel some heat from satellite, the term monopoly pretty aptly describes the situation—a market with many buyers (African-Americans) but only one seller (BET). While scholars such as economist Thomas Sowell have argued, "… where there is no power to exclude, there is no economically meaningful monopoly …" (Sowell 1994: 108). Others maintain that with about six corporations that control most radio, publishing, television, and film, "[u]ltimately what you're talking about is fewer choices, fewer journalists in the field, fewer foreign news bureaus, fewer news stories, fewer programming choices available … Diversity of channels does not give you diversity of content" (Ben Bagdikian quoted in Lasica 2002)—a point of which finds validation in what happens in the transforming media industries.

Johnson was not the only or the first African-American trying to gain entry into the potentially lucrative but expensive television business. In 1975, William V. Banks became the first black owner of a broadcast television station, WGPR-TV Detroit. In 1978, William T. Johnson joined two others to start KBLE-TV in Columbus, Ohio, the first black-owned cable television system in the nation.[24] Media entrepreneur John H. Johnson of Johnson Publishing also invested early in the promise of cable. Reminiscing in his autobiography *Succeeding Against the Odds*, Johnson said:

> When Chicago was wired for cable, I was one of the thirty-nine investors who agreed to put up $5 million in a joint venture with Continental Cable. But Continental executives wanted us to invest and leave the operating to them. This was unacceptable to me and other Black investors. The situation ultimately worked to my advantage. For Continental later withdrew from the Chicago market, and I am one of sixteen Black investors who own sizable shares in the company that is wiring the whole city (J. Johnson 1989: 334).

In 1982, entrepreneur Percy Sutton, owner of several radio stations nationally, sold his Detroit radio station to finance a joint venture with the black-owned Unity Broadcasting Network to purchase a cable television system. It began operations as Queens Inner Unity Cable System with the partnership of Warner Communications (Walker 1998: 323).

Since BET's launch, other cable network competitors have attempted to enter the fray such as the World African Network (WAN) in the mid 1990s. Based in Los Angeles and New York, the World African Network promised a new vision of Africans in the diaspora. The channel itself fell under the umbrella of the aforementioned Unity Broadcasting Network, started in 1987. Under the helm of Eugene Jackson, Unity served as a vehicle for the *Miss Collegiate African American Pageant* and subsequently, the black Greek stepping competition, *STOMP*.

Unlike BET, the World African Network was to operate as a premium channel. Premium channels require additional monies from its subscribers beyond the basic cable service due to their lack of advertisers. This reliance on subscriptions elevates its status—HBO for example. Once launched, it would stand as the only premium channel directed at an ethnic–based audience. WAN pledged programming that paired and compared Hollywood productions with exclusive African–American productions; promoted daily themes (such as "Diva Day" and "Echoes of Our Ancestors"); and focused on news and information about African-Americans. According to its 1993 company literature, the World African Network would unify African people worldwide by providing entertaining, informative, and culturally sensitive programming. Originally scheduled for a June 1994 launch, WAN failed to materialize as a cable channel.

The Major Broadcasting Cable Network (MBC Network) launched in June 1999. It offered MBC News, promising more depth and focus on African-American stories. MBC changed its name in 2004 to the Black Family Channel and brought in filmmaker and actor Robert Townsend as president and CEO. Citing new directions in the network, the change was to "redefine television by producing innovative and engaging family programs for black America. The Black Family Channel will continue the mission to solidify its position as the cable destination for the African-American viewer" (BFC 2004). The change also reflected principals of branding articulated by Al Ries and Laura Ries. Since the company

could never occupy the cachet
and familiarity of "first" as
BET held that honor, it could
be the "opposite of the leader"
(186) and do it differently (Ries
and Ries 2004: 191). Thus, the
Black Family Channel expressly
targeted one aspect of African-
America—25- to 54-year-olds
and the black family as a unit.

Figure 2.7b   Black Family
Channel logo.

As of 2005 according to the
Cabletelevision Advertising Bureau, Black Family Channel had
an estimated 14+ million viewers. Employing a similar marketing strategy as BET, Black Family Channel continued to push for
more subscribers and cable system space. The network's founders
were attorney Willie Gary, boxer Evander Holyfield, former baseball player Cecil Fielder, broadcaster Alvin D. Jones, and entertainer Marlon Jackson. These black cable capitalists realized that
this time, folks would not as easily come on board. In other words,
BET's betrayal and failure to live up to its promise gets replayed
on television daily. Despite all their efforts, on May 1, 2007, the
company announced that it would discontinue its cable presence
and move to the Web.

New Urban Entertainment (NUE-TV) launched in 2000 and
attempted to reach "a more sophisticated" African-American audience with a "mix of news, comedy, feature films, and inspirational
programming" (NUE-TV company literature). Yet even with the
backing of music mogul Quincy Jones, the network never achieved
the necessary $100 million start up cost to secure a national pres-
ence—this failure included withdrawal of support from Radio
One—as discussed below. The lack of funds combined with cablers'
decision not to put the network on their systems forced its founder
Dennis Brownlee to close the network in 2002.

The latest black entry to the cable television landscape is TV
One. Parented by a joint venture between Radio One, the seventh
largest radio chain and Comcast, the nation's largest cable opera-
tor, TV One entered the cable fray in January 2004. It became the

Figure 2.7c   TV One logo.

first *legitimate* potential competition to BET due to its secured national presence on Comcast cable systems. Run by Alfred C. Liggins III (with his mother, Catherine L. Hughes, founder of Radio One, in the background), the network aimed to be "in African American media what Univision (UVN) has become in Hispanic media" (quoted in Yang 2004).

Targeting the 25- to 54-year-old market, TV One offers more adult-oriented programming than BET. Said its president Johnathan Rodgers: "For a lot of people, the concept of programming for African-Americans was satisfied by simply having one channel … But when you looked closer at BET, you saw its audience was younger-skewing. BET is a marvelous channel for young people, both black and white. But what about the rest of us? There was no home base for African-American adult audiences. I want to be that home base" (Larson 2005). Emmy-winning producer Tim Reid (with his New Millennium Studios) is the senior executive supervising producer in charge of making original movies and series with Rose Catherine Pinkney as executive vice president of programming and production.[25] After three years of operation, TV One estimated its viewership at nearly 38 million. Corporations such as Lowe's, Ford, Allstate, Dell, Nabisco, Chevy, and UNCF advertised on the network. It has received marginally good reception from African-American reviewers such as Ronda Racha Penrice of AOL Black Voices. Yet despite its promise, both Johnson and Lee, at least in early 2004, refused to see them as competition (Yang 2004). TV One is predicted to break even within its first five years.

Although this may change soon, no cable network thus far has succeeded in gaining enough capital, cable space, or subscribers to effectively challenge BET. According to Paul Kagan Associates, in 1999 BET maintained the highest operating margin among basic cable networks. This was likely due to its reinvestment of only 16% of its total revenues into programming. In the final analysis, despite the presence of "good" intentions and marketing jargon, new channels need a funding base—a base that ultimately affects their ability to act in the audience's interest. Some argue that with viewers' ability to choose what they watch (or link to with the Internet) commercials may face obsolescence. Yet because advertising drives these new industries, as it does the old ones, assurances of commercial participation prevail. Like everything else, advertisers morph with the medium. According to Michael Rogers, *Newsweek Interactive* creator: "There's going to be a lot more full sponsorship, in the sense that you won't be able to get a service without sitting through an ad" (Krantz 1993: S29). Macro Media's George Canter added: "That's assuming you'll be able to tell the difference between the advertising and the programming ... the Holy Grail ... is embedded advertising ... The ad becomes part of the program—or vice versa" (Krantz 1993: S29). This transformation found demonstration already by such things as the Chick-Fil-A Peach Bowl of 2005 becoming just the Chick-Fil-A Bowl in 2006 or product placement pervading most reality programs and many other traditional narrative genres as well. So in seeming violation of the 1890 Sherman Anti-Trust Act—one expressly about monopolies—having no competition implies that mitigating factors exist to make BET successful—factors that include an extremely gracious and silent African-American community, an additionally gracious but vociferous black press, and a little musical form called rap.

Coverage of BET

Black Enterprise magazine (*BE*) serves as the preeminent and only publication to promote and examine black business and more significantly, African-American progress in corporate America. Since its inception in 1970, founder, chairman, and publisher Earl G. Graves Sr. has used the magazine as a vehicle for publicizing African-American corporate positions, advancements, and potential places of employment. According to the official website, its target readership is the African-American "fast-growing, upscale consumer market." Studies show that clearly, *BE* is the only vehicle to regularly feature African-American business. However, its effectiveness is hampered by the target market—black business leaders who comprise a very small percentage of the overall number of business leaders in this country.[26] While the magazine has *always* featured African-American owned businesses, its emphasis on entrepreneurial endeavors took *center stage* only in the 1990s.

BE shifted its focus from corporate advancement to entrepreneurship as evidenced by its January 1997 cover examining Generation X's choices to eschew corporate America in favor of entrepreneurship. Furthermore since 1994, the December issue of the magazine has been devoted almost entirely to the entertainment industry and in this period, the magazine began to address the entertainment industry, particularly hip hop, as a viable area of engagement and employment.[27] In fact, a sizable proportion of all *Black Enterprise* stories since 2000 have been about African-American movers and shakers in the entertainment and sports arenas. As shown previously (Figure 2.1), BET's Johnson graced *BE*'s March 2003 cover with the caption "Slam Dunk! Billionaire Bob Johnson Acquires an NBA Franchise." While not appearing for BET, the profitable run and sale of the network gave Johnson the financial wherewithal and the circle of contacts to bid successfully for the basketball franchise.

Ironically, Johnson has been on only three *BE* covers since BET's 1980 inception—the May 1992, the March 2003, and the June 2007 covers. Yet from *BE*'s editorial perspective, given the many brief articles throughout the years, Robert Louis Johnson is the "captain of capitalism." When attempting repeatedly to question someone on *BE*'s editorial staff about their choices via email and phone, I received a polite run-around. BET was *BE*'s 1997 company of the year. It is clear not only from the *BE* perspective but also from articles housed in publications from the *Wall Street Journal* to online news services that BET has always been considered and lauded as a black-owned business with all the rights and responsibilities endowed with that three-word term—despite its rumor of illegitimacy.[28] The black press, despite fairly extensive programming criticism, largely coddles the big elephant for its first twenty years.[29] But the most significant aspect of BET's growth comes from its unacknowledged partner—the hip hop industry.

Figure 2.8 The Boondocks. (The Boondocks) (2004) Aaron McGruder. Distributed. by Universal Press Syndicate. Reprinted with permission. All rights reserved.

The Resonance of Hip Hop

Beginning in the 1990s, hip hop overtook mainstream culture. The mainstream press covered this transition in terms of its impact on audiences, its transformation of the music industry, lyric opponents and advocates, the marketing usage of, and its affect on the music business' bottom line. In the academy, courses like "Hip Hop and Hollywood," "Hip Hop: Politics and Popular Culture in Late Twentieth Century United States," "Power Moves: Hip Hop Culture and Sociology," "Race, Politics, and Rap Music in Late Twentieth Century America," and just plain "Hip Hop Culture" appeared in university class schedules. A deluge of both scholarly and journalistic books filled the pages of Amazon.com on the history, economics, and activities of hip hop. These works praise and criticize, offer biographies, insider information, and visioning for the role of this truly new cultural marvel. As both an art form and a business, hip hop allowed expression and commerce (a hustle and flow if you will) to meld. African-Americans grounded this wave and certainly occupied the central space of visualization in its birth, transformation, and dissemination.

A general consensus exists about hip hop's early history and development as shown in Havelock Nelson and Michael A. Gonzales's *Bring the Noise* (1991), Tricia Rose's *Black Noise* (1994), William Eric Perkins' *Droppin' Science* (1996), Nelson George's *Hip Hop*

America (1998), Alan Light's *Vibe History of Hip Hop* (1999), and S. Craig Watkins's *Hip Hop Matters* (2005). In addition, literally thousands of other single-authored books, anthologies, scholarly and press articles chronicle this new pop. The development of hip hop hinged on its participants' passion of music, creativity, and style. The Boogie Down's sets fostered community—the turntables, the speakers, the use of light pole electricity, the young and old all looking out windows at the park.[30] This type of socialist forum and valuation of oral tradition has a history in African-American communities and within its cultural production. It was nurtured by the tangential connection African-American and Latino youth felt toward disco and their exclusion from rock and pop. Much of the impulse, background, and context of hip hop foregrounded cultural insularity and motivational exuberance. Yet the invocation of capitalism—both by record executives as well as BET—turned this organic—not pure—but organic impetus on its head. While hip hop's impact is undeniable, its relevance continues to be debated.[31] Yet, what makes hip hop so critical to discuss here is its relationship to the growth of Black Entertainment Television.

Over its 27-year history, BET has played into and presented the largest and most consistent platform for African-American visioning. As hip hop grew, so did the network—not in direct proportion but with a definitive correlation. When BET began, seeing black performers on television certainly was not a new phenomenon but extremely infrequent. However as hip hop developed, its de facto space for national visualization became BET. Journalist Brett Pulley offered: "BET became the center stage where black America could witness this profound cultural shift on a daily basis. Viewers began to regard BET as their very own outlet" (Pulley 2001). Beyond the nation, Pulley argued that BET put the insular musical form of rap on a world platform. Or in other words, said writer Nelson George, the music video made the "culture mythic" (George 1998: 97). Thus ultimately, representation, or lack thereof, played a foundational part of hip hop's drive.

Many black entertainers—even beyond hip hop artists—agreed with this assessment. In its self-published reflection, *Celebrating Twenty Years: BET Black Star Power*, Board of Directors member

Denzel Washington maintained: "BET has presented a complete picture of us to the world ... whether in news or entertainment, BET has provided opportunities to create, to lead, to soar. It has proven that 'Black Star Power' exists on both sides of the camera" (quoted in BET Editors 2000: 7). Whether or not one agrees with this characterization of the network, clearly BET provided a consistent platform for and benefits from black music performance unrivaled then and now.

More crucial to the connecting of BET to hip hop, pioneer and entrepreneur Russell Simmons maintained that BET has been "critical to the expansion of hip-hop culture." He further stated: "You've got to look to them to preserve those art forms in their most honest forms ... The early artists have had integrity in the way they deliver their art forms, and there is a lot of commercialism and influences that change it from its core. BET will protect its core" (quoted in BET Editors 2000: 26). Beyond the obvious critiques that emerged from such an assertion, Simmons' sincerity came into question as his Def Jam label and BET partnered to purchase the website 360hip-hop.com in 2000. Furthermore, others like hip hop feminist scholar and filmmaker Rachel Raimist argued: "Hip hop hasn't really been touched by BET ... [BET only offers] a thin sliver of commercial rap" (Raimist Interview 2005).

Yet despite its support from and of black entertainers, it seems to me that Robert L. Johnson's BET actually exemplified the pimp metaphor that circulates so liberally in contemporary pop culture—the current iteration of it, courtesy of hip hop. The pimp, formerly just a man who orchestrates prostitutes and manages their pay, became a man (or entity in this case) recognized for his conspicuous display of material wealth, reputation, and ability to give shout outs. In addition to the management of prostitutes, Ice-T's "Pimptionary/Glossary" defined pimpin' as having a "fly, cool lifestyle, which [may have] nothing to do with prostitution" (Ice T 1994: 199). Taken straight from the narratives of Iceberg Slim, the pimp has developed into a twenty-first century Horatio Alger, Shaft, and John Gotti all rolled into one—and in the case of BET, one phat money-making machine.

Thus, in the way that communications scholar Christopher Holmes Smith described the hip hop mogul, he captured the paradox of the business practices and success of BET and its correlation with pimpin when he wrote:

> ... the rapper's upwardly mobile ascent is not tethered to a sense of either individual propriety or communal accountability in the same manner as is the ascent of a CEO for a publicly traded company ... he always stands a good chance of convincing his target market of a satisfactory return on their psychic and material investments, and he can continue to be representative of mass expectation of the good life without being responsible for its fulfillment (Smith 2003: 80).

Through both its predominant programming and the lifestyle of its founder, BET guaranteed a life of fabulousness. This life was there for all black folks' taking if you only watch, believe, and imitate.

The duplicitous relationship between pimp (mogul/BET) and prostitute (consumer/audience) reigns throughout hip hop not only because it promises more but actually produces less—only a few Diddys, Jermaine Dupris, Jay-Zs, and Master Ps—but more critically, because of the plantation-like structuring of the music business itself. Essentially four conglomerates control U.S. music distribution: Warner Music Group, Universal Music Group, Sony BMG Music Entertainment, and EMI Group. Distribution is the sole way that consumers become acquainted with artists—awareness facilitated primarily through radio air play and music video. BET has harvested the fruits of these mostly disenfranchised, contractually-enslaved artists-laborers, without compensation, linking it economically to hip hop. Moreover, the BET Network itself has suffered from similar sorts of sharecropping accusations in its practices of low wages, low budgets, and generally low expectations beyond accruing profit.

Furthermore, like the founding of BET, hip hop ironically has received its most commercial valuation and validation from whites, limitedly in the beginning and overwhelmingly since the 1990s. Sociologist S. Craig Watkins talked about the value of hip hop and white consumers in his text *Hip Hop Matters*. He explained:

Since the introduction of SoundScan in 1991, a new logic has dominated hip hop's corporate identity. Though the movement's creative
and entrepreneurial elite will never admit it, their efforts since the
early nineties have focused primarily on the young white consumers
who make hip hop a lucrative culture industry ... [Within this realm,
the] focus on Eminem's whiteness is, in actual fact, an expressed
anxiety about blackness—particularly the perception that black
street culture is spreading into spheres of white domestic comfort,
privilege, and consumer culture" (Watkins 2005: 108–109).

In her work on BET as a super text, media scholar Ayanna Whitworth-Barner argued: "BET facilitates the racial formation of the
wigga by validating the nigga. On a macro-level the network has
involved our [economic] structure, capitalism, to defend its creation of the wigga; on a micro-level, BET involves stereotypes that
are already set in place [for] America to push the race envelope by
exploiting both blacks and whites" (Whitworth-Barner 2004:12).[32] In
a 2005 focus group with predominately white students at the University of Arizona, their impressions of BET gave credence to this
theory.

One 18-year-old female remarked: "I love rap. It's my favorite
music in the whole world, and I know I'm the whitest white girl in
the whole world ... I watch BET all the time ... I love how it's like
black right, black power" (U of Arizona focus group April 2005). The
students interviewed take BET's music focus and the imagery from
music videos as the personification of black culture. In other words,
hip hop has become the embodiment of contemporary blackness—
an embodiment forged through claims of accessibility and cooperation as integral to its articulation and definition. Co-optation is a
fundamental right or rite of passage for all who choose to engage it.

Writer Nelson George observed: "The buppies of ... black music
departments of the early to mid-'80s and programmed radio stations were still putting time into Michael Jackson clones or the latest act from Minneapolis ... They didn't understand, respect, or
support hip hop" (George 1998:59). While this mindset persisted
for the initiation of most black musical forms, it is ironic (or perhaps

typical) that it holds sway with black executives who should know better in the late twentieth century. Additionally, cinematic narratives' employment of hip hop artists or themes abounded post the 1989 release of Spike Lee's *Do The Right Thing* and the 1991 releases of *New Jack City* (Mario Van Peebles) and *Boyz n the Hood* (John Singleton). Narratives as disparate as *Love Jones* (Theodore Witcher 1997), *Save the Last Dance* (Thomas Carter 2001), and *Brown Sugar* (Rick Famuyiwa 2002) to *8 Mile* (Curtis Hanson 2002), *Four Brothers* (John Singleton 2005) and *Hustle and Flow* (Craig Brewer 2005), all coalesced around the sights and sounds of hip hop.

According to the Recording Industry Association of America, in 2006 the genre of rap and hip hop represented 11.4% of all consumer music purchased (www.riaa.com). R & B and urban represented another 11%. So collectively, black music, (or music mostly identified with African-American artists), accounts for nearly 25% of all music purchased, with the African-American population still sitting around 13%. This figure validated the idea that in terms of capitalist potential, music presented itself as a viable outlet for African-American youth. Business scholar Juliet E. K. Walker maintained that entrepreneurs of the hip hop industry were the "first black generation to capitalize on its cultural expressions for economic reward beyond the entertainment industry" (Walker 1998: 328). She suggested that the recording industry, more than radio, more than television, more than film, "has provided blacks with the best means of advancement into high management positions" (Walker 1998: 321).[33] Journalist Cora Daniels positioned hip hop as savvy business when she commented:

> For all of hip-hop's "keepin' it real" bravado, it is in essence a hybrid business because the goal is always to be large! To get paid, by any means necessary. That means moving beyond the "hood." And regardless of hip-hop's foolishness (for a quick peek turn on BET), hip-hop is business. It is one of the nation's leading exports, with sales of more than $5 billion abroad including music, fashion, and movies. Therefore, hip-hop entrepreneurs are businesspeople, and big ones (Daniels 2004: 166).

BET taps into whatever current thing pops in African-American culture. In this time frame, it has been hip hop. And, they were certainly not alone in this. The spread of hip hop has been aided by corporations hawking their wares on the bodies of black and brown poor to get to white and suburban youth. In *No Logo*, journalist Naomi Klein argued that in the world of super brands like Nike, Hilfiger, and DKNY, "cool hunting simply mean black-culture hunting" (Klein 1999: 74). She cited Nike's aggressive strategy to this point. "The company has its own word for [observing and copying black style]: *bro-ing*. That's when Nike marketers and designers bring their prototypes to inner-city neighborhoods in New York, Philadelphia, or Chicago and say, 'Hey, Bro, check out this shoe,' to gauge the reaction to new styles and to build a buzz" (Klein 1999: 75). This word of mouth, man-on-the-street impulse forwarded hip hop in the same way BET spread and tried to position itself in the lives of African-Americans. Furthermore, Maven Strategies President Tony Rome believes: "Hip-hop's endorsement of different brands gives [corporations] a cool factor and representation among youth. They gain credibility by being mentioned in songs" (quoted in Graser 2005). But more to the vision BET seemed to follow, journalist Marc Graser added, "Advertisers are only eager to leverage the power of hip-hop as a marketing tool and generate exposure for their brand among the music genre's young urban consumers" (Graser 2005). This point in particular brings Dávila's assertion regarding the making of a Latina market back to the forefront. The BET branding mantra captured this conundrum well. But perhaps Jay-Z's line in Kanye West's "Diamonds from Sierra Leone (Remix)" captures it best. He declared, "I'm not a business man; I'm a business, man."

Now That's Black

Activist Ron Daniels' memory of community support for BET was echoed at the tail end of ML's (Paul Benjamin) diatribe in *Do the Right Thing* (Spike Lee 1989). ML commented, "I'll be one happy fool to see us have our own business right here. Yes, sir. I'd be the first in line to spend the little money I've got." Beyond feelings of stagnation, some wonder aloud why black business owners such as BET should care either way whether or not blacks like their products when, by and large, they fail to patronize them. In other words, as my uncle Billy Joe Cain insists, "Negroes don't support nothing" anyway. Perhaps it makes sense that Robert L. Johnson's next major business venture was in athletics. The NBA and NFL display African-American bodies performing three-quarters of every year—without accounting for the college and high school televised iterations of these sports. The connection between entertainers and athletes has become translucent and examined extensively within scholarly and popular discourses.[34] What receives only limited mention is the strengthening link between representation, entertainment, and commodity construction and production. The embrace of and attempt to flip the commodification of human beings as a sign of black progress resonates in the building and branding of Black Entertainment Television. One hundred and forty-four years ago, it was called slavery; in 2007, they call it business.

Chapter 3

I'm Rick James, BitchHHHH!
BET Programming

We don't want to be a video channel. Music will cheapen the product.

—Robert L. Johnson (circa 1980–1981)

Our goal is to make BET the predominant source for advertisers to reach the black consumer.

—Robert L. Johnson (October 1, 1984)

Our primary mission has always been to showcase music. So why would the dominant African-American network not be steeped in music?

—Robert L. Johnson (October 1, 2002)[1]

The above epigraphs succinctly illustrate duplicity as the foundation of the Black Entertainment Television network, and admittedly I am deeply conflicted about the most visible and contentious area of BET—its programming. Many aspects of it literally make my skin crawl. Seeing video after video after video of near-naked, very young women, gyrating, begging, crawling, pleading for some attention from some fully clothed, unattractive brotha just makes me mad. Yet I'd be a liar if I said here that I never watch it—both for scholarship and pleasure's sake.

As scholars Dan Rubey, Andrew Ross, and Tricia Rose have argued elsewhere, there is something very captivating, engaging, and quite fun about watching energetic, toned bodies move in ways that most past twenty-five only remember or entertain in the privacy of the home.[2] Despite the FCC and organizations such as the Parents Resource Council's crackdown on the depiction of sexuality on television, we regularly encounter similar imagery on MTV, VH-1, MTV2, billboards, magazines, music videos playing in malls, gyms, hair salons, university cafeterias, barber shops, dorm rooms, and on the Internet. Plus, no other venue offers the constant instant visual gratification that BET does—black folks all the time. So much so that some studies conducted in the early 2000s concluded that black folks were actually now *over*-represented in television given their 13% population figure, a conundrum I address shortly. So I must acknowledge my struggle when trying to understand and contextualize what this programming means, ascribe value to how people have taken it up, and discern what audiences want to see. In this chapter, I examine the programming provided by BET Holdings, trace its development, give close textual analysis to some of its offerings, and dissect the actual practice of branding black bodies for profit.

Framing the Parameters

The programming of BET must first be assessed within the frameworks of capitalism and the edicts of black business that have been articulated in the first two chapters. I invoke the interlocking ideas of two scholars, political theorist Manning Marable and philosopher Louis Althusser. In *How Capitalism Underdeveloped Black*

America, Marable wrote: "The logic of the ideological apparatuses of the racist/capitalist state leads inextricably to Black accommodation and assimilation into the status quo, a process of cultural genocide which assists the function of ever-expanding capital accumulation" (Marable 2000: 9). In other words, Marable used aspects of Louis Althusser's manifesto, "Ideology and Ideological State Apparatuses," to deconstruct the way ideologies, in this case the media, work to make capitalism palatable to people who are habitually excluded from its purview, demonized, and made to believe that shit is sugar.

Specifically, Marable's work proffered that media helps capitalism appear more welcoming and accommodating to African-Americans by providing their actual visual representation while at the same time stripping these same black folks of their cultural capital. Meaning, what once was considered the uncontested (or at least acknowledged) province of black innovation, (music, dance, fashion, language manipulation—Elvis, the Beatles, and Michael McDonald notwithstanding—and style), has now become open, imitatable, and bankable to and by mainstream society, largely with the help and encouragement of BET and other music television programs as well as with the commodification of hip hop. It is not that white folks have ever *not* been a significant part of the financial piece of creative capital in the U.S. However, the new century finds that the innovative part—dominated by black folks—receives input from a vast myriad of voices, (more and more "blacksperts," "niggerologists," and "I Know Black People" contestants), often diluting and stankin' up the pot.[3]

And this iteration of white insertion is different than what occurred with vaudeville and minstrelsy. At least those performances were positioned "somewhat" as parody—unlike the contemporary versions where wholesale co-optation is employed. This new, primarily one-way, fluidity, largely promulgated by the transformation in the television industry and its programming, finds among other things lack of talent no longer an impediment to fame and at least some modicum of success. Because of BET's choice to program mostly music videos, the network and Johnson were touted as sellouts, traitors, and betrayers. Yet for almost its entire existence, BET was the only game going.

Moreover, the significance of representation cannot be overstated, especially for those who fail to receive it sufficiently or broadly. The benefits of visual representation had received consistent and extensive research. Examining representation, especially linked along race and gender lines, provides a central focus in television studies while influence in communications studies dominates that discipline's research agenda. Specifically in communications, quantity, quality, and effects of blacks in media (mostly white scholars thinking about black folks), find validation in publication and scholarly discourses.[4] In terms of impact scholarship, programming (perceived as positive or negative), and narrative inclusions and exclusions find a great deal of comment as well. Television Studies centers on programming—textual analysis, implementation of critical theory, and industrial and cultural consequence.

Cultural theorist Stuart Hall called representation an "essential part of the process by which meaning is produced and exchanged between members of a culture" (Hall 1997: 15); Scholars Ella Shohat and Robert Stam believed that within hegemonic discourse, representation becomes allegorical—"every subaltern performer/ role is seen as synecdochically summing up a vast but putatively homogenous community" (Shohat and Stam 1994: 183), or in other words, the significance of each discreet, individual representation of blackness, in this case, often reaches epic proportion as a sign of *the* one and only black race. Media scholar John Fiske took the overwhelming preponderance of images—a hyperreality—as a sign of dissolution of meaning. He maintained that images overwhelm "any neat distinction between representation and reality, between fact and fiction. [They] refuse ... to allow 'truth' à place in reality alone" (Fiske 1994: 62).

African-Americans and others across class and gender see representation as a key component to understanding, equality, and black progress. For example, in a 2005 closed-door retreat of Hollywood participants (executives, policy makers, actors, academicians, and trade personnel), the central rationale for the confab was to discuss the status of people of color in Hollywood and collectively, what could be done to change, improve, and grow it. The tragic paradox of this discussion and debate (and others like it across disciplines) was that while many continued to nuance the viability of representation and monitor its progress, others (especially people of color) found themselves in a time period where representation "appeared" to be the only ground that *could* be contested.

Capitalism, privatization of prisons, inequitable schools and schooling, cocaine use, war, deconcentration of poor, and corrupt political processes continued to materialize and increase as the status quo of U.S. existence—the a priori reality—areas that few had, it seems, the belief, energy, or know-how to change. So as sociologist Darnell Hunt maintained, popular television serves as "a key cultural forum in which we imagine the nation and negotiate our places in it" (Hunt 2005: 22). These reasons and other equally important ones make the programming of BET significant and crucial to examine.

BET Programming—An Overview

In 1980, Black Entertainment Television stood as a much-needed and desired platform for visioning African-American imagery in general and black artistic talent specifically. Its initial programming consisted of older, African-American populated theatrical releases. Beyond these, Johnson's investment into airing black college football and subsequently offering *Bobby Jones Gospel* on Sunday mornings transformed the television possibilities for African-Americans. The larger vision for the network was to provide a space for black folks to see themselves—their stories and their lives on the small screen—beyond mainstream news reports.

Yet according to journalist Brett Pulley, Johnson initially harbored skepticism about programming his network with music and music videos. In noting the success of MTV, however, he recognized a business opportunity because MTV initially maintained an exclusive focus on rock videos—a province of white musicians. With limited choices of programming featuring African-Americans anywhere on television, Johnson acquiesced to those encouraging him to capitalize on the possibility of airing black music videos—despite his assertions post (recall chapter epigraphs). Thus, BET's

Figure 3.1   Donnie Simpson on the *Video Soul* set.

first music program launched one year after its founding in January 1981 as *Video Soul* with host and then BET production head, Virgil Hemphill. By 1983, BET televised six hours of music videos via *Video Soul*, and popular Washington, D.C. radio disc jockey Donnie Simpson was hired to helm the program (Figure 3.1). Simpson became the first African-American and one of the nation's first all-around v.j.'s (video jockey), introducing familiar black artists and visual renditions of their songs on *Video Soul*. Cameo (before "Word Up!"), Midnight Star, Shalamar, Atlantic Starr, and Earth, Wind and Fire all contributed to the black tele-visioning of soulful (but in house) America. That same year, BET moved to a 24-hour schedule. As the network developed, it expanded its video offerings through different types of music shows, increased its infomercials, and maintained its black college football games and gospel Sundays. However, it did little else.

One of the most pervasive criticisms of BET over the years has been its lack of original programming. In fact, Johnson is quoted as saying to his staff, "We don't have to reinvent the wheel. We just have to paint it black" (quoted in Chait 2001). As industry scholar Barbara Selznick suggests, original programming offers several benefits to brandcentric cable networks. Original programming allows networks to create a library of programs that can be run cheaply into the future, a secondary market revenue stream, and a way for a network to stand out (Selznick 2001: 4). Nevertheless, BET consistently framed its lack of original work in terms of cost. Johnson argued: "Once you put [original programming] on BET, there's no ancillary markets to sell the programming to try to recoup costs ... and the advertising marketplace won't support it enough to turn a profit" (quoted in Umstead 1996: 62).

In his investigation of what international television executives think of African-American situation comedies, for example, industry scholar Timothy Havens lent support to Johnson's assertions. Havens found that: "In their talk of ethnic and universal African American series, we can see that a pervasive rhetoric of Whiteness underwrites American distributors' definitions of universality" (Havens 2002: 388). So in this regard, Johnson's concerns had merit. The international television market has longstanding racialized perceptions of African-American narratives and their viability beyond the borders of the U.S., especially white Europeans. Havens noted, however:

> Some non-European buyers, selecting from the same program offerings, locate different textual features that they believe resonate with their target audiences' unique preferences. Latin American and Middle Eastern buyers from general entertainment channels identify the working-class settings, humor, and communication styles in African American sitcoms as valuable. A South African buyer claims that all of these textual features, as well as the history of African American political struggle, help her connect with her target audience. Each of these instances shows buyers activating textual markers of Blackness that differ from those intended by American distributors (Havens 2002: 394).

While the mindset of white European and white American distributors certainly impacted BET's ability to conduct business abroad, it seemed that an equally insidious hindrance worked against originality—profit margin and greed. Remember John Malone's mantra in chapter 2? I offer this interpretation because by the 1980s, secondary television markets existed in the Caribbean, Canada, and the continent of Africa. And more importantly, by the

1990s, U.S.-based cable networks such as MTV, Lifetime, and even Superstation WGN could have served as potential ancillary markets for original programming.

But with this observation, it is not as if BET has had no original programs; it's just that most of the original programs BET airs are ones featuring music videos—from early ones such as *Video Soul* (1981–2000), *Rap City* (1989–present), and *Video Gospel* (1989–present) to later and more popular ones such as *Caribbean Rhythms* (1996–1999), *Cita's World* (1999–2002), and *106 & Park* (2000–present). While the substance of these programs is music videos, in between the videos they interject light host banter, entertainer interviews, and cultural commentary—some of which will be explored later. Over the years, BET has produced some limited public affairs (news and religious) programming, entertainment programs, and a comedy series. Beyond these, it cablecasts syndicated comedies and dramas that feature black characters and black themes shown previously on broadcast and cable networks. Young people watch the network for its music (some in almost a radio-like situation), for new dance moves, fashion, or for new hair styles. They also, in many cases, enjoy the idea of hosts and guests that are popular to their specific generation. And while the interviews may not necessarily be "challenging or stimulating," they provide at least surface insight and information about young, black entertainers (Spelman focus group November 2004).

Yet since its sale to Viacom, some insist that BET's programs largely emulate those of its corporate mate MTV. This claim finds substantiation by looking at some of its programs. MTV's *TRL-Total Request Live* (1998–present) corresponds to *106 & Park* (2000–present); *Cribs* (2000–present) on MTV becomes *How I'm Living* (2001–2003) on BET; and the longstanding *The Real World* (1992–present) on MTV finds its counterpart as *College Hill* (2004–present) on BET. Even NBC's *The Apprentice* (2004–present) finds itself revisited in BET's *Ultimate Hustler* with Damon Dash (2005). Twenty-first century television privileges selling formats domestically and abroad. Thus the adage "nothing sells like excess" finds resonance in television's quest for audiences. However, not dissimilar to the way Mattel made Christie and Curtis as corollaries to

Barbie and Ken, the new BET programs appear, at the moment, to be just dipped in chocolate, "painted black." And arguing that a certain cultural flavor infuses these BET programs is not enough. African-Americans populate MTV, VH-1, and UPN already.[5]

Twenty-five years post its inception then, BET announced a full slate of original series beyond music and talk shows. Vice president of programming development Robyn Lattaker-Johnson maintained, "I'm not here to take proven formulas and put brown faces in them ... I'm not going to do the black *Bachelor*. If we do a dating show, it's not going to be a derivative" (quoted in Wallenstein 4 April 2005). This must mean once they get rolling with this new thing. Because in fall 2005, BET's pledge to do more original programming aired as reality programs *Blowin' Up: Fatty Koo* (another Puffys' *Making the Band* 1, 2, or 3 on MTV), *Remixed* (one of many make-over programs), and *The Ultimate Hustler* (Damon Dash in an *Apprentice*-like situation). *The Cousin Jeff Chronicles* (later changed to the *Jeff Johnson Chronicles*) promised Jeff Johnson hosting mini-documentaries with topics such as women in music videos, the AIDS epidemic in black and brown communities, and life in South Africa; however, this show was to air only four times per year. These programming additions call for a glimpse into the ongoing non-music original programming on the network—both as an illustration of its trajectory and its tensions. Non-music video original series on BET have included: *Bobby Jones Gospel, Comic View, Lead Story, Teen Summit, Our Voices with Bev Smith, Live in L.A., Oh Drama!*, and *Hey Monie*, among others. While not the totality of their original non-music video programs, I focus on a few of these series for their longevity and their importance in helping to shape the network brand.

The longest running entertainment program on all of cable, *Bobby Jones Gospel*, emerged on BET almost from its beginning in November 1980 (Figure 3.2a). Introducing the format to a Nashville network affiliate in 1976, Jones's program combines performances of gospel music with some celebrity testimonials, minimalist preaching, and of course Jones as director. Bobby Jones hails from Tennessee and earned bachelor's and master's degrees from Tennessee State University and a doctorate from Vanderbilt.

Figure 3.2a   Dr. Bobby Jones.

He is touted for almost singlehandedly exploding gospel music on a national and international stage. He is credited also with opening up traditional black churches first to gospel music itself, it having been associated with uncultured black folks, and second, to contemporary artists such as Kirk Franklin, Mary Mary, Tonex, Yolanda Adams, and Tye Tribbett, all of whom include r & b, rap, and hip hop aesthetic sensibilities into their music for Jesus. Jones reflected: "Had it not been for the will of God and Bob Johnson, I think it would have been extremely difficult for our music to survive the way that it did. Even though we had plenty of radio, television opened up another major door for the rest of the world. Generally, people did not listen to gospel music on the radio unless they were gospel music advocates. It was confined. But when we opened up that television market to the rest of the world, that's history" (quoted in R. Williams December 2004). According to Jones's own website, *Bobby Jones Gospel* is the highest Nielsen rated show on BET and has been for most of its existence.

While *Bobby Jones Gospel* anchors Sunday mornings on BET, other programming has been created around it. *Lift Every Voice* (2001–present) features extended interviews with gospel artists—talking about their background, careers, music, and lives. *Video Gospel*, introduced and produced by Jones, features gospel music videos and is one of the few programs in the country to do so. Jones seeks to use these programs (and his annual gospel retreat) as platforms for education. Very much in line with educational uplift discourses historically circulating in African-American culture, Jones insisted:

> If you can sing, wonderful, but learn the techniques that will make you even more profound. If you play the organ, the piano or the keyboards, then good, but then study it. Don't just study it by ear. If you're a great writer, learn something about English and grammar. Learn how to write professionally. If you want to be a business person in gospel music, mentor with someone and study. I seek the same thing for myself, because I know very little. When the retreat comes, I immerse myself in every one of those activities so that I can continue to grow. If I am called to be a good leader, a good leader must be knowledgeable (quoted in R. Williams December 2004).

And in 2006, BET introduced a new original program called *Meet the Faith*, hosted by former CNN correspondent Carlos Watson. This show attempts to marry religion, activism, and social consciousness in a talk format. Yet talking with college and high school students around the country, very few invoked the Sunday lineup as part of what they watch. In fact, a few non-black interviewees thought the programming was oxymoronic. One said: "I think it's really odd. Like, BET talks about subjects they talk about and then on Sunday we go to church." Another added, "I could see if it was just in the morning or something, but all day?" However, Jones contended that "they needed it, BET ... to kind of counterbalance the kinds of presentations that happen there" (quoted in *News & Notes with Ed Gordon* 1 November 2005). *Bobby Jones Gospel* thrives as church attendance continues to grow, and a staggering 85% of African-Americans claim that religion is very important. The program is cheap to produce, yields solid Nielsen cable ratings, and in many ways serves as one of the few tangible and broad connections to traditional African-American sensibilities that BET airs.

Teen Summit entered black households in 1989. The talk show series tackled teen concerns with teens as hosts speaking to a teen audience who gave both commentary and credence to what was said. It included appearances by popular and upcoming entertainers, therapists, and scholars waxing eloquently on topics such as teenage pregnancy, dress, and racism. The program was hosted initially by Belma Johnson but later used a series of hosts, co-hosts, and posse members over the course of its fourteen-year run, the most famous being Ananda Lewis, who left the series abruptly to become an MTV v.j. in 1997.

During its tenure, the series won six NAACP Image Awards. In a personal interview, one former posse participant remembered, "I knew people who watched it faithfully every single Saturday afternoon" (*Teen Summit* interview May 2006). Beyond giving insight into pressing teen issues, it also provided tremendous opportunities for the young people who appeared on the program. The posse member elaborated, "The exposure and the opportunity that BET gave me is unprecedented and unheard of in the industry ... You [appear on] a national show for a national audience ... It doesn't happen outside this arena" (*Teen Summit* interview May 2006). Yet the program failed to generate substantial profits. However, it had the support of then vice president of corporate affairs Sheila Crump Johnson, who solicited Kaiser Permanente and the Centers for Disease Control to sponsor the series.

As part of its attempt to show corporate social responsibility, BET offered *Teen Summit* through the cable industry's "Cable in the Classroom" effort. However, as the following notice implies, this gesture was half-hearted. An online listing provided by a nonprofit group, The Education Coalition (TEC), stated:

> BET recognizes the importance of taking responsibility for youth by providing teachers with the best educational resources available. BET on Learning, the network's Cable in the Classroom umbrella effort, airs Teen Summit commercial-free *the last Sunday of each month at 3 a.m. ET.* Support materials include: *YSB* and *Emerge* magazines. [Italics mine]

Educational and informational resources produced by BET, *Teen Summit*, *YSB*, and *Emerge* no longer exist. While it aired, *Teen Summit* failed to generate substantial viewer numbers, at least according to Nielsen. However, the cancellation in 2003 took people by surprise and enraged them. *Teen Summit* had very little competition across the television landscape. Contemporary live action programs targeting black teens (or any teens for that matter) neglected this population and could only loosely include programs such as those on Nickelodeon and Disney or even such attempts to reach this audience like *Soul Train* or MTV's *Real World*. Most nonfictional programs of its ilk were locally produced—alongside increasing websites focused on teen concerns. Television programming that addresses youth social concerns finds little opportunity in the commercial universe of the twenty-first century unless it has a good laugh track, as rhetorician William Broussard observed. Instead, adult-themed fictional narratives are projected onto teens by way of programs such as *The O.C.*, *Buffy the Vampire Slayer*, and most daytime serials that find common and increased life in both broadcast and cable landscapes. While this is no laughing matter, other programs on BET are all about being funny.

Comic View appeared on BET's schedule in the fall of 1992. Recognizing the success and possibilities of HBO and Robert Townsend's *Partners in Crime* (1991), the syndicated *It's Showtime at the Apollo*

Figure 3.2b *Comic View* logo.

(1987–present), and HBO's *Def Comedy Jam* (1992–1997) as well as the viability of humor in black life, BET initiated this series with then up-and-coming D.L. Hughley as host. The program featured new comedians from all over the U.S. who performed about a ten-minute standup routine (which was edited down to five to seven minutes). Unlike the Apollo series, the live studio or club audience did not judge the comics. Instead, the crowd was shown to generally appreciate the performances, at least as implied by their edited on-screen laughing faces. The program host opened with humor and also told jokes between each performer. Sometimes jokes from various comic performances were packaged around a central theme and re-aired; for example, jokes about love making. Many of the performers were quite funny and covered territory familiar to many black communities. In the tradition of "playing the dozens," the comedians staked out the ground of intra-community common knowledge. In other words, if you get it, enjoy. If you don't, oh well.

Yet even for many black folks, the humor on *Comic View* revived the pain and promise of the derisively called Chitlin Circuit. The Chitlin Circuit originated in early twentieth century theater. Developed because of the U.S.'s overt racism that mandated blacks' exclusion from many places, each performance in the circuit was aimed at African-American audiences. Some argue that this audience was not necessarily interested in being challenged or integrated. Accordingly, they sought a few good laughs and maybe, an inspirational message. One theater artistic director, Rudy Eastman, suggested, "Pure escapism is one of the reasons these shows are so popular. The characters are familiar. These are people that you know, you see them in your neighborhood. [These plays are] not about suffering and not about 'the man,' they're about being good people and being religious" (quoted in Lowry 24 July 2004).

Beyond this aspect, others believe that the series has grown continually out of the box and not in a progressive way. For example, one focus group student remembered the program this way:

> I don't like *Comic View* anymore. Some people do, but I remember I was watching it with my mom; and there was this one joke. The lady said, "What would you do for a Klondike bar?" ... The joke was that she would let her uncle molest her ... and people were laughing ... And it was like, you don't take offense to that. .... That really turned me off about the whole thing (Spelman focus group November 2004).

The mise-en-scene of the program in some measure catered to this type of transformation as well. The New Orleans version of *Comic View* included numerous women dancers attired in Las Vegas-type showgirl outfits. Nameless, their only role was to open and close the show and periodically provide in-between entertainment. Beyond the performers' part of the show, audience members also played a role. As one focus group participant observed, "It's funny ... what goes down with the comedy show. They'll put these beautiful women up front and everybody else toward the back! The whole time they're all zooming in on their breasts. It doesn't really matter what the comedian is saying, as long as you tune in to Aiesha's breasts" (Spelman focus group November 2004).

In this same tradition (and desire minus religion), the fourteenth season of *Comic View* appeared in 2005 for sixty minutes most weeknights on BET. Over the course of its run, *Comic View* had been expanded, re-edited, telecast, and sold in discreet forms directly to consumers. CEO Debra L. Lee said of the program, "Black folks just like it ... As much as we say we want PBS, that's what we watch—comedy, music and sitcoms. It's entertainment. It's like white folks watching *King of the Hill*, *Friends* or *Seinfeld*" (John-Hill 17 March 2002). While Lee compared inequitable programs, her impetus of citing comparable inroads into particular communities was well grounded. *Comic View* earned an average .8 rating—one of the highest for the network—which was approximately 450,000 households.

Paradoxically, BET has been charged on more than one occasion for underpaying (or failing to pay at all) its *Comic View* performers, as referenced in chapter 2 with AFTRA and D.L. Hughley's complaints. Some suggested that even the movement of show location from Los Angeles to Atlanta to New Orleans was done to inhabit less union-conscious space. Yet at least one former BET insider insisted that comedians appearing on BET failed to understand how cable works in general and the disparity between union wages and one-time allocations. But more importantly, this same insider maintained that the hosts of *Comic View* got paid! Either way, clearly *Comic View* propelled Hughley's career as well as that of comedians Cedric the Entertainer and J. Anthony Brown. In addition, it gave many women comedians such as Sommore, Laura Hayes (Miss Laura), Sheryl Underwood, Montana Taylor, and Adele Givens opportunities not afforded them in any other televisual space. Women worked as both *Comic View* hosts and regular performers. This fact should not go unrecognized. In the same year *Comic View* began, Russell Simmons' *Def Comedy Jam* emerged on HBO with host Martin Lawrence. The series became another platform for black comics, and many of them moved fluidly between the two programs. *Comic View* continued to exist in spite of Johnson's perceived disdain for certain aspects of the black community—aspects the comics frequently targeted. It served as a BET staple and as a hallmark of its "authenticity"—its connection to "real" black communities—an area which will be addressed later in this chapter.

BET Tonight talk news program came into being as part of a larger project to increase the amount of news BET produced. In this 11:00 pm weeknight showcase, interviews with prominent African-Americans took place across generation, profession, and gender (although skewed heavily toward men regardless of their life outlook benefiting African-Americans ala Clarence Thomas). Before it, BET's first foray into news was two-minute segments in the middle of *Video Soul.* In 1986, it blossomed into *BET News,* a weekly half-hour digest covering news pertinent to African-Americans. Journalist Tavis Smiley joined BET in 1996 as executive producer and host of *BET Tonight.*

Smiley had already been a member of the black radio community for five years when he joined BET—having created one-minute critical commentaries on the state of black America called *The Smiley Report* in Los Angeles, and serving as commentator for *The Tom Joyner Morning Show.* African-Americans outside of BET's target demographic acknowledged the news programming as one of the few (and some, the only) reasons why they tuned in to the network at all. Not only to see high profile African-American interviews or black major events (Million Man March, etc.) but also, more importantly, to see the likes of Julianne Malveaux, Chaka Khan, and Russell Simmons (before his mainstream success and before calling Smiley an "Uncle Tom")—entertainers, politicians, and activists important to black America but not necessarily recognized by other Americans.

While BET news programming initially centered on African-American and African diasporic concerns, it became more about the news of the day, especially entertainment news, as defined by majority media outlets like CNN, the Associated Press wire service, and *The New York Times*—all conveyed by a young black anchor, Jacque Reid. In order to increase its advertising and subscriber base, BET canceled *BET Tonight with Ed Gordon* along with two other long-standing public affairs programs, *Lead Story* and *Teen Summit* in December 2003. Two years later, in 2005, at its first television upfront announcement, ten-year old *BET Nightly News* was canceled to make way for news briefs throughout the day—MTV-style. At the end of 2005, the network announced the hiring of former CNN pop culture correspondent Touré, former editor-in-chief of *The Source* magazine Selwyn Hinds, and writer and filmmaker Nelson George. BET president of entertainment Reginald Hudlin described the hiring of the Brooklyn-based trio as pivotal to the next phase of BET news and public affairs programming. Touré would serve as host, writer, and consulting producer for BET News; Hinds would assume the role of interim executive producer for the daily BET news briefs, periodic BET news specials, and *Meet the Faith*; and George became consulting producer on all BET news and public affairs programs (*Call and Post* 17–23 November 2005). While these perspectives promised to add a certain critical insight to BET's heretofore invisible news division, I wondered would it be a vision that differed markedly from the masculinist vision already emanating from the network—despite the presence and control of women?

In 2006, the BET News division created *The Chop Up*, a "weekly dissection of the people, places and issues rumbling in the hearts, minds and souls of Black folk." Airing Sunday mornings and Wednesday evenings, its online literature positioned the new program this way:

> "The Chop Up" will be passionate and progressive, a show built from the DNA of BET's youth-driven audience; the same audience that powers media shifts and trends the world over. "The Chop Up" will be fast-moving with pulsing visual, tonal and audio cues. And it will be interactive, seamlessly incorporating the BET demographic into the show with viewer-sponsored podcasts and web-based polls facilitated through BET.com. Anchored by a rotating cast of BET News talent, "The Chop Up" represents BET's successful grab of the holy-grail chased by news organizations all over America: how do we keep the 18–34 audience informed without boring them to death. In essence, how do you stay fly yet substantive? Tune in to "The Chop Up" for the answer (bet.com July 2006).

Only with time will the existence and direction of the news division gain total clarity. However if keeping young people from boredom is a central goal, the direction looks bleak for critical engagement, thought, and transformation, especially in light of BET's 2007 upfront to advertisers.

The 2004 fourth quarter ratings from Nielsen Media Research showed Nick-at-Nite as the top cable network among black viewers across all demos. The reason for these figures, according to Doug Alligood, senior vice-president of special markets for BBD&O in New York, was repeat episodes of *The Cosby Show* and *The Fresh Prince of Bel-Air*. Among African-American viewers aged 25 to 54, BET ranked in second place, followed by Lifetime, TNT, and ESPN (Larson 4 April 2005). However, in 2005 BET ranked number one in African-American households, with TNT, Disney, Lifetime, and Nickelodeon following very closely behind. The overwhelming preponderance of programming selections by black women, for example, centered around African-American narratives and characters. For this group, 2006 choices included: *The Parkers*, *Soul Food*, *Girlfriends*, and *Hey Monie* on BET, *Moesha* on Noggin, *Missing* on Lifetime, *That's So Raven* and *The Proud Family* on Disney, and *Eve*, *Half and Half* and *Girlfriends* on UPN (two of these were canceled with the consolidation of WB and UPN for fall 2006). With these numbers validating once again African-Americans' desire to see people who look like them on television and in a certain type of format, BET's choice to program music videos the way it did remains curious. Thus examining the programming of music videos more closely may yield some greater insight to these decisions.

Music Videos on BET

Record companies supply music videos free of charge to music video networks—ready-made promotion for and exploitation of their artists. Yet this free resource has virtually transformed the way music enters the lives of listeners. As mentioned in chapter 2, 2004 found BET citing its target audience as 18 to 34. BET vice president of public relations Michael Lewellen argued: "Most of the complaints coming from certain pockets of the community are from those who've always felt that BET should be all things to all people. No network can be all things to all people" (quoted in Ross 27 February 2003). But at any given time prior, BET argued both for trying to serve all of African-America and only targeting the 12 to 24 demographic of music-buying youth—depending on which advertiser and/or constituent group considered buying the network. This leads me to conclude that narrowcasting for an ethnic audience may be only a first step in both defining a market and gaining a wider (often white) audience with common interests that advertisers like and want.[6] So I investigate here what music videos are to the people and advertisers BET claims to target.

In a macro view, "music video" as a generic term receives substantial critical and everyday interrogation. Music videos are noted for their innovative visual and aural techniques; creating entertainers who otherwise might not have succeeded; their deemed detrimental impact on teens in the areas of sex, relationships, racialization, gender construction, and attention span; and their pervasiveness. For example, communications scholar Debashis Aikat's 2004 study found that music videos appearing on BET.com and MTV.com contained a considerable amount of violence. The two most-identified violent musical genres, hard rock and hip hop or rap, also had the youngest target audiences (Aikat May 2004). For many in the baby boomer generation, music videos have not provided the world with much progressive imagery. However for listeners of popular music, music videos offer a window for visualizing and idolizing artists who otherwise may not have been encountered. Ostensibly replacing the live performance, music videos provide an avenue for fantasy creation that a live performance cannot emulate (except in the few cases of mega-stars such as Tina Turner, Prince, and Janet Jackson, or a stellar awards program).

Yet University of Houston focus group participant Kurt Richardson and others argue that BET serves simply as a practice field for musical artists. He believed that Viacom is "basically using BET as a training ground or a minor league for entertainers in terms of [if] they can sell on BET or hit the black audience. Then they put 'em on MTV and they know they're a proven commodity" (U of Houston focus group February 2003). In other words, once an artist receives the support of the predominately black teen and young adult audience, she might be recruited to the big leagues (MTV and VH-1) where she really could achieve Black Star Power, accorded this status by white audience support. Looking at two of the most popular programs for airing music video proves instructive.

BET offered *Video Soul* as its first foray into music video exhibition. Keep in mind, MTV started only in 1981, so this was quite new ground across the television landscape. Most music videos appearing on the network were simple visual illustrations of song lyrics with minimal special effects. Donnie Simpson proved a soothing, sophisticated, and easy-on-the-eye complement to the nation's black singers and musicians as he appeared daily with his James Brown's "Gonna Have a Funky Good Time" theme song. Concentrated almost exclusively on r & b, this program gave welcome recognition to black folks' cultural treasures. For example, the first video played was George Clinton's "Atomic Dog."

Because *Video Soul* aired for sixteen years, at least three different generations embraced it. The older set associated the program with the initiation of the network, the ability to connect artists' faces with songs beyond album covers, *Right On* magazine, and *Soul Train*, and hearing soul music on television. For younger folks, *Video Soul* invoked memories of the Coca-Cola Top Ten Countdown (with a big Coke machine as part of the set), specific music videos, and entertainers such as Bobby Brown and Whitney Houston (separately) appearing behind the bell-ringing sliding door—*Star Trek* style. Simpson believed that *Video Soul* wielded a tremendous impact on the world of television and African-American representation. He comments on this as BETJ (formerly BET on Jazz) began airing old episodes of the series as *Video Soul Gold* in 2006:

> BET served as a catalyst in serving an entrée to getting Black videos played on MTV. We certainly influenced MTV. That was pretty significant. I think back now how popular BET was, especially in my travels in the Caribbean. It was amazing. I remember doing *Video Soul* in St. Thomas for a week. When I got off the plane, they had a

50-piece steel drum band playing the theme song from *Rocky*. I'm waving my hands side to side like the president. The reception was unbelievable. It was a real rock star kind of thing (quoted in bet. com/BETJ, 1 March 2006).

The dearth of competition, the quality of entertainers, and the reach of the program allowed it to flourish. However as the music changed, so did the need to reflect a newer aesthetic—from host down. BET canceled *Video Soul* in 1997, and a few years later replaced it with *106 & Park* (Figure 3.2c).

106 & Park, the program and address for BET's most popular program with its cited target demographic, began on the network in 2000. Copying not only the format but also the aura of MTV's *TRL*, the program differentiated itself by con-

Figure 3.2c   *106 & Park* logo.

centrating exclusively on hip hop and a bit of r & b. From its initiation through the middle of 2005, the co-hosts were A.J. Calloway and Free. The two sparred with each other, the studio audience, and the program guests. They also did some on-location hosting and represented the network (and themselves) at various events (including in Charles Stone III's 2002 film *Drumline*). The program features top ten countdowns, studio audience competitions, artists' performances, and of course, the centerpiece, music videos.

While *106 & Park* clearly parrots MTV's *TRL*, ratings suggest that BET's version resonates more with viewers. Many University of Arizona focus group participants chose *106 & Park* over its competitor because of length of song airplay. One person commented: "BET is really like, music, and you get to really feel the music while you're watching it. You don't get interrupted" (U of Arizona focus group April 2005). Others believed that MTV turned cheesy with all of its reality programs and was overdone; thus they turned to *106 & Park* for the comfort of music. Said another respondent: "MTV is so scripted and so commercial, and BET, you can just watch it and you feel like you're with them and their friends" (U of Arizona focus group April 2005). In July 2005, Free and A.J. departed simultaneously under undisclosed circumstances. On billboards and blogs around the Internet, viewers expressed their unhappiness with this change. In addition, *106 & Park* shed its uptown location for a midtown spot in 2002, leaving Harlem civic leaders disappointed as it, at least symbolically, dealt a blow to Harlem's black business growth. A change as significant as the hosts departing left a bad taste in the mouths of viewers. Nevertheless, black, brown, and white young people continued to watch it.

BET's Programming—A Metaphor

In 2000, BET inaugurated an awards program to honor African-Americans within entertainment, sports, and the larger black community.[7] With its fourth iteration of the BET Awards program in June 2004, it hoisted the theme of "Bigger and Better." Comedienne and actor MóNique served as the literal physical embodiment of this theme, and according to *Billboard*, the awards program at the time became the highest rated show in the network's history.[8] Three and one-half hours long, the program netted a 4.61 rating (or 5.6 million viewers), up seven percent from the year prior (*Billboard* 10 July 2004).

With such high numbers and its content, I use the 2004 BET Awards program as a metaphor for and case study of BET's overall programming. Suggestive of the most clichéd example of black family gatherings that are plagued with the cousin no one wants to be bothered with, (illustrated well in the "Family Reunion" episode of *The Bernie Mac Show*), the awards program exuded the feeling of down home. It operated as if it was an indoor, exclusive space for African-Americans who know "how we do." For example during the final hour of the program, MóNique got rapper Lil' Jon in check from the stage. After being addressed several times throughout the show, she finally said to the audience, "Yaw, take your birth control pills please—every single day." Funny stuff to be sure, but on an awards program that in the next instance honored Danny Glover for his contributions to humanity? Foregrounding a specific class and cultural aesthetic as well as tapping into the consistent diss black entertainers receive on major (and minor) awards programs, the 2004 BET Awards show reveled in the confluence of black excellence and simultaneous mediocrity, dozens playing, and presumed relevance. But as cultural critic Marc Anthony Neal and I note, where else can you see Slick Rick, Janet Jackson, Ron Isley, Angela Bassett, Yolanda Adams, Carl Anthony Payne II, and Danny Glover all in the same space?

Beyond the on-display factor, Neal believed that this award show and others like it allow blacks to "[relish] in those cultural insiderisms that no amount of crossover hip hop will ever give non-blacks access to ... " (Neal 29 March 2001). This sense of family and familiarity was thick, but insider or no, my own generational skin must be prickling, since the original super freak pissed me off by his comments during the show. Or maybe the cause of my ire was the glaring contradictions pervading through most of BET's program-ming—programming characterized, according to Johnson, by qual-ity and innovation (despite his own lewd proposal during the 2005 BET Awards to stay on his post if Beyoncé would give him a lap dance).[9] The paradoxes inherent in mainstream, capitalist represen-tation played themselves out across the bodies of African-Americans on BET and were exemplified within the 2004 BET Awards.

Case Study One

In addition to the mainly misogynist videos that run all day, a prime example of BET's sustained disdain and contempt toward women came within the performance of Rick James and Teena Marie at the BET Awards show. Once two of the hottest r & b artists, their performance memorialized the passage of time. Beyond provid-ing the camera personnel with many physical challenges in try-ing to shoot their rather erratic choreography, their mode of dress harkened back to their heyday (and hey shapes). At the end of the performance of their much-loved song "Fire and Desire" and post announcement and acceptance of Beyoncé's award as best female artist, James (seemingly hot in his velvet ensemble and quite possi-bly high) grabbed the microphone (Figure 3.3). He exclaimed: "And for the girl backstage, for that girl back stage, make it perfectly clear. Never mind who you thought I was. I'm Rick James, Bitchhhhh!" With that, James swaggered off the stage in presumed triumph.

Figure 3.3   Rick James—BET Awards 2004.

Rick James *is* the original "super freak"—one of the central artists who, in 1982, took MTV to task for not playing black music videos. His 1980s music success was legendary (as was his battle with cocaine, abuse of women, and law entanglements).[10] With his pronouncement at the awards show, both men and women in the audience leaped from their seats howling, some in shock, others with their fists pumping the air and hands clapping in support of his masculinized reclamation of self and position in the world of black music. Quite frankly, the crowd's response was more jarring and disturbing even than James's comment, because this narrative and performative scene were both enacted against a nameless and unseen woman.

The devaluation of women on cable is not the exclusive province of BET or even cable television. In fact, it is so much the norm of television (and film and music and magazines and plain American culture), that it seems redundant to even mention it. Nonetheless, because BET provides the most consistent forum for visualizing African-American women and girls—and visualize in all parts it does, I cannot *not* talk about it. Some suggest, my students especially, that James simply mocked the skit of comedian Dave Chappelle and Charlie Murphy who, on the *Chappelle Show* (Comedy Central 2003–2005), devoted a whole episode to James (Figure 3.4).

In this episode, the real-live Rick James confirmed his drug-induced behavior over the years by being repeatedly shown saying, "Cocaine is a helluva drug." Rick James's alter ego character

Figure 3.4   Dave Chappelle as Rick James.

(played by Chappelle) walked around constantly saying, "I'm Rick James, bitch," slapping folks (women and men) indiscriminately but demeaning women in general and Charlie Murphy in particular for his skin color, "darkness is spreading". However, what failed to be critiqued in this extended joke is that James, a notorious woman-izer and drug abuser, reclaimed his virility by debasing and checking women. And despite artists Eve, Missy Elliott, and Meredith Brook's assertions, being called a bitch does not empower or compliment in the twenty-first century. Whenever a term has been used for deni-gration and carries a denotative meaning as something not human, its reclamation potential remains quite limited. Like this example, the music videos of BET provide few spaces for African-American character building or even whole-ness. Women largely serve as set decoration and examples of male success. Paradoxically, however, BET consistently pushes women to the forefront of both its origi-nal programming and its mana-gerial staff.

Whether it's Bev Smith (Fig-ure 3.5) hosting *Our Voices*, Sherry Carter (Figure 3.6) on

Figure 3.5   Bev Smith.

Figure 3.6   Sherry Carter.

Video Soul, Ananda Lewis (Figure 3.7) on *Teen Summit*, Jacque Reid (Figure 3.8) as the *Nightly News* anchor, or Free (and later Julissa Bermudez) on *106 & Park*, women found significant visual space on the airways of this network. Behind the scenes also seemed filled with a preponderance of women who helped guide the company's growth, and one, Debra L. Lee (Figure 3.9), since 2005 served as CEO. Nonetheless, the quantity of female employees has done little to undercut the pervasiveness of rump shakers within the predominant music video programming format.

The anger and disdain directed toward women in general and black women in particular, have reached epidemic proportions in popular culture. While both Powell and Martin led the FCC's attempt to transform the television landscape in terms of sexual explicitness, violence, and language (most often offensively directed at women), cable remained outside of its purview. Furthermore, and insidiously, the paradoxical representation BET offers is not confined to human women.

One of the most fascinating characters emerging from BET was an animated woman named

Figure 3.7   Ananda Lewis.

Cita (Figure 3.10). Appearing from 2000 to 2002, this well-endowed female figure spent two hours per weekday introducing music videos and dispensing cultural advice on women, work, and rap all within *Cita's World*. Cita conveyed sassiness with an urban (southern roots) way of speaking that caused both enjoyment and angst among African-American cultural commentators. Neal maintained: "As a cyber-creation, Cita employs an 'authentic' black femininity to reinforce patriarchal norms within black life and culture as represented within mass culture"(Neal 2001: 166). This character, along with most of BET's programming, raised questions of authenticity—what it means and what place it serves in contemporary discourses within television and black culture.

Figure 3.8   Jacque Reid.

The search for and articulation of the authentic occupies central space in many aspects of contemporary U.S. academic and everyday discourses. Literary scholar Wahneema Lubiano positioned authenticity within its relationship to essentialism. She argued:

Figure 3.9   Debra Lee.

Figure 3.10   Cita clone.

... to be authentically "African-American" or "Black" has, at various
times in history and in the present, meant and sometimes means to
be rhythmic; or to have a predilection for playing craps, drinking,
using, and/or selling drugs, or raping white women; or being a jungle
savage; or being uninterested in marriage; or being on welfare—the
list goes on and on. The resonances of authenticity depend on who
is doing the evaluating ... The categorical imperative is essentialist,
whether imposed by dominance or volunteered for under the terms
of Euro-American political or African-American cultural hegemony.
If we fail to problematize the notion that being African-American
always means *only* being embattled, that African-American film is
political only insofar as "someone" empowered to make the evalua-
tion recognizes its political "reality" and calls the shots on its trans-
gressiveness, and that "authenticity" is always already known and can
therefore be proven, then we have fallen into the trap of essentialism" (Lubiano 1991: 269, 270).

Historian Marilyn Halter asserted that seeking authenticity is
"very much related to nostalgia for an idealized and fixed point in
time when folk culture was supposedly untouched by the corruption that is automatically associated with commercial development
... Although commercialism stands as the archenemy of cultural
purity, corporate interests have nonetheless begun vying with one
another to claim their particular output as the most authentic in

the marketplace" (2000: 17, 18). Performance artist and scholar E. Patrick Johnson called authenticity "yet another trope manipulated for cultural capital" (2003: 3). In spoken word artist Saul Williams's "Coded Language," he penned: "Statements such as 'keep it real,' especially when punctuating or anticipating modes of ultra-violence inflicted psychologically or physically or depicting an unchanging rule of events will henceforth be seen as retroactive and not representative of the individually determined is" (S. Williams 1999). And anthropologist John L. Jackson Jr. theorized about what he calls the intersections of authenticity and sincerity. He wrote:

> Sincerity was once about things, and authenticity about relations between people. In the present, their connotations have been reversed ... Racial sincerity and authenticity are both ways ... for locating *the real* in (and in the intentions of) everyone around us. The difference is that authenticity theorizes this as an unbalanced relationship between the powerful seer and the impotently seen ... Sincerity, however, is an attempt to talk about racial *subjects* and subjectivities. Race is not singularly and exclusively about authenticating others—or, more specifically, it is about authenticating others who concomitantly escape solitary confinement within the prescripted categories that others impose (J. Jackson 2005: 15, 17).

These discourses of authenticity impact the perception of what is programmed on BET, and in particular, the reception of Cita. Much of Cita's critical commentary was directed toward women but referenced ideologies of men. To that end, in the BET-published book *Cita's World*, for example, Cita assessed Lil' Kim this way: "Lil' Kim and Ms. Cita used to be real tight ... But once the little one got a record deal, she changed. She went and bought some discount boobs, got some rainbow-colored wigs, fake eyes, and she started buying clothes four sizes too small. Word, I think she started shopping in the children's section the way some of them outfits looked on her. Cita just gonna preach the truth and keep it real" (Howard 2001: 128). Yet the reality she claimed came from not only a fictionalized character but also a hyper-real figure in her animation. The realness of her testimony, her actuality, possessed a level of double falsity. She could be considered a twenty-first century niggerologist.[11] Her comments, though positioned as quintessentially contemporary, revealed the twentieth century bourgeoisie underlying prescriptions for behavior, dress, and gender—this commentary hidden within the body and voice of a twice fictionalized, female character.

Industry scholar Kevin S. Sandler wrote that animation became a way for a cable network to stand out—to brand itself. It seems that the implementation of Cita may have been initially no more than a unique addition to an established music video program (*Jam Squad*). Due to her popularity, however, the following year the program was renamed *Cita's World*. Clearly this virtual woman registered with not only viewers but also business interests. Thus BET's plan to introduce three animated series in its 2007–2008 season. Furthermore, some suggest that miniaturization may be the way people can deal with changes in technology. Cita's positioning clearly staked ground in the battle of authenticity. In this case, she invoked the meaning and value of ghetto fabulousness. Thus beyond gender, Jackson theorized that ghetto fabulousness is actually the excess of authenticity. He contended:

> Ghetto fabulousness, when at its most fabulous, epitomizes a consumerism and commercialism that revels in knock-offs and wears them, sincerely, against the grain of societal expectations ... Global fabulousness would not survive without this low-end global commodification of trademark infringement, without such brash disregard for international trade laws. Ghetto fabulousness uses this underside of the global to challenge its own confinement, to declare the social margins quite central to the people who live there, even as they struggle for more access to a global mainstream" (J. Jackson 2005: 59–60).

Recognizing Jackson's interpretation, I further that ghetto fabulousness, or fabulousness of any kind, exists as an embodiment of the warring factions within the consciousness of black folks. The double consciousness so eloquently identified by W.E.B. Du Bois goes beyond race to include the terrors of class division, the oppressions of gender distinction, the ravages of generational hierarchies and displacements, and the consistent friction between black identity and self-worth. Ghetto fabulousness also goes beyond style. It reflects the privileging of white accoutrements and ideologies as the quintessential destination of choice. Whether it's Lil' Kim's infatuation with the designs of Marc Jacobs, Lil' Jon rapping about liquor,[12] or even the mansions, Hummers, and diamonds that pervade music videos, the overarching goal is the possession of wealth (or more accurately, the impression thereof). Even when Ludacris, T.I., or Master P rep for the "dirty south" and its associated iconography (poor living conditions and poor black people), their prominent display of bling, cars, and sweat attire (among the ruined neighborhoods they shoot within) point to other worlds—better ones, *white* ones.

When searching for Cita on the web in 2004, the company Oddcast emerged. Oddcast produces virtual hosts for corporations. At a now-defunct link for BET, www.staging.oddcast.com/bizdev/sandy/stephen_hill.html, the company apparently constructed a whole product presentation designed for the network and directed toward Stephen Hill, executive vice president of entertainment and music programming. In this pitch an apparently out of breath, black, Barbie-figured female character told Hill that she (and others like her) could fulfill all his virtual host needs at BET. As her breasts heave, she rhythmically and decidedly introduced him to a wide variety of black-like/light women—all similarly endowed with different skin tones, hair designs (length and color), and with slightly different vocal intonations. Problematically, this creepy compendium of women of color may be the wave of the future—with them existing alongside real-live ones featured on programs such as BET's *Uncut*.

Case Study Two

After the announcement of upcoming talent on the 2004 BET Awards, the program's host, MóNique, was introduced. With the pronouncement of her name, MóNique and a plus-sized women's posse stood in silhouette repose as bass and finger snapping commenced. Once they easily sashayed down a pyramid of steps, the sound of a record remix and singer Beyoncé's "Crazy in Love" began.

Figure 3.11   MóNique at BET Awards, 2004.

In the music video for this song, the singer demonstrated her hip hop dance skills—rapid torso movement, swiveling hips, and sensual pulsing. MóNique set out to emulate this visual fun time and accomplished the goal impressively (Figure 3.11). The camera movements exhibited the beauty of these big black women. The dancers brought the crowd to their feet as much for the impressiveness of their display as the shock of it. In some ways their dance acumen should not be surprising, as other heavy hoofers such as Fred Berry (Rerun from *What's Happening*), have demonstrated these skills in the past. Nevertheless, this performance, coupled with MóNique's in your face "now there" to Beyoncé, laid the foundation for the remainder of the program. While African-Americans continue to value the often-bigger bodies of black women, (a view that is changing in part due to continued social assimilation), the outfits and performance of MóNique and nem pointed to a heightened sexuality that had nothing to do with black cultural appreciation.

Unfortunately, it seems to me, their dancing display tied black women's sexuality to animism, although often cited as connected to the dances of the African continent. In fact, the performance more reflected the late twentieth century strip clubs of popular culture—an ethos that danced BET's *Uncut* into existence.

Thus the corollary to this performance in BET's programming was the music video program *Uncut* that began in September 2000. *Uncut*, one of BET's most popular and controversial video shows,

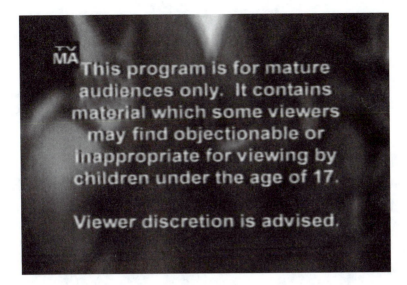

Figure 3.12   *Uncut* disclaimer.

appeared on its schedule as a vehicle for more sexually charged
and narratively risqué videos. Airing at 3:00 am EST, the program
originally presented music videos by unknown or limitedly known
artists. As the program gained a wider audience, videos by popular
artists like Jay-Z, Lenny Kravitz, and Snoop Dogg aired as well.
Said BET senior vice president Stephen Hill, "*Uncut* is for adult
eyes only [see Figure 3.12, the disclaimer that ran before the program aired]. Any kid up at 3 o'clock in the morning, their biggest
problem is not BET" (Moody 5 April 2004). Touché. Yet even the
disclaimer lured not only adults but males in particular of all ages
with a seductive and breathy female delivery of the statement.

On *Uncut*, the soft pornography of the music videos further
blurred the lines between pornographic adult entertainment and
basic cable programming. And while these genres and expectation
of these genres differ, significant similarities exist between them.
Music videos of *Uncut* robbed both black women and men of their
humanity. Beyond disembodiment and the elevation of discreet
body parts, no courtship narratives, no tenderness, in other words,
no love existed in this realm. Writer John Stoltenberg described sex
clubs and the falsity of gender in a way that directly applies to most
of the scenarios of *Uncut*:

There's ... the kind of sex you can have when you pay your money into a profit system that grows rich displaying and exploiting the bodies and body parts of people without penises for the sexual entertainment of people with. Pay your money and watch. Pay your money and imagine. Pay your money and get real turned on. Pay your money and jerk off. That kind of sex helps the lie a lot. It helps support an industry committed to making the people with penises believe that people without are sluts who just want to be ravished and reviled—an industry dedicated to maintaining a sex-class system in which men believe themselves sex machines and men believe women are mindless fuck tubes. That kind of sex helps the lie a lot (1990: 271).

It reduced women to the quintessential product—so much for power to the p****.

As popular culture across the board became more graphic lyrically, images reciprocated (or perhaps initiated) a similar response. So from Marvin Gaye's "Sexual Healing" (1982) with its images of naughty nurses and Gaye's on-stage performance, audiences were offered 50 Cent's "In Da Club" (2003): "I'm into having sex, I ain't into making love ..." where the million-dollar 50 retooled his body into a machine that all women (and possibly some men, too) desired. The positing of BET as the destination of choice promoted and provided for this transition of music lyrics and imagery despite its assertion of "it's not our fault." All that is left is the actual sexual exchange: money, women, poles, and perceived power. And as illustrated within documentaries such as *The Show* (Brian Robbins 1995), HBO's *Pimps Up, Ho's Down* (1999), *Hip Hop Videos: Sexploitation on the Set* (VH1 2005), and *Beyond Beats and Rhymes: A Hip-Hop Head Weighs in on Manhood in Hip-Hop Culture* (Byron Hurt 2006), that piece of the business clearly already plays. The shifting (or outright disavowal) of blame and the refusal to take responsibility forecasts a world increasingly devoid of any ability to see one another as more than objects—sexual or otherwise. Not even attempting to explain how a program such as *Uncut* forwarded Black Star Power or quality, I turn to what followed the program, tele-evangelism.

Case Study Three

The 2004 BET Awards opened with a duet by acclaimed producer and rap artist Kanye West and gospel singer Yolanda Adams. Rising from the stage floor, Christ-like on a cross-laden pulpit, West sang and rapped about wanting Jesus to walk with him (Figure 3.13). In this version of the song, replete with an African-American white-robed choir, dancers, and rapid edits, West was paired with Adams, who added a little background and soul-stirring emphasis to the rendition.

The front row audience of young women bounced with exhilaration as their young male counterparts stood in cool repose, either simply bopping their heads or adding a light hand clap. The fairly lengthy performance merged what seems to be contradictory or at least incompatible impulses—gospel and hip hop. But West and Adams bridged the gaps of generation, holiness, and secularity to situate the theater space as one inclusive to all of African-America—sinners and redeemed alike.

Discussed more extensively in chapter 4, BET's late night programming has always consisted of either infomercials or evangelists. Both supplied BET with maximum profit for limited work. This peddling of goods and salvation came through a myriad of aesthetic choices and performances. Showing how to make money, how to cook more efficiently, how to look more fashionable, how to feed the hungry, and how to gain prosperity through Jesus was

Figure 3.13   Kanye West "Jesus Walks" 2004 BET Awards.

reflected in everything from cheesy indoor sets to elaborate out-door locations. Even the 1993–1994 well-produced Rio hair info-mercial fiasco aired on BET. While infomercials dominated BET's late night in the early part of its existence, white and black television ministers represent the seller of choice in the twenty-first century.

The quality of these productions varied. Minister Creflo Dol-lar's program featured multi-camera setups, fonted scriptures, and expertly edited talks intertwined with audience responses and pro-motions for Dollar's CDs, DVDs, and conferences. On the other hand, other ministers might inhabit smallish congregations sur-rounded with dull browns and blues. In one case, the minister's healing messages (the laying of hands) were peppered with he and his female assistant standing before a 1950-ish wallpapered space, together reading fan letters—extremely low tech and low-budget, yet on a national network. More often than not though, *Uncut* was followed by Robert Tilton's *Success-N-Life*.

Tilton, a white Southern Word of Faith minister, was originally based in Dallas and came to national prominence in the early 1990s. Beyond his continuing entanglement with the legality of his spiri-tual corporation, Tilton's methods of appealing to would-be believ-ers (and especially the African-American ones of BET) were more than humorous, they were insulting. The juxtaposition of black and brown booties bopping against a white (disgraced) southerner claiming the word of God for black souls was more than just jarring. If nothing else, the two programs' positioning suggested a general disregard and disrespect for its target audience in favor of generat-ing revenue. When BET representatives were questioned about the religious programming, they rejected any responsibility for what aired. They suggested that the ministers were funny and that per-haps viewers should acquire more discernment. However, as my fourteen-year-old goddaughter Parey Hunter frequently observes, "That's just not right," in Jesus' name.

Case Study Four

Regardless of one's assessment of the 2004 BET Awards program, few can dispute its high production values. The expert facilitation of multiple cameras all around the theater, onstage (and from the aisle) choreography, lighting, special effects, and video clips (of both nominees and special acknowledgments), rivaled any other presentation of its kind. Black entertainers from film, television, and sports blended fluidly to keep viewers engaged and auditorium guests excited. The program also moved smoothly, with minimal presenter banter and curtailed awardees thankfulness. The quality of this program stood in opposition to its other made-for-the-network programming, BET Films.

BET Books, a compendium of short novels under the imprint of Arabesque Books, was purchased in 1998 as a venue for BET to enter the world of filmmaking. Created in 1994, Arabesque Books published 250 titles by 2000. BET decided to invest in film production as part of its brand outreach strategy. Its first foray into these waters was as investor of actor and producer Tim Reid's *Once Upon a Time When We Were Colored* released in 1995. The film tells the story of a black family that survives and thrives despite the racist reality in which they live. Playing on only 345 screens, it earned $2.2 million (blackfilm.com). More recently, BET produced the feature film *Diary of a Mad Black Woman* (2005), directed and acted in by Tyler Perry. This film, directly from Perry's "chitlin circuit" plays, grossed $50.3 million by the end of its run. But with the purchase of the Arabesque Book imprint, BET embarked on full-scale film production for the network itself in 1999.

Nina Henderson Moore, executive vice president of news, public affairs and program acquisition, maintained: "The original 10 Arabesque Films were historic in that they represented the largest single slate of African American-themed films ever produced" (quoted in "BET Pictures" 19 October 2000). She further stated: "BET's commitment to showcasing African-American talent in front of and behind the cameras is stronger than ever before … We've constructed a successful formula at BET Pictures that leverages a diverse and influential pool of African-American and other resources to create product that is compelling, entertaining, and of the highest quality possible. We're applying this formula to our made-for-television productions, as well as our theatrical releases …" (quoted in "BET Pictures" 19 October 2000).

Spending nearly one million dollars per film (or less—one-quarter of what HBO spent at the time and 1/50th of what an average theatrical release costs), Johnson believed because "blacks are underutilized, many fine actors will gravitate towards our production" (quoted in *Economist* 10 April 1999). The BET Pictures films made to date include *After All* (1999), *Incognito* (1999), *Intimate Betrayal* (1999), *Rendezvous* (1999), *Hidden Blessings* (2000), *Masquerade* (2000), *Midnight Blue* (2000), *Playing with Fire* (2000), *A Private Affair* (2000), *Rhapsody* (2000), *Commitments* (2001), *Fire & Ice* (2001), and *One Special Moment* (2001). Two involved well-respected director Julie Dash (*Incognito*) and cultural commentator Nelson George (*One Special Moment*) as evidence of their ability to attract quality black talent. Long-time media participant Roy Campanella II produced the initial ten films.

Yet most of the actors appearing in these narratives fell into one of three categories: 1) experienced actors with limited mainstream (white) exposure; 2) B-level actors or; 3) new faces. Similar to the books upon which these films were based, the films shared the commonality of inexperienced production skill (not necessarily value but experience or possibly talent), formulaic plots, and uneven performances. The rhythm of several of these films suggested a television serial rather than a discreet film project. In many of the narratives, for example, the usage of wipes to transition scenes posed a distracting shift in television narrative. Furthermore, with films such as *Masquerade* and *Rhapsody*, for example, several instances of BET Holdings product placement surfaced—a copy of *Emerge* magazine being read prominently by the lead male character (Cress Williams), the magazine *Heart and Soul* became a part of the narrative inasmuch as the lead female character (Simbi Khali) wanted to become its competitor,[13] and Lenore's (Gina Ravera) video was mentioned several times as garnering airtime on BET in *Masquerade*. Audiences who quickly identified the aesthetic of these films derisively labeled them a "BET movie." This type of assessment has dogged the network its entire existence. As perceived by several Clark Atlanta focus group participants, "BET looks like it was shot in somebody's basement! ... [It] is kind of bootleg" (Clark Atlanta U focus group 2004).

Nevertheless, BET boastfully promoted itself as the only one invest-
ing in black film production on this level and scale. And given the
films' legs (repeat airing on the network, home DVD sales, etc.), BET
received a good return on its investment. Yet it is its programming
that not only audiences but media critics as well find problematic.

Media Commentary of BET

One of the most vocal media critics of the network has been car-
toonist Aaron McGruder, who waged a highly successful critical
campaign against BET in his comic strip *The Boondocks*. Syndicated in 1999, McGruder constantly lampooned Johnson, the
network's programming, its ideology, and everything else within
BET's purview. In the 1980s, comic books received new life as
adults became a viable market for a medium once considered the
province of children.[14] By extension, McGruder's newspaper strip
flourished as well. This cartoon series and the national attention
it received disturbed Johnson so much that he wrote an editorial
against it in the *Washington Post*. He claimed in part that the journalist Paul Farhi elevated McGruder and "his irresponsible and
simple-minded comments to a level of a bona fide critic of all that
BET Holdings has accomplished in its 20-year history" (*Washington Post* 11 December 1999). Others, such as cultural critic Mark
Anthony Neal, maintained that McGruder represented the post-
soul intelligentsia.

One of McGruder's more cutting comic strips appeared on the
heels of Johnson's attack of him. McGruder responded to Johnson with the strip that in essence gave him an in-your-face black
booty salute as a symbol of BET's contributions (or lack thereof) to
African-Americans (Figure 3.14). The strip illustrated the disdain
between the two.

Beyond widespread dissatisfaction with its programming in general, one of the most insightful commentaries about BET, black representation, and responsibility emerged within a Disney's children
series *The Proud Family* (Bruce Smith, creator 2001–2005). In episodes addressing television and television viewing, "The Man," an
extremely tall, well dressed, and disembodied (headless) black man,

Figure 3.14   Boondocks BET booty salute. (The Boondocks) (2000) Aaron McGruder. Distributed by Universal Press Syndicate. Reprinted with permission. All rights reserved.

enters the frame and narrative as the one in control (Figure 3.15). However, he consistently takes no responsibility for the questionable programming that airs on his network.

For example in the episode "Hooray for Iesha," the entire narrative satirized the programming strategies of both UPN and BET. The Wizard, black owner of the local channel WCOD, cancels *Iesha* (which could also be UPN's *Moesha* and BET's *BET Tonight with Tavis Smiley*). The Wizard tells the disappointed children that they shouldn't boycott him because he is simply a "tool of the man" at the station. He urged them to protest the parent company, UBC.

Figure 3.15   The Proud Family.

The main character Penny Proud (voiced by Kyla Pratt) climbs an outdoor billboard to protest the cancellation. And after weeks of her camping there and extensive press coverage (by the same station), the network renews *Iesha* (a double parody in that it reflects real-life singer and actor Brandy Norwood).[15] The episode teaches several lessons about the business of media—product placement, demographic targeting, and the role of advertisements. Yet one of the most important insights is the duplicity of ownership—lessons that are readily translatable to BET.

Blackness on Demand

The programming of BET illustrates the triumph and the tragedy of the nation's first network targeting African-Americans. The pride African-Americans felt in watching Robert L. Johnson succeed materially cannot be dismissed; neither can the success of BET's programs in forcing other networks and advertisers to consider African-Americans in their programming. As filmmaker and president of entertainment Reginald Hudlin maintained, "BET is the largest black media company in the world." Furthermore, he suggested:

> And our goal as a brand—and that includes everything from online to wireless to the cable channels—is to be a repository of all black culture ... Black culture is pop culture, and it's a global commodity. And right now, there isn't a one-stop shop. Particularly with the merger of UPN and WB, there's going to be a lot of desperate eyeballs hungry for black product. We want to be the premiere destination for consumers of black entertainment. (quoted in Frankel 24 February 2006).

Yet as television scholar Deborah Jaramillo argued:

> Visibility and fairness are not and *should not* be the only issues brought to the minorities-on-television discussion. First off, cultural validity should not fall in line with patterns and degrees of consumption. Latinos and African Americans have not *made it* when they have been targeted. They have been deemed to be marketable, and

that is not the same thing as being on the receiving end of a deep and sincere level of cultural understanding and acceptance (Jaramillo 2002: 5).

Beyond shortsightedness and greed, why is it that BET only in late 2000 began to do serious original programming—programming beyond music video shows and *Teen Summit*? As discussed earlier, Johnson gave two reasons for not creating more original programming: 1) lack of ancillary markets for the kind of programming that BET would produce and 2) lack of advertiser support. However, especially on the second point, how is it then that BET acquired the syndicated shows from virtually every broadcast network—which clearly, at least to some degree, had been doing the kind of programming that is thought to be appealing to demographic black and supported? Its 2005–2006 original programs, *College Hill, Season of the Tiger*, and *Ultimate Hustler* all fell into the media-making mode of observational documentary. In this realm, the frame of reference works for audiences as a fictional narrative but is positioned as the "what is." Wrote media scholar Bill Nichols: "We look in and overhear social actors ... The viewer experiences the text as a template of life as it is lived ... Observational cinema conveys the sense of unmediated and unfettered access to the world" (Nichols 1991: 42-43). Yet for Generation Xers, these "reality programs" are their contemporary soap operas and life lessons. The constant promos, cliff hangers, conflict (drama), and perceived realness create an appealing mix for young adults.[16] This programming wave promises revenue (assuming a sellable idea) but will the foci BET selects move beyond what currently exists? In other words, will docudramas like *Season of the Tiger* (2006) be perpetuated, or will *Lil' Kim: Countdown to Lockdown* (2006) become the norm?

Sociologist Herman Gray distinguished productions made about, by, and for black folks versus those that are made just *about* them (Gray 2000). Beyond the visual accoutrements alluded to in chapter 2, in many ways BET is a nonfiction *Boomerang*. Knowing this, it becomes difficult to comprehend BET's programming choices given that most of its staff are African-American—a point they stress. Presumably, anything that it makes should be considered an insider production. Nonetheless, BET's programming begs the question of what good is an insider creation when it reifies (or just plain duplicates) the racist and one-dimensional characterizations found in any outsider creation? Furthermore, as one student observed, although BET is supposed to be "all that," it fails still to program 24 hours. It presents infomercials (products or praises) on at least five hours daily—this after twenty-seven years. But maybe this gives validation to the wicked economic structure of television. The privilege of artifice—certain class mindsets—allows one to pretend uncritically and without consideration of the ramifications on the lived life.

One of the best segments of the 2004 BET Awards program was the tribute to twenty-five years of hip hop on wax. The Sugar Hill Gang kicked it off followed by Melle Mel and Grand Master Flash, MC Lyte (briefly), Slick Rick, Doug E. Fresh, and Public Enemy. These artists kept the audience on their feet as they reminisced on the foundation of the cultural phenomenon, especially Doug E. Fresh. The performances gave old heads (the Wayans brothers, Hill Harper, Russell Simmons, Kristoff St. John, Malinda Williams, Lisa Raye, myself at home) an opportunity to sing lyrics from the 1980s and early 1990s heyday of rap. This same occurrence (to a lesser degree) occurred with the lifetime achievement award presented to the Isley Brothers.

Although presenter and actor Mekhi Phifer introduced Public Enemy as the group that showed what hip hop could be about, the crowd seemed less "with them" than the other performers. Over the years, BET programmed exciting and important events in black America. Even each award offering improved—indeed to be bigger and better (well, minus the 2006 installment). However, the accolades bestowed upon Johnson and the BET network fail to fully account for much of the programming that has passed for quality entertainment.

In 2007, while reaching 80 million households, a great proportion of BET's programming remains music videos. And after twenty-seven years of operation, it is just beginning to capitalize on its core participants' placement as innovators in American society. Meaning, despite its new heightened corporate ties, it is still unwilling to take risks on new art forms or new (or just plain broad) conceptions of blackness. The voluminous competing and complimentary discourses that define black innovation, black programming, and black identity narrow into seemingly one thing for BET—profit. And perhaps it is its failure to address the aforementioned issues that—paradoxically—limits both the cultural *and* economic viability of BET's product.

Chapter 4

The Impossibility of Us

BET Impact

Young Woman: I'm not going to lie and say I'm any better than anybody else. I went to a predominately white school, and I went to public school. And when I went to public school, what is the first thing I started doing? I started watching BET because that's how real black people act. If you ain't from the ghetto, if you ain't smoking weed, if you ain't drinking, then you ain't black. (Commotion) ....

Young Woman: I'm not saying that's true, but that is what people believe and that is what people think about rap artists or whatever ... the majority of people that buy rap artists' CDs ... are white kids, because this is how they think black people do.

Young Man: That's true ...

Young Woman: When you turn on BET, what is it that you see? ... How does it affect you? Think about it! Be real. Get out of the "Oh, I watch it because of the duh duh duh." Be honest about it.

—Clark Atlanta U focus group, November 2004

What will the Latin American or African child learn of America from our great communications industry?

—Newton Minow, former FCC Chairman,
1961 "Vast Wasteland" speech

During the 2005 BET Awards program, co-host Will Smith told a personal story of his visit to Mozambique (Figure 4.1). While there, young people called him by name, and he saw the names of Tupac and Jay-Z written on a tin "shack." But what struck him most was a young boy telling him, you all are impossible. Through a translator, Smith queried further and the boy explained that in his mind, African-Americans do the impossible. He could not understand how, as a 13% minority, something like a BET even existed. Smith concluded his remembrance with: "For all of us to be here to acknowledge the impossibility that we are, just does my heart good" (BET Awards 2005).

In many ways, the young boy made an astute observation. African-Americans manage to survive and succeed despite every circumstance hurled against them. In the case of BET, as Megan Mullen noted in her cable text, its very "founding … involved a combination of a narrowcasting vision and the ability to make do on extremely limited funds" (Mullen 2003: 123). Yet it is this existence of BET that highlights the paradoxes of living while black in

Figure 4.1   Will Smith at 2005 BET Awards.

the twenty-first century—contradictions that can overwhelm when considering discourses and real-lived actualities of those posed by the young woman and her Clark Atlanta classmates in the opening epigraph. Through its business structure and programming, BET facilitates a deepening of these conundrums inasmuch as it constructs and promotes an essentialized blackness that both allows for self-visioning and imposes limitations. And while paradox has been thought of as any surprising or counterintuitive claim, its contemporary meaning suggests, at least according to philosopher Peter Suber, "a concept or proposition that is not only self-contradictory, but for which the obvious alternatives are either self-contradictory or very costly" (Suber www.earlharm.edu, n.d.). I offer this latter definition here because much of what has been discussed in previous chapters covers aspects of BET that are not only self-contradictory but also exact a high cost across African-America. Taking up issues both inside the BET network and out into the streets, this chapter explores what impact BET has made on black America and the larger world that receives many of its ideas of African-America from this company. I believe that while its impact is significant, its progressiveness and potential are being squandered.

One of the critical ideas BET sells to audiences is its potential to impact African-America, African-American communities, and the larger media landscape. Many believed in 1980 (and still) that salvation and equity for African-Americans came through blacks' ability to produce and distribute programming—programming that reflected the dreams, issues, and lives of black America. As noted at the end of chapter 3, scholars such as Deborah Jaramillo argued that people mistakenly assume "economic viability equals cultural force" or conversely, I suggest, cultural acknowledgement provides power. She contended, "Unfortunately, this conflation of economics and culture has been naturalized in the discourse surrounding greater visibility for ethnic minorities on television" (Jaramillo 2002: 5). However, as media scholar and journalist Kristal Brent Zook maintained, "What we, as black people and Americans, should really be upset about is the lack of alternative voices in the mainstream media as a whole" (Zook 23 December 2002). Yet despite the acknowledged limits of representation to do much more than "represent," the value of Robert L. Johnson's mainstream capitalist success outweighs protests.

In terms of its psychic impact, BET proves phenomenal. Many older African-Americans concede that having this black-owned entity to represent the race is a crowning achievement. Being able to sell it for billions of dollars and then buy a national basketball franchise also gives black folks a psychological boost. At least two scholars even argue for BET's value as a culturally-endowed product. For example, Alice A. Tait and John T. Barber suggested that not only is BET on target with preserving African cultural sensibilities, but its business practices are actually "liberational." They argued that in BET's " … focus on black music and other culturally creative forms, it honors an important African ancestry … BET stands as a tribute and legacy to future generations of African Americans" (Tait and Barber 1996: 195). They maintained further that while "BET's programming does not strongly reflect the collectivist action of African Americans … [It] does, however, perform the collectivist function better than the networks and other African American-inspired programs" (Tait and Barber 1996: 196). Yet beyond the emotional feel-good, and perhaps model of a successful business endeavor, the representational, economic, and political relevance and value of the network seem negligible, or better yet, bittersweet. Thus in order to interrogate the implicit binaries within the impact BET makes, I turn first to an examination of what exactly scholars mean when they invoke the term impact.

Impact Studies

Communication studies scholars look at impact as effects and influences—so much so, they refuse to even invoke the term impact.[1] For this text, however, impact implies a broader scope. It takes into account a greater range of implications, occurrences, and narrative logics. I use effects and influence studies of communications scholars to buttress arguments on BET's impact; yet only limited scholarship of this kind has been published. In fact from extensive database research, only four scholarly studies have centered the network in its 27-year plus history.[2] Most other studies that included BET were ones conducted on the impact, work of, and consequences produced by music videos. On this particular topic, a deluge of scholarly and journalistic material exists—including chapter 3 in my *Shaded Lives: African-American Women and Television*. The bulk of these findings, especially since the turn of the century, concluded several things: 1) music videos often create a "dream world" where male, child-like sexual fantasy plays out; 2) music videos reinscribe the -isms of the world by hierarchically and binaristically positioning women and men, heterosexuals and homosexuals, whites and others against one another; 3) women (particularly women of color) live in service to male entertainers; and 4) the more exposure to music videos, the more likely viewers are to conform and confirm traditional beliefs about gender, race, and sexuality.[3] I refer to these studies again as I explore music videos as BET's major programming choice. But here, it's important to underscore the pervasiveness of this area of inquiry.

Other impact research has looked at the cable industry—regulatory debates, shifts in audience consumption patterns (in terms of content, frequency, and context), and transformations in technology. Yet even in these areas, Black Entertainment Television remained a limitedly cited reference. Even in general books on cable television, BET received not much more than a parenthetical mention, a cursory glance at its existence. A part of the inattention, it seems to me, can be attributed to racial disregard—the same reason Nielsen keeps distinct tabulations of the television viewing choices of African-Americans (and now Latinos)—because these groups don't watch the same programs as white Americans. Scholars, unfortunately, are not vastly different in their viewing preferences. And while scholarship on cable television is just beginning to flourish, especially in media studies, analysis of networks such as MTV (several texts, in fact), Nickelodeon and CNN have existed for over a decade.

Beyond actual cable programming, the rationale for all television programs' existence, advertising, received considerable examination—examination in terms of its impact, quantity, and quality of images across identity categories.[4] According to at least one 1995 study, commercials on BET contained African-Americans at about twice their actual population, situated one-third of their characters in segregated settings, and provided BET audiences "with an opportunity to view blacks in naturalistic social situations, offer[ing] commercials that depict blacks as central characters, and contain[ing] substantially more ethnic targeting cues" (Elliott 1995: 83). Yet by a 2000 study, white-dominated commercials appeared to be prevalent on BET—whites becoming overrepresented in this black-identified world (Entman and Rojecki 2000: 174).

Furthermore, in a 2006 study, results showed that of the nearly 1,100 advertisements on BET, WB, and Disney televised one week in July 2005 from 3 to 9pm, more than half were for fast food and drinks. Approximately 66% of the fast-food ads aired on BET, compared with 34% on WB and none on Disney. For drinks (like soda), 82% were on BET, 11% on WB and 6% on Disney; and for snacks, 60% were on BET, none on WB, and 40% on Disney. The study, published in the *Archives of Pediatric and Adolescent Medicine*, provided separate research as well: one study indicated that children consume an extra 167 calories, often from advertised foods, for every hour of TV they watch; and another suggested that even preschoolers grow fat from watching more than two hours of daily TV. BET vice president of communications Michael Lewellen responded to these findings with the assertion that because BET's current target audience was blacks aged 18 to 34, its programming "does not target children" (*Wall Street Journal* 3 April 2006), and thus the results failed to apply to or concern BET. Yet it flew in the face of reports on the obesity crisis and general poor health of African-Americans as well as BET's own health initiative, "A Healthy BET." While this section gives an overview of the way impact is assessed and some of the categories it engages, looking at specific ways in which the impact of BET is measured across various identity, collective, and national lines provides evidence. Thus, I begin with its audience.

BET Audiences

In 2005, a Nielsen Media Research report claimed that African-Americans watch 40% more television than all other groups—specifically, 11 hours and 4 minutes per day. It stated further that African-Americans maintained a higher percentage of homes with multiple television sets, with cable plus and cable premium channels, and with video games. Additionally, these same homes possessed a lower percentage of Internet connection (Steadman 2005). Findings such as these provided by Nielsen and others do three things: 1) highlight the disparities in the nation's viewing consumption; 2) presume a numerically sound assessment process; and 3) insidiously perpetuate a looming stasis or magic number that will provide balanced representation. With this balance, these studies and similar discourses suggest a "no color lines" world—one created by and perpetuated within Hollywood—would become manifest, although not extended beyond the Adams exit on the I-10 freeway there. And beyond watching more, a 2006 *USA Today* article noted that black households continued to principally watch programs with black narratives and characters as central. The Nielsen study concluded: "Distinct viewing patterns and distinct viewing choices of African-Americans offer programmers and advertisers the opportunity to reach this audience in different ways" (Steadman 2005:40).

The BET target audience can be characterized in a myriad of ways beyond the 18 to 34 years purported by the network. However, the characteristics of African-American, young, and primarily urban reflected at least the iconography of those who appeared on the network. University of Houston collegiate Fred Walker talked about a historical feeling of family and accomplishment with BET. He mused, " ... if you wanted to see your favorite artist you would go to BET so it was more like a family thing growing up ... it felt like it was a black thing. And now because [of BET's mainstream success], for the time being, it seems to be more popular to be black" (University of Houston focus group February 2003). When BET sold to Viacom in 2000, adult black communities responded in dismay. It incited discussions of control, pointing to the omnipresent "the Man" as colonizing black folks' stuff, and African-American progress in the U.S. Ironically, a few years later many young people didn't even realize BET was no longer black owned. For example in the 2004 Omaha focus group, my question of what BET meant to them yielded the following exchange:

R1:   It means black people doin' somethin' good. It ain't just white people that got they own stuff.

R2:   White people own BET, idiot.

R3: Yeah, white people own that.

R1: Oh, for real?

R2: Yeah, they sold it to Viacom. It ain't black owned.

R1: Oh they did? Never mind then.

—Clair youth group July 2004

This lack of ownership knowledge (and in some regard, lack of it mattering *much*) impacts the ways in which black business mantras circulate in the twenty-first century. Communications scholar Emmanuel K. Ngwainmbi posed the question: "How can potential consumers and business partners in the [African-American] and [African] communities be persuaded to purchase and use products and services produced by Black entrepreneurs, when slavery and colonialism have continued to dominate the Black consumer's thought process?" (Ngwainmbi 2005: 4). In a restaurant review of Minneapolis' Midtown Chicken Shack, the writer remarked that BET always aired in this space as part of the ambience and as a complement to the excellent food served. The restaurant advertised three commercials per week on BET. "Above the television is a little framed double portrait of Malcolm X and Martin Luther King Jr. (Malcolm also stands guard in a portrait over the cash register), and the table in front of the television tends to act as the community table, where people gather to discuss misfortunes … " (Moskowitz 2001).

This business and others around the country like it believe that BET holds sway with consumers at some very basic identification level. And despite black disparagement and lessened support of black-owned businesses for a multitude of reasons, including perceived quality of products, quality of service, and quality of environment, many still give lip service and actual pocket tribute to the need for black businesses—BET included. Yet understanding how much (or how little) advertisers value the African-American audience continuously (the key factor in this process), I pose an opposite question: What is BET's worth to black consumers?

One testament to how well regarded BET is for reaching black America by both black and white audiences comes through its acquisition of high-profile political interviews. Because of its long-term "only" status, BET became the de facto site for a person to clear his name before *the* African-American community. In 1992, for example, former Washington D.C. mayor Marion Barry talked with BET's Ed Gordon from his Pennsylvania jail cell after being convicted for cocaine possession. Barry reasoned, "I knew the reporter would understand the true nature of what was going on in my life at the time" (quoted in Waxler 22 April 1996). This perceived understanding was clear in an exchange between a Clark Atlanta focus group participant and me when I asked about what they watched on BET.

Young Woman: *BET News* is good because ... you'll be able to get it [what's going on] from a black perspective.

Interviewer: Do you think it's a black perspective? What generally do you find makes it a black perspective?

Young Woman: ... it may not necessarily be, like, black reporters, but there may be something [going on and] BET is going to tell you how it's relevant to you, how it affects you in a way that you hadn't thought of.

—Clark Atlanta U focus group November 2004

In another network coup, O.J. Simpson granted the first televised interview about his murder acquittal to Gordon in January 1996. While he offered little new insights, due to his simultaneous hawking of his tell-all video, in BET's *O.J. Simpson: Beyond the Verdict with Ed Gordon* Simpson defended his lifestyle choices. He asked: "Where should I go? Back to Africa? ... I am black. I was raised black. When I give money, I give to black causes ... My mother taught me that it's your character that counts, not your color" (quoted in *O.J. Simpson* 1996). His life associations notwithstanding, it was to BET, back to black folks, where Simpson came to reaffirm the veracity of the jury's findings of his innocence. And in December 2002, Mississippi Republican senator Trent Lott attempted to retain his claim to the majority speaker seat by also talking with Ed Gordon—hoping that by appearing on the channel that presumably *all* black people watched, he could find redemption for his comments made in a pubic space. During the 100th birthday party for South Carolina segregationist Senator Strom Thurmond, Lott suggested that if Thurmond won his bid as head Dixiecrat, "We wouldn't have had all these problems over the years." If this had happened, BET would likely not exist.

Beyond interviews, BET provided exclusive footage of the 1996 memorial for black U.S. Secretary of Commerce Ron Brown. BET televised the *entire* Million Man March in 1995 and the 1996 funeral of the Honorable Barbara Jordan. Screening these momentous and historical events in America made a case for the viability of BET to a wider range of black Americans and as an access point for white ones. Beyond C-SPAN in a couple of these cases, BET was the only television space to provide connection, exude reverence, and lend importance to the stories and lives of African-America.

In his 1992 *Blacks and White TV*, historian J. Fred MacDonald surmised that since only 39% of African-Americans subscribed to cable in 1989 and with the slow pace of wiring in major black hubs, "even when cable is made available to African-American households, many [will] find it unaffordable" (MacDonald 1992: 269). Yet fast-forward to 2007 where African-Americans obtained cable in a larger proportion than anyone else. In many households, cable appeared to take a weighty priority. If according to 1999 Census figures, the average African-American household earns $29,423 yearly and the average expanded basic cable household bill is $28.92 (NCTA), cable costs represent 1.18% of black household' expenditures. These are 1999 figures with 2006 ones finding the average cable bill running around $41.00—not including premium networks and taxes (Kagan). This shows that if nothing else, the desire for television (specifically cable television), connectedness, and representation continues to penetrate the minds and priorities of black audiences.

While grappling with how to get at the actualities of BET's impact on audiences, I encountered an article about the border—specifically, the U.S. and Mexico border. The literature of this

encounter—both popular and academic—is voluminous and specific as is the legislation surrounding the questions these discourses
address. Yet what intrigued me, beyond the racism of it all, was the
idea of psychological border crossings and its resonance with many
BET audiences. Let me explain. In "Cultural Mourning, Immigration, and Engagement: Vignettes from the Mexican Experience,"
psychology scholar Ricardo C. Ainslie reflected on his immigrant
status—as one who belongs but is not firmly at home—coming to
a place that is foreign, yet strangely familiar. This led him to focus
on borders that are "historical, social, and psychological boundar-
ies, rather than a discrete geographic boundary ... [immigrants and
others] whose struggles are linked to psychological crossings that
rupture a subjective sense of clear delineation" (Ainslie 1998: 284).
I believe that the idea of psychological border crossings works as a
powerful framework for some of BET's audiences.

If it is as Robert L. Johnson remembered: "I used to tell operators that Black Entertainment Television was colorblind, and in fact,
we consciously programmed the network so that it would appeal
to, or at least wouldn't offend, a broader audience" (*Advertising
Age* 11 April 2005: B8). White folks are not only a partial target
for BET's advertisers but are also invited to cruise, to sample, to
explore, to mask black culture. These invited interlopers, (and all
others), entered into this arena as special guests. Invoking world
history, when the Arawaks welcomed the Spanish and the Wolof the
French, their invitations read, "Come co-exist with us, trade with
us." These groups failed to recognize the belief system, potential
atrocities, and purpose of their guests' visits. Furthermore, neither
of them said "Come, become us." However, BET ignored significant
lessons such as these in favor of building its brand on the bodies of
blacks to make available to all consumers, and Johnson appeared
color blinded by the profit potential. What these crossers received,
coming over to the black side, was an opportunity to live, explore,
and evoke a certain blackness without the physical consequence or
psychological permanence—or as cultural critic Greg Tate's book
title succinctly stated, they got *Everything But the Burden: What
White People Are Taking from Black Culture*.

In the same vein, BET called for African-Americans, Caribbean-Americans, and other hyphenated-black folks living in the U.S. and black folks abroad to indulge in a specific, constructed aspect of black life—positioned as the quintessential and authentic blackness spot for those in the know. Differences in class, generation, and region addressed some of the disconnections and contentions produced by BET; however, the term cultural dislocation aptly embodied this polarity. So the Clark Atlanta student's feeling of cloaking or putting on her blackness like a coat is as real for her as a college-educated and more-broadly identified African-American in the target demographic as it is for any other not-targeted group member.

Cable scholar Megan Mullen contended: "One way BET mollified concerns about its stereotypically low-income population was through an appeal to some 'crossover' market segments, especially teenager and young adult white viewers. While this probably was more of a cost-cutting measure than a deliberate attempt to widen its demographic niche, the effect is apparent in the fact that BET is one of the longest-surviving basic cable networks" (2003: 159). Yet, observed Steven Goodman, executive director of the Educational Video Center, "Our society has generally responded to inner-city teenagers in two ways: to punish them more harshly—whether in the classroom, community, or courtroom—than any other demographic group, and to market their urban youth culture more pervasively" (Goodman 2003: 24). This combination of criminalization, cooptation, and crossover forged an unholy alliance. The bodies of the poorest and less advantaged become the property and fetching price for McDonald's, Chevy Tahoe, and Robert Tilton's healing for Jesus all televised on BET. Thus, the importance of black BET audiences seemed to be in direct proportion to the selling price for their cultural *Essence*.

Buffoonery and Booty Shake

Essential notions of blackness—notions that over time UPN and the WB regurgitated well—pervaded BET's non-produced but aired sitcoms and music videos alike. Said an anonymous black broadcasting executive, "Bob Johnson has marketed and branded

BET as the spokesperson for African-Americans—all of them. So white Americans think BET represents and is the voice of Black America, not teenage black Americans. A lot of black Americans resent that. They know it doesn't represent them" (quoted in Ross 2003). Similar to the criticism that targeted the earliest television programs featuring black characters, the programming of BET panders to mainstream (and increasingly in-house) expectations.

Its connections to the past are well rehearsed. When in a description of the radio and television series *Amos n' Andy* David Hinckley noted:

> Amos drove the Fresh Air cab, while Andy stayed in the office, 'layin' down to think' or 'restin' my brain.' Had Andy been just a deadbeat, there would have been no story. But he was a deadbeat with the American dream of easy money, which made him the regular mark of George Stevens, the Kingfish. The Kingfish was the leader of Amos 'n Andy's lodge, the Mystic Knights of the Sea, and he always had a get-rich plan, and it always involved scamming $5 or $10 from Andy while Amos was out. What the schemes had in common was they all failed (Hinckley 2002: 25).

Hinckley's insight into this 1950s television program (which began on 1920s radio) resembled the output of BET, and unfortunately made a painful link to the legacy of Eurocentric "ideology" pervading the behind-the-scenes control of this formerly black-owned entity. Reminiscent of the critique filmmaker Marlon Riggs made in his documentary *Color Adjustment* (1991), plantation humor, minstrelsy, and performance are recycled in service to capitalism on BET.

Spike Lee's *Bamboozled* suggested a minstrelsy ethos of contemporary television—laying the charge squarely at the feet of UPN and WB. In the film, white television executive Dunwitty (Michael Rapaport) immerses himself in blackness—his office art, his intonation, his black wife. Near the end of the film, he goes even further by donning blackface to view the minstrel show taping. He asserts to black television writer Delacroix (Damon Wayans): "Brother Man, I'm blacker than you. I'm keeping it real" (*Bamboozled* 2000). Lee discussed the construction of this character, saying "Culture should be appreciated by everybody, but for me there is a distinction between appreciation of culture and appropriation of a culture. People like Dunwitty ... are dangerous because they appropriate black culture and put a spin on it as if they are the originators of it. There's a big difference" (Lee quoted in Crowdus). While Lee's concerns and linkages ring valid, if he really wanted to do a thorough critique and throw down the gauntlet, he would have indicted BET with the same charges in the film.[5] Truth be told, the majority of programming on the network for black folks provides the racial sanction and legitimacy for FOX and CW to construct and capitalize on a unidimensional and racist conception of blackness.

I argued in *Shaded Lives* that representation continues to be contested ideological ground and quantity of images remain an issue despite the seeming plethora available. BET initially maintained that it provided programming unavailable elsewhere. Yet what it meant was that it provided a space for visioning black folks consistently. Since the early 1980s, it aired various off-network programs such as *Sanford and Son* (NBC 1972–1977), *The Jeffersons* (CBS 1975–1985), *Thea* (ABC 1993–1994), *Generations* (NBC 1989–1991), *In Living Color* (Fox 1990–1994), *The Parkers* (UPN 1999–2004) and many others. As noted, these programs migrated from broadcast television and other cable networks. So while black folks could see almost everything BET aired elsewhere, they could not see them at the ready nor could they view or listen to the sounds of African-America except on BET, at least not initially. Ironically, Johnson seemed surprised that he needed to rebuke charges of disdain from black audiences in offering these series. He exclaimed: "People loved these shows when they were on the networks ... When they're on the white networks they're called classics. When they're on BET, they're called 'tired ol' reruns'" (quoted in Pulley 2004: 131–132). However as early as a 1978 report on how blacks use television, the researchers found that: "The qualified acceptance of shows that feature blacks suggests that the available programs are more relevant and popular than they would be given meaningful alternatives" (Booker T. Washington Foundation 1978: 114). It seems part of the human condition to want and need a reflection of self—somewhere. While BET offered that, it replicated the distortions of mainstream representations. Moreover, music videos' impact, as the primary programming offering on the network, more than syndicated programs, sits as a critical site of exploration.

Sociologists, anthropologists, psychologists, media and educational scholars conducted extensive studies on the ways in which music videos influence and inform the lives of their audiences. Referenced earlier, these investigations assessed the impact of music videos on youth and violence, sexuality, gendered relationships, intra- and interracial relationships, and self-esteem. In a 2005 investigation, for example, the researchers found that black adolescents' exposure to music videos helped shape their ideas about gender and sexual relationships—creating "expectations of adversarial dynamics and of mutual disrespect" (Ward et al. March 2005: 161). "Highlighting appearance and status over intellect and emotion," wrote Ward, "these characterizations, in most cases, imply that the only source of power available for a woman is the use of her body and sexuality" (Ward et al. March 2005: 161). Other works such as Carol Vernalis's *Experiencing Music Videos: Aesthetics and Cultural Context* (2004) focused on and celebrated the music video form as a distinctive artistic medium or in an earlier work, *Dancing in the Distraction Factory: Music Television and Popular Culture* (1992), Andrew Goodwin analyzed the industrial and economic, aesthetic, and music component of music television for audiences.

Music videos transformed the way music enters people's lives and the ways that performers do their jobs. Yet, they have not killed radio as many predicted—an important part of black America's living experiences. Some have argued that black people consume radio very differently than others. In fact, radio VP Ronald T. deCastro believed: "Music television is a complement to radio. We help them, they help us" (deCastro 2006). With music videos, audiences get to see and hear people that they normally wouldn't hear on radio. However, music videos gutted the concert industry and changed the way the recording industry conducts its business. Plus, as business scholar Juliet E.K. Walker maintained, " ... despite their contribution in revitalizing the American recording industry and their numerous personal and financial achievements, blacks did not emerge as the principal beneficiaries of the crossover of black music into white markets" (Walker 1998: 322).

Beyond academic and industrial critiques, the impact of music videos found expression among audience members themselves. For example in November 2001, the National Pan-Hellenic Council, the umbrella organization of the nine U.S.-based black sororities and fraternities, discussed boycotting BET because of its programming. Keep in mind that by this time, BET had been in business for over twenty years, with essentially the same focused programming. However, it had been less than one year since its sale to Viacom. The council had meetings with Johnson in September of that year. Post the meeting through email, the heads of these organizations released to its memberships a draft of a letter addressed to Johnson stating in part:

> As discussed with you and your staff, we believe that BET does not operate in the best interest of the African American community ... Your responses to our concerns were not only unacceptable but were also insulting. We raised concerns with you about the type of videos shown on BET that have a negative influence on our community, particularly our youth. We believe that these videos are an exploitation of African American youth (NPHC 2001).

By November, however, they decided against activating this boycott in favor of meeting with the BET staff on a consistent basis to discuss concerns. This belated communal response illustrated the clinging of many to both notions of black redemption (hoping that Johnson's capitalist actions would be subverted by awakening some sympathetic racial consciousness) and the aversion to bringing a brother down.

In a later example, 2004 witnessed Spelman College students protesting rapper Nelly's scheduled visit to their campus largely in response to his video "Tip Drill" (Figure 4.2). The lyrics and corresponding video discussed and visualized the rapper's need to find a tip drill—a woman to insert his (and his crew's) penises.[6] This desire was demonstrated in the video by sliding a credit card along the crack of a black woman's behind. The brouhaha of the protest (not really the actual video) made national news and reignited

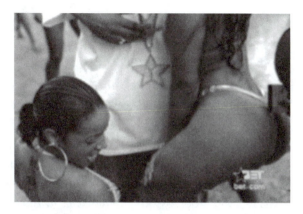

Figure 4.2   Nelly's "Tip Drill" video as seen on *Uncut*.

debates about representation, images, hip hop, and misogyny. The young, African-American women of Spelman felt that these types of videos, largely found on BET's *Uncut*, were now over the top—explicit, hypersexual, and harsh. In fact, two Spelman focus group participants voiced their observations on the *Uncut* program this way:

Respondent 1: "I remember like earlier it was like, local artists and stuff like that. It wasn't so much naked people—and it was more like untapped stuff, like people who weren't necessarily known. And you saw a lot of local people, like you saw 3–6 Mafia and all good stuff like that."…

Respondent 2: "Now it's just naked people …"

Respondent 1: "It's not just nudity, it's like vulgarity" (Spelman focus group November 2004).

Their critique reflected the feelings some African-Americans harbor about all of BET's programming. Their comments suggested not only negatively transformed visual imagery but also BET's impact and viability on the lives of citizens, both in public and private spaces. Clearly a good deal of its programming and business actions proved regressive or at a minimum, disrespectful, especially in terms of the ongoing classist discourses that grounded BET's claims for black veracity.

The Firing of Tavis Smiley

Because U.S. audiences have limited input on the choices, scheduling, or longevity of BET's programming (or any television network's for that matter), they fail to act much on transformations they dislike. So when in March 2001, *BET Tonight* host Tavis Smiley was abruptly dismissed from the network, the response from the audience was unexpected and unprecedented. Smiley's contract was due to expire later that year, yet the apparent contentious relationship between he and Robert Johnson proved combustible. Unfortunately for BET, Smiley possessed alternate platforms to voice his displeasure with this decision. As an ongoing commentator for *The Tom Joyner Morning Show*, a nationally syndicated black radio program, BET was quickly taken to task over the radio airways.

Communications scholar Catherine R. Squires wrote about the continued relevance of black media and black audience activism. She assessed black talk radio station WVON but her comments also applied to the *Tom Joyner Morning Show*: "WVON exists in response to the poor public service Blacks feel they receive from mainstream media providers. Its commercial success rests on listener loyalty, which can only be had through public-minded programming, awareness, and celebration of black culture and through a commitment to community service" (Squires 2000: 91). In the article "Black Talk Radio: Defining Community Needs and Identity," she contextualized the contemporary scenario: "In the mainstream public sphere, Blacks, like other nonwhite groups, are considered 'special interest,' not included in the category of everyday citizens. Hence, conversations concerning issues that are pertinent to the entire body politic are often considered relevant only to members of the class considered 'typical' citizens: whites" (Squires 2000: 85). In this vein, Joyner urged his listeners to phone, fax, and email Viacom regarding the Smiley atrocity. According to reports, hundreds did just that.

To address this deluge of audience complaints, Johnson made an uncharacteristic appearance on the network in a one-hour special edition of *BET Tonight* with space for audience calls and reporter Cheryl Martin as host. The bizarre special found Johnson asserting his control of the network, his continued authority to make decisions, and his plan for the network. When one caller asked Johnson if he had become a "front man" for Viacom, he replied: "I'm absolutely calling the shots ... I make too much money to be a front man." In effect, Johnson insisted, "I am still the H.N.I.C." At stake was not only his credibility as a business man, but his cred as a black man in charge. Despite this airing, the protest persisted. To finally resolve the matter, Johnson arranged a conference call between himself, Joyner, Mel Karmazin, and Debra Lee. Joyner agreed to calm the masses, to quiet the storm, in exchange for a promise of greater resource support for BET from Viacom. Karmazin said: "Whatever [Johnson] wants to do to make that network better, he has my support" (quoted in Pulley 2004: 204). In many respects, this scandal propelled Smiley toward more status and acclaim than he could have possibly attained remaining with BET.[7] More pertinent to this text, it pointed to the willingness of black audiences to get with "the Man" yet unfortunately, to disbelieve the now frequent occurrence of public and professional black-on-black attacks. This incident spoke also to one of the assertions BET made about its influence on the community—the idea that BET put people to work.

Community Impact

As discussed in chapter 2, BET began with the financial and operational support of TCI yet relied on and cultivated the loyalty of black folks to support black business and black representation. BET promised that through its existence, a more diverse media universe would surface; a bigger and better black America would emerge because BET was there to sponsor such a transformation. BET forwarded a sense of community in line with Rev. Dr. Martin Luther King Jr.'s vision of a "beloved community" where he advocated for non-violent change and brotherly love. BET asked its audiences to coalesce around and laud its blackness through the network as a testament to black solidarity and strength.

One way BET purported to benefit black America was through its claim to boost the black economy. Lampooned below, the network alleged that it employed more African-Americans than any other television network (see Figure 4.3a). While the veracity

Figure 4.3a The Boondocks (The Boondocks) (2000) Aaron McGruder. Distributed. By Universal Press Syndicate. Reprinted with permission. All rights reserved.

of this assertion is hard to verify, looking at hard numbers of the television industry sheds light on its truth possibility. According to research reported by the Gay and Lesbian Alliance Against Defamation, African-American characters made up 14% of the 2005–2006 scripted network schedules. The 2005 WGA "Hollywood Writers Report" found that most people of color's stories on television were found within comedies. In the 2004–2005 season, for example, seven of the top-10 shows for African American writers aired on UPN, including each of the top five shows that included *One on One* (71%), *Eve* (69%), *Second Time Around* (69%), *Cuts* (63%), *Girlfriends* (56%), *All of Us* (43%), and *Half and Half* (31%). "Not surprisingly then in 2004, Viacom ranked second among conglomerates and large independents in terms of the employment of minority writers (the total number of television writers working for Viacom in 2004 was 705. 16.5% of these, or 116, were minorities), trailing only the now defunct Carsey-Werner, where 18% of the writers were minorities" (WGA 2005). Clearly, BET contributed to Viacom's number but in a way that might seem the most evident. First beyond BET, Viacom owned CMT, MTV, VH-1, CBS, and others which all contributed to its numbers of minority employees. Second, because BET did not have any scripted BET-produced shows, the need for WGA writers and PGA producers was limited. In the 2005–2006 BET schedule, for example, the original series beyond music video programs included: *Bobby Jones Gospel*, *Comic View*, *College Hill*, *Remixed*, *Lil' Kim: Countdown to Lockdown*, and *Season of the Tiger.* Most of these operated squarely in the genre of reality TV.

Reality television, the darling programming choice of twenty-first century television due to its revenue return, employs minimal writers, producers, and all non-actors. Media scholars Susan Murray and Laurie Ouellette defined reality TV as "an unabashedly commercial genre united less by aesthetic rules or certainties than by the fusion of popular entertainment with a self-conscious claim to the discourse of the real" (Murray and Ouellette 2004: 2). This nod to the real and BET's propensity to work within a very tight economic framework made reality television an ideal choice for the network. And while it did not afford known actors, writers, and producers to roll like their colleagues at other networks, it did provide an opportunity for many not likely to be seen and heard other places to do so.

In fact according to many, the BET Network served as a training camp for blacks who might not otherwise gain entry into the television arena. Many students from Howard University and others from schools in the Washington, D.C. area received their start in television with BET. As one former executive insisted, most African-Americans in entertainment television passed through BET. BET overall has shown loyalty to its workers, especially in the beginning. However this insularity had its drawbacks. For example one former worker believed that because many of the employees of BET had never worked anywhere else, they lacked standard business etiquette: "I found a lot of informal [and inappropriate] jokes ... [the staff] was handled very loosely" (former employee interview 2006). Additionally, while some insiders argued that the salaries were adequate, others say that the salaries do not compare to the industry. One suggested that BET's attitude was like, "look, we made you. We can treat you like we want" (former employee interview 2006). Furthermore, in-house discussion about talent was derisive and "extremely unprofessional."

In addition to the uncertain number of black employees and working conditions, Johnson took questionable stances regarding workers' rights. He stood firm against his employees unionizing, and in one instance he reduced the hours of BET workers who joined an electricians' union. A federal judge subsequently ruled this action illegal. Yet Johnson justified his actions by accusing the unions of racial bias, saying "I don't see them taking part in the NAACP's threatened network boycott. I don't see them writing open letters to the networks about their lack of black representation. Why do they pick on BET? Why not ABC or NBC or Fox?" (quoted in Chait 2001).

Outside of its own in-house strategies, another way BET exemplified its commitment to black communities was through its engagement in televised and social programs that informed and supported African-American knowledge and understanding of issues concerning the group. For example, the network partnered with the Kaiser Family Foundation and a number of other corporations to launch "Rap-It-Up" in 1998.[8] Designed to promote HIV and AIDS awareness, the campaign encouraged African-Americans to get tested for HIV and to practice safe sex. In partnership with Topics Education, a classroom-based curriculum of ten lessons was designed to target 9th and 10th grade students in urban health classrooms across the country. The overarching campaign consisted of not only on-air spots but also the curriculum, special programming, sexual health resources online, teen forums, and an informational toll-free line. As highlighted in a 2005 interview with CEO Debra L. Lee, "the network has had more than one million calls from viewers during its most recent awareness campaign" (Alexander Fall 2005: 37). One Clark Atlanta focus group participant recalled the "Rap-It-Up" campaign as "very informational in terms of sex education. Not a lot of stations have that kind of sex education for blacks." In November 2003, BET launched "Speak Now" in partnership with the National Action Network to increase voter awareness, registration, and participation in the 2004 election. It included PSAs on BET and BET Jazz and local events/partnerships. In another effort, BET started "A Healthy BET" (Figure 4.3b) initiative in 2004 with singer Kelly Price as spokeswoman.

Figure 4.3b   A Healthy BET logo.

According to its website:

The *A Healthy BET* campaign began in January 2004 with a nation-wide fitness challenge. Healthy BET is a national campaign devoted to promoting healthy eating and lifestyle habits to reduce the occurrence of obesity among African Americans. To strengthen the campaign, BET has teamed up with General Mills and together they will leverage their strengths in brand recognition, product quality and consumer influence.

A Healthy BET Campaign included celebrity and real life PSAs, programming vignettes, a nationwide fitness challenge, community forums on nutrition and fitness, a journal or brochure, a toll-free information line, and a dedicated website.

The primary target for Healthy BET is African American women 18–54. According to the American Obesity Association, African American women and young girls are at highest risk. According to AOA, 78 percent of African American women are overweight; 51 percent are obese. The secondary focus of Healthy BET is overall awareness throughout the Black community regarding healthy living, prevention, and nutrition (bet.com n.d.).

This laudatory program, however, flew in the face of many of the advertisements on the network, as discussed earlier. According to Pulley, much of the social welfare drive and philanthropy for the network came from Johnson's former wife, Sheila Crump Johnson, who served as vice president of corporate affairs from 1990 until she was fired at the end of the decade. Similar to its overall business strategy, BET managed to craft all of its corporate, consciousness-raising programs as communal affairs—even its push toward individual gain.

Black Wealth

A part of the premise and press of BET has always been about wealth accumulation. Far from the race men of the past such as Du Bois, Washington, or Garvey who insisted on individual progress as tied to the larger public uplift, contemporary ideologues use race as a tool for personal advancement. The mantras of wealth accumulation emerged in many forms and in many spaces. For example, a top five focus of rap lyrics is the acquisition of riches; *Black Enterprise* magazine initiated an ongoing "Black Wealth Initiative" to direct African-Americans toward money; and how-to acquire wealth books from Dennis Kimbro and Napoleon Hill to Jesse Jackson and Jesse Jackson Jr., all constructed money-making proficiency as central to black survival and progress. Even within the late 1990s black erotic literature by authors such as Reginald Harris, Zane, Tanarive Due, and Sapphire, a maddening focus of these narratives was explicit details of not juicy sex but instead, accoutrements of material success—the kinds of cars driven, houses bought, and clothes worn— an "erotics of capitalistic ethos" or "materialphilia" as cultural theorist Deborah Elizabeth Whaley called it (revisit chapter 2)! A part of BET's paradox has been its programming and major black stars' grounding in stories of poverty, crime, and dysfunction but overarching and explicit elevation of money. BET's focus on wealth pervaded a significant aspect of its outreach.

For example in August of 2002, BET partnered with the Consumer Federation of America and the Bank of America Foundation to form "Black America Saves." Through the BET.com Black America Saves web page, consumers could obtain "helpful" information on saving and building wealth, estimate their net worth, and enroll as a Black American Saver. Accordingly, savers received a free subscription to the quarterly newsletter *American Saver* and free advice over the phone or Internet from a registered financial planner. CEO Debra L. Lee surmised: "This may be the first generation of black Americans who are able to accumulate wealth ... The community just needs to focus on it more" (*USA Today* 2005). And on the website, she suggested: "Black wealth is a new concept for our community ... [It] is a concept that's uncomfortable for us" (bet.com). This thinking was certainly top down, reflecting Johnson's conservative and individualistic ethos.

In fact over time, Johnson developed into a significant black face for conservative political and classist causes—many of which were directly antithetical to the growth, development, and uplift of African-American people. For example in 2001, he publicly supported the repeal of the Estate Tax as a benefit to African-Americans. In a widely circulated published letter that he and several other black businessmen signed, Johnson claimed:

> The Estate Tax is particularly unfair to the first generation of the high net worth African Americans who have accumulated wealth only recently. These individuals may have family members and relatives who have not been as fortunate in accumulating assets who could directly benefit from their share of an estate as heir. Elimination of the Estate Tax would allow African Americans to pass the full fruits of their labor to the next generation and beyond (*Washington Post* and *New York Times* April 4, 2001).

Yet a 2002 Pew think tank found that overall, African-American net worth was a paltry $5,988. Thus the tax that Johnson wants to repeal ultimately benefited less than one-half of one percent of African-Americans. And Johnson had been clear, his efforts were for his family (implied immediate), period. So second cousin Joe was s.o.l. Later in 2002, Johnson championed the privatization of the Social Security system as a Bush-appointed commission member—a commission charged with transforming the program. Johnson reasoned: "African Americans who contribute to the Social Security system and payroll taxes also have one of the highest mortality rates, so in the end, they may not receive the full benefit of what they put in Social Security" (quoted in *The Black Commentator* 3 October 2002). So instead of an assured retirement income for however long one lived, Johnson advocated investing—entering the game of chance as a sound method of estate planning for wealthy and minimum-wage earners alike. In this same time frame, he purchased seven Homewood Suite hotels and was named "Humanitarian of the Year" at the T.J. Martell Gala. These actions made clear that at least Johnson never needed to worry about Social Security regardless of the predicament in which the change might put many of the network's audience. Moreover, the advocacy of wealth not only pervaded Johnson and BET's overall worldly discourses but non-secular ones that appeared on the network as well.

BET and the Black Church

In traditional black Christian doctrine, prosperity often linked to sin (See Matthew 6, 1 Timothy 6, and 2 Kings 5). Yet as early as 1917, labor leader Asa Phillip Randolph connected the value system of money and Christianity to hypocrisy, writing: "the church is the recipient of large contributions from the financial rulers of the South and naturally preach the christianity of profits" (Randolph 1917: 7). Randolph's making capitalism a religion of its own found resonance in today's business espousals. Writer Harry Cox argued: "The Market makes available the religious benefits that once required prayer and fasting, without the awkwardness of denominational commitment or the tedious ascetic discipline that once limited their accessibility. All can now handily be bought without an unrealistic demand on one's time, in a weekend workshop at a Caribbean resort with a sensitive psychological consultant replacing the crotchety retreat master" (Cox March 1989: 23). More importantly, the philosophy of material prosperity through Christ found illustration in BET's Sunday and late night lineup.

Black Entertainment Television provides the only sustained national visualization of African-American Christian experiences. In fact, as discussed in chapter 3, BET's longest running program is *Bobby Jones Gospel*. A part of BET's consistent program offerings, beyond r & b and hip hop music videos, remained its Sunday morning gospel—live (taped) programs, Christian music videos, and late night religious infomercials of preaching and performance. Some contended that the appearance of this Sunday line-up is problematic—remarking that booty shaking all through the week and then church on Sunday just seems wrong. Others argued that this confluence of programming simply replicated the paradoxical (and often hypocritical) tendencies of black Christians, the black church, and quite frankly, Christianity at large. Yet with its institutionalized programming binary, BET directly impacted the growth of and highlighted the dilemma within black communities' contemporary Christianity and the representation thereof.

BET helped television evangelism grow—especially in terms of African-American ministers' participation in this arena. While televangelism existed since the 1960s with ministers such as Billy Graham, Pat Robertson, Frederick "Rev. Ike" Eikerenkoetter, Jim Bakker, Jimmy Swaggert, Charles Stanley, and Frederick Price forging the path, BET created a platform for these practitioners and many others to specifically reach African-American Christians and potential converts. Beyond targeted programming, a key part of BET's infomercial paradise—BET Inspiration—had been a litany of white and black ministers around the U.S. who sought to lead viewers to Jesus. Twenty-first century black ministers such as Creflo Dollar of World Changers Church International and Eddie Long of New Birth Missionary Baptist Church followed in the footsteps of some of these ministers to evangelize the gospel of prosperity.

In fact, most national televangelists follow some variation of the Word of Faith gospel—a gospel some derisively associate with prosperity ministries. Ministrywatch.com evaluated Word-of-Faith supporters and decriers as follows. Supporters might say it appears to be faith-based; offers broad ministry outreach; emphasizes strong teaching ministry; emphasizes responsibility of giving; multi-ethnic ministry; willingness to tackle tough contemporary issues such as racism; emphasis on accountability to God for work; and emphasis on excellence. Critics, on the other hand, are apt to describe it as: approach to Scripture is extreme, unbiblical; doctrinal distortions involving creation, Christ, salvation, godly living are not found in Scripture; distortion of Biblical teaching concerning giving, stewardship; overly provocative, divisive teaching on delicate issues; harshly defensive responses to balanced criticisms of teaching and ministry methods; equating of excellence in Christian life with ostentatious appearance and lifestyle; and false teaching, heretical, and apostate.

Associated with this "Word of Faith" movement, Dollar's ministry has appeared on the BET network for a number of years, and in the twenty-first century is seen daily. Known for his dynamic style, Dollar started his ministry in 1986 with eight people and now claims a congregation of over 23,000. His *Changing Your World* television program is seen in the United States and internationally. Many of Dollar's followers believed that his Rolls Royce, private jets, million-dollar Atlanta home and $2.5 million Manhattan apartment confirmed the validity of the "prosperity gospel" teachings. Critics, however, suggested his lavish lifestyle was proof of nothing more than the generosity (and foolishness) of his congregants.

The ministries of Bishop Eddie L. Long of New Birth in Lithonia, Georgia (Georgia's largest church), also appeared on BET for several years as well—terminating its cablecast with them in 2006. According to New Birth's staff, leaving was an executive decision, although the ministry continued to be cablecast on the now defunct Black Family Channel. Like BET's Johnson, Long supported many of the efforts of the Bush administration including federal funding for faith-based programs and anti-gay marriage. Yet critical of Long's positioning, Reverend Timothy McDonald of Atlanta said: "If you look at the black pastors who've come out with the faith-based money, they're the same ones who have come out with campaigns on the gay marriage issue" (quoted in *Church & State* October 2005: 16–17). Yet Bishop Long pooh-poohed any bad faith due to his political stances or his compensation when he said: "You've got to put me on a different scale than the little black preacher sitting over there that's supposed to be just getting by because the people are suffering" (quoted in Blake 28 August 2005).

Similar to many of the white ministers of old such as Swaggert, the Bakkers, Robert Tilton, (in addition to contemporary ones where Tilton still reigns), African-American ministers Lyons, Dollar, and Long have all faced accusations of financial impropriety (or in the case of Lyons, found guilty of such) with their million-dollar ministries and "ungodly" wealth. Yet Dollar and many lesser nationally known black ministers still exist on BET's Sunday lineup along with its overnight schedule. Other mega church ministers showing on BET included T.D. Jakes, *Get Ready with T.D. Jakes* (Dallas since 1993), Paula White Ministries (Tampa), and Marilyn Hickey, *Today with Marilyn Hickey* (Denver). In fact, finally in 2001, amidst longstanding criticism, BET decided to eliminate its infomercial programming—although it replaced this programming with the selling of religion as overnight time filler.

Apart from fiscal malfeasance, many criticized BET for airing people such as Tilton and Benny Hinn, whose spiritual legitimacy have been called into question on several occasions and fronts. Their viability relies heavily on the contributions of poor people—particularly people of color who have very little to give. In response to these and other issues, BET insisted that it did not bear ultimate responsibility for what aired because the network was not involved in the production of these shows (Bender 2000). In a 2000 *salon. com* article, then BET Director of Corporate Communications Rob Santwer maintained that most of their religious programming was acquired. They bought packages of preachers from Rosenheim Associates of Connecticut. This company served as a clearing house for preachers. According to Rosenheim, ministers wanting to minister and advertise on BET had to send their tapes and proposals to them first. Next, BET got them, reviewed them, and made the decision of whether to place them on their lineup. With a yea vote, Rosenheim placed the ministry on a waiting list for a 52-week contract with time slots Monday through Sunday 4:00 to 9:00 am and Sunday 5:00 to 11:00 pm. In May 2006, BET's time slots were completely sold out.

Yet, as journalist Stephen Bender asserted, that sort of "we don't produce it" argument" didn't work for *Nike* when the company tried to deflect criticism for its "independent contractor" sweatshops" (Bender 2000). And, it doesn't work for BET either, despite the non-taking to task of this type of programming by religious communities or non-religious ones. BET approved all ministers appearing on the network. Perhaps it was the weight of a continually transforming world and the religion of globalization that kept the nay-sayers and well wishers alike silent and potentially, prosperous. One of the central confluences between BET and the mega church ministries that it airs is the idea of ownership and vision. The black church stands as the greatest and most enduring ownership and black-directed spaces and opportunities within African-America. It continues to be the one place that blacks control. Pre-2000, BET existed as another central, sacred space for the pride and strength of ownership and control. Post Viacom, it functions to help illuminate paths to black capital righteousness.

The New Millennium Colonization: Globalization?

When former FCC Chair Newton Minow gave his 1961. "Vast Wasteland" speech to U.S. broadcasters mentioned at the beginning of this chapter, the media landscape looked very different. In the new century, television and cable are controlled by just a few multinational corporations. Programs are designed with syndication, DVD sales, foreign sales, and ad webcasting potential in mind. Branding mantras pervade every aspect of the vertical and horizontal system of media enterprises with an eye always toward the global marketplace. In fact, according to industry scholar Kevin S. Sandler, "Solid brand equity is a new form of currency (together with ratings) that is exchanged between networks, audiences, and advertisers" (2003: 91). As an extension of a country's economic reach into the marketplace of another, brands reflect the beliefs and values of the country of origin—the dominant place being the U.S. Some argued "brands are simply another form of United States economic and cultural hegemony" (Haygood 2004: 4).

Discussions of media-induced cultural imperialism have circulated since the 1960s. Largely based on the writings of communications scholar Herbert I. Schiller, the heart of this argument portended that imported media (largely from the U.S.) had a strong and frequent detrimental influence on the culture of local viewers. This theory faced contest by numerous concerns—one in particular suggested that the cultural and imperialist paradigm failed to "realize the ability of the media entrepreneurs in Southern countries to use and adapt new technologies for their own innovation" (Karim June 1998: 5). Yet a correlation continued to exist between what came from the west and its replication in other spaces. In fact, two studies focusing on the adoption of U.S. values by individuals in Trinidad and Belize found moderate to moderate–strong effect, respectively (Elasmar 2004: 6). Moreover, communications scholar Michael G. Elasmar argued that the "contentions of [cultural imperialism] are at the roots of all international legislation to protect indigenous cultures from influence through foreign television" (Elasmar 2004: 7). Scholar and women's development activist Peggy Antrobus contended that globalization has become a new form of colonialism (Barbados Curriculum Transformation Conference 16 June 2000).

Communications scholar Joseph Straubhaar made a case for audiences possessing both various states of mind and familiarity with the country from which the media text emerged in informing how a program or network would be received. He suggested that imported media may provide a sort of "cultural capital" for an audience watching, clearest with "language ability ... but also includes education, travel abroad, familiarity with the ways of life of other countries, education abroad, work with international companies, and the kind of family life which is produced by and reinforces these kinds of advantages" (Straubhaar 2003: 105). For example in a study on the impact of American music videos on Botswana youth, the researchers concluded that while the students with home televisions watched substantial amounts of American music videos, they still lacked a deeper understanding of culturally-specific language and symbol usage. Furthermore, they found that American entertainers might actually be replacing the importance of African entertainers for a younger generation of youth (Lloyd and Mendez 2001). Nonetheless CEO Debra L. Lee envisioned BET globally when she stated: "I want [BET] to say to people what Motown did and what Ebony did: that this is the showcase for African-American culture. We're for all people, but we showcase African-American culture" (quoted in Alexander Fall 2005: 38).

BET shifted the star on its logo from the left to the right to de-emphasize the star power and focus on its audience (Figure 4.3c). It has also taken up a new slogan "It's My Thing" to help shift African-Americans' perception about the network's focus—"drawing from 'It's a Black Thing' for recognition as a black network but retreating from actually saying this in order not to alienate white audiences."[9]

Figure 4.3c   BET—"It's My Thing" logo.

While it seems that people are completely conversant with BET, their loyalty is much more about the representations than the network itself. These findings provide evidence to entertainer Will Smith's observations at the beginning of the chapter.

Given the lack of films and television programs featuring African-American lives distributed abroad,[10] BET has emerged as a central source of information about U.S. black folks. Via satellite,

BET enters homes in the Caribbean, Canada, Europe, and the continent of Africa, among others. In Canada specifically, BET stands as part of a national specialty cable package—ethnic programming distinguished—that is segregated from mainstream outlets. However since its appearance there in 1997, unlike other networks that program abroad, little has been done to make BET particularly Canadian. Journalist Clifton Joseph of the CBC noted: "BET came here invoking black solidarity to get the support of local blacks … When it had our backing, it abandoned us and then bombarded us with jive-talk images" (quoted in Jones, V. 19 February 2001). This strategy should ring familiar. Yet, said BET's vice president of special markets Roslyn Doaks, "The CRTC doesn't require BET to have any Canadian programming. None. And we have never promised anything to anyone. But, of our own initiative, we do showcase Canadian talent like what's her name? Deborah Cox" (quoted in Jones, V. 19 February 2001).

An assessment of BET's possible programming translation came from communications scholar Karim H. Karim when he wrote:

> Creative artistic and cultural programming appears to be a low
> priority in commercially-based ethnic broadcasting … Whereas the
> Black Entertainment Television reaches out to the African diaspora
> (and other viewers) in North America, the production values of most
> of its programming can hardly be distinguished from that of other
> networks. Given the paucity of media content for specific ethnic
> minorities, their members seem to become reliant on commercial
> ethnic broadcasters. The primary problem does not appear to be
> cultural imperialism, but the loss of cultural integrity in the struggle
> for commercial success within national borders and beyond" (Karim
> June 1998: 8).

This loss, this lack of cultural integrity, exacts a toll. Ostensibly, it furthers the merging of capitalism and self-worth. But more insidiously, it normalizes and encourages the status quo of disdain for African-Americans worldwide. As communications scholars have theorized, "if a local viewer perceives an imported TV program to be produced by an outgroup, then prior information about that group (knowledge, beliefs or attitudes) will influence the manner with which this viewer will process the content of the TV program" (Elasmar 2004: 16). In other words, if the preponderance of information about a foreign country or people is derogatory, viewers will not only look for examples that confirm their prejudices but also find it very difficult to change their ideas if their assumptions are not refuted or augmented by other substantial positive information. It seems to me that seeing BET's *Uncut* on Easter morning (as it aired in 2006, or any other time for that matter) will not promote a whole lot of thought transformation about black Americans.

Media studies scholar Frank Ukadike has written about homes that have access to cable networks via satellite in the African continent. Viewers in the continent receive direct to home satellite predominately from South African provider Multichoice. However, the receipt of this type of service is primarily limited to the wealthy. For those with fairly constant access, the Internet provides a great vehicle and opportunity to visualize and interact with the world. In the online world, African-Americans are depicted as virtually cultureless. Black women in particular are usually whores and sexually desired—potentially frigid but never virginal.

Bet.com provides its own talk-back space for consumers of the network and distinct online information. Black Entertainment Television finds some critical attention and reference in these spaces—although it's never clear about the veracity of the writers. In 2007, black participation on the web hovered around 61%. BET.com was included in any top five websites frequented by African-Americans listing. With the decreasing costs in computers, competing Internet providers, and increasing entertainment potentialities of the web and other platforms, black participation is forecasted to increase. Yet as former college president Delores Cross argued, "merely having access to a box—an information box—does not necessarily mean that you have improved, or that you're more literate, or that you're better able to solve problems in the community ..." (quoted in Young 2001). The Internet provides a space for the equality of perspectives. Regardless of background, education, economics, race, or gender, it allows for and foregrounds the right to expression. On the bet.com message board, mediated conversations about programs, music, and random personal topics reigned. Similar to the way the Internet functions for diasporic communities, identities emerge (Karim June 1998).

Sociologist Herman Gray noted that "black American cultural representations sustain their global appeal—circulating, borrowing, aligning, and appropriating a wide array of traditions, formations, memories, and desires—is deeply disturbing and problematic for some members of the black Atlantic diaspora" (Gray 2005: 16). While BET provides a unique entry way and connections to some of black America, it is centrally American and as such maintains the same problems connected with all other North to South flows of media in the world. Tellingly, when Viacom decided to tap the continent of Africa as a market, it turned to MTV. MTV launched its 100th channel and the continent's first music channel, MTV Base, in November 2004. At least from its website (www.mtv.co.uk/mtvbase/), the majority of programs feature African-Americans with an inclusion of a few artists from the continent and Caribbean. What this suggests about the target, affiliation, and corporate understanding of Black Entertainment Television is that while BET may know black people, Viacom (and the white executives at MTV) know business better. And ultimately, business know-how trumps cultural connection, understanding, and content.

The greatest impact of BET has been along the axis of culture and symbolism. Its programming and business maneuvers have been watched, criticized, and then, copied. Its community initiatives have foregrounded wealth building as the best way for black folks to negotiate living in the U.S. with weight loss and worship as secondary necessities. However, these efforts have received less emphasis and much less imitation. Talking with students of Obafemi Awolowo University in Ile-Ife, Nigeria in late 2006, one student questioned me about the future of African representation with the types of images emanating from BET as a model. All I could tell him was that right now, these representations are considered a symbol of black success.

Chapter 5

It's Your Turn

Black to the Future

...the solution of letting a few of our capitalists share with whites
in the exploitation of our masses, would never be a solution of our
problem, but the forging of external chains ...

> W.E.B. Du Bois, "What the Negro Wants" (1944)

To take the culture industry as seriously as its unquestioned role
demands, means to take it seriously critically, and not to cower in the
face of its monopolistic character.

> Theodor W. Adorno, "The Culture Industry:
> Selected Essays on Mass Media" (1991)

Fuck right. It ain't about right; it's about money.

> D'Angelo Barksdale (Larry Gilliard, Jr.) in *The Wire* (2003)

About one year before her death, Evelyn Inell Cain-Smith, my mother, said to me repeatedly, "I've done what I can; it's the young folks' turn." Her position came from someone who lived life as an activist—one who believed that everyone can and should make a difference—that exposure and opportunity meant everything. So in invoking her sentiment, her appeal, I recognize that crucial considerations are needed to negotiate and revise progressive African-American representations, commercial and non-profit media, and capitalism. But beyond that, less talk and more definitive actions are needed to address both the systematic inequalities embedded in U.S. society and the decisions made by its citizens. Due to their historic lack on television, marginalized audiences are high, bamboozled if you will, with the assurance of enhanced representation and voice and by extension, equity and fairness. Yet as chronicled so eloquently in *Dancing in September* (Reggie Rockbythewood 2000) and *Bamboozled* (Spike Lee 2000), the lure and demands of representation are often quite corrupting.

As discussed in chapter 2, the March 2003 issue of *Black Enterprise* magazine ran a cover story of Robert L. Johnson's purchase of the Charlotte NBA franchise (see Figure 2.1). The article, "Slam Dunk," exalted Johnson's business acumen, talent, and viability as an African-American entrepreneur. Soliciting quotes from lawyer Johnnie Cochran, Alabama businessman Donald V. Watkins, and sociologist Harry Edwards as validation, *Black Enterprise* saw Johnson's purchase as emblematic of the breath of air needed and a next step for black folks. BET functioned as the backdrop and evidence of his winning ways, and Johnson's 13-year old son (minus his daughter) appeared within the article as representative of the next generation of successful capitalists.[1]

Ironically or paradoxically, the June 2003 *Black Enterprise* "Letters" section included an offended subscriber, James Frazier of Staten Island, who wrote in part:

> I wonder how many 10-year-old black boys will put aside their schoolbooks to shoot baskets with the hope of [becoming] a professional basketball player. Mr. Johnson has proven he is not interested in the black community, especially black children. BET made

Mr. Johnson a billionaire, and he repays us with rap and hip-hop videos ... When will *BE* stand up for the black community and stop portraying Robert Johnson as a black role model? (*Black Enterprise* June 2003)

Black Enterprise editors responded to the charge with: "We feel the more relevant question is, how many black boys [and girls] can we inspire to put down their basketballs and hit the books with the hope of becoming a billionaire who can afford to buy a major sports team" (*Black Enterprise* June 2003)? Based on the editors' comeback, whether it's basketball or the books, black youth should focus on getting into the billionaire's club—ala Bob Johnson's model.

In getting to those riches, *Black Enterprise* and other such oracles consistently promote the idea that more black businesses will increase African-American employment and reduce the economic distress of black inner cities. Yet according to economist Andrew Brimmer, prospects for firms owned by blacks are forecasted at only "moderately optimistic," and moreover, will only attract a small proportion of the income of the black community (Brimmer 1998). Furthermore, the insistence of black business development presumes that 1) black folks aim to locate their businesses in cities (as opposed to suburbia or the web) and 2) these businesses will provide goods and services needed in these communities. The ideology calls for black corporate workers to transfer their knowledge and expertise from majority white firms to black ones that can profit from that same experience. In other words, black folks should use some of that CAU, Wharton, and Harvard MBA education along with that IBM, Coca-Cola, and HP training to make small businesses like *The Omaha Star* and Paschal's[2] better and more profitable. Yet despite prophesies like Brimmer's, the contemporary solution to black achievement is forwarded as black business development, black capitalism, and white upper class aspirations. And by these standards, BET has fulfilled all the requirements.

Over its history, critics invented many apropos and sometimes harsh characterizations for the BET acronym such as "Black Embarrassing Television," "Butts Every Time," "Black Exploitation TV," and "Black Entertainment Tragedy." African-Americans expected

BET to be a place where all viewers, especially themselves, could listen with their eyes—could envision an understanding of the material conditions, choices, variety, and experiences of black culture as structured and lived within the U.S. If the Diaspora received attention as well, it's all good. Yet BET is not, was never designed to be, a radical alternative to cable or broadcast television representation. Its industrial parameters and cultural ideologies, business decisions, and programming plugged into an already constituted system of practices. This meant that BET conformed to existing television advertising-supported norms. And with its incorporation into the Viacom family of businesses, the narratives it tells have begun to wholly resemble its step-siblings—business imperatives privileged above all else.

In this final chapter, I revisit the various paradoxes that have shaped BET's past in order to situate its future trajectory. As many citizens continue to bemoan the "crisis" in education, the "crisis" about the war, the "crisis" of unemployment, and the increased devaluation of human life "crisis," most operate in a modus of complacency and paralysis. While ridiculous amounts of U.S. life demand attention, I, however, devote this space to recommending actions for change in just one arena—television audiences' thinking about, envisioning of, and acquiring the will and power to make representation matter differently—with BET as the learning tool.

Media Movement

As expressed in the preceding chapters, the foremost criticism of BET as a media enterprise rests with its programming. While some reviews of the network address what African-Americans expect or want to see, most critiques offer limited instruction or direction on how to get it. Yet many academics, activists, students, homemakers, and entertainers have been engaged in trying to change the world of media. From poet and activist Nikki Giovanni to journalist Farai Chideya to rapper and activist Sistah Souljah to feminist scholar Valerie Smith to media makers such as Ben Caldwell, Spike Lee, Zeinabu irene Davis, Cauleen Smith, Rachel Raimist, and Pablo Toledo, each take up media from their corner of the visual universe in order to make a difference in black, brown, and world communities. The key connection between all of these workers is their recognition of the possibilities and power in both individual effort and collective action. While many folks and organizations work to transform the media landscape in terms of either macro issues (consolidation, commodity construction, and cost factors) or micro ones (media literacy and media production), few specifically address African-American viewers and consumers, a space where some illumination seems necessary.

In 1972, writer and social historian Lerone Bennett Jr. penned what he called the "Black Agenda of the Seventies" regarding black media. This plan included:

- A National Commission on Black Communications linked up with local units, to monitor and challenge existing media. The commission could also develop expertise, synthesize experience, and encourage the development of new black media on a cooperative management basis.
- Black-owned or black-operated TV stations, preferably on a noncommercial basis, in five or six key cities.
- Additional black-owned radio stations.
- Noncommercial radio stations at black colleges and universities.
- A substantial increase in the number of black executives in local and national radio and TV stations.
- A national wire service with a black orientation.
- At least two black members on the Federal Communications Commission.
- A new orientation and a significant increase in the amount of relevant material in black-owned media (Bennett 1972: 223).

In 1980, the nation got BET. And by 2006, the U.S. hosted three black-themed cable networks (BET, TV One, and Black Family Channel); three black men sat on the FCC over a thirty-five year span (Benjamin Hooks, William Kennard, and Michael Powell); 240 black-owned radio stations existed (almost all commercial, though) with several nationally-syndicated black radio programs including *The Tom Joyner Morning Show*, *The Steve Harvey Show*, and *The Whoopi Goldberg Show*; noncommercial radio and cable stations operated from several HBCUs, and Black PR wire service provided needed information on black America.

Despite these accomplishments, what media advertisers will buy, market penetration, and consumer demand remained the hallmarks of television success. And after more than 25 years of successful programming (at least in the case of BET), the increase in advertiser CPMs (cost per minute) for black-owned networks is still prompted by only two things: a lack (of programs) that address a black audience and/or the spillover from mainstream networks. With the merger of the WB and UPN and the CW devoting only one night to African-American–cast comedies in 2007, the broadcast market has returned to a level of black representational absence that typified television before the mid-1980s. Keith Bowen, executive VP for advertising sales and marketing for TV One remarked: "There is less diversity in television than there was three years ago" (quoted in Friedman). While this should mean a capital bonanza for a savvy network, when asked why doesn't the CW, for one, program a second night, their entertainment president Dawn Ostroff responded that "as a broadcaster, we aim to bring a variety of disparate and successful programming to our young-adult audience" (quoted in Friedman). Al Anderson, chairman of Atlanta's Anderson Communications, believed: "It all comes back to the same question: Do [advertisers] recognize that blacks aren't dark-skinned white people? ... If you look at the top 200 advertisers, you'll find that more than half have no black [advertising strategy] at all" (quoted in Stilson).

What should be painfully clear by all of this and the preceding chapters of *Pimpin' Ain't Easy* is that while almost all of the things Bennett called for now exist, the representational landscape transformed into something much broader and much more complex than could have possibly been envisioned in the early 1970s—lessening the impact of his black communications agenda. And since it should be clear also that the media realm will continue to not only expand but also flourish, one way of confronting its duplicity is by understanding how it operates—becoming media literate. Media literacy is a world educational tool, used differently and for various purposes depending on its geographic location. It suggests that the audience (as consumers) needs to critically engage with and understand how media, media production, and media decision making work in addition to how ideas are conveyed.

While almost two-thirds of parents say they are "very concerned" about inappropriate media content according to a Kaiser survey, just 15 percent use a V-chip to control access to programming, and 40 percent are not even sure of whether they have one. Meanwhile, more than 40 percent of four- to six-year-olds have a television in their bedroom. For older children, that share is almost 70 percent. And one-third of children six and under live in homes where the television remains on all or most of the time—whether or not anyone is watching it. The simplest solution for those who have cable: get the V-chip; use the V-chip; turn off the television; and remove televisions from bedrooms (children and adults alike).

In terms of media production, video producer and media studies scholar Sut Jhally argued in his documentary *DreamWorlds II* (1995) that the context of viewing must be changed. For many young people, images of criminality, mayhem, and death fill their television screens with black and brown outline. These scenes serve as either a catalyzing force or a depressing reminder of the status quo. Simultaneously, other images stream across screens blaming these same folks for society's failings. Television affects a continuous denigrative dance that feeds upon itself. So while it is largely the young who wage insurrections, they are fueled by the fifth estate. Using cultural specificity as both a resource and a tool of empowerment, programs that reflect connection and relevance to populations beyond booty shake offer a modicum of alternative television viewing.

In children's programming, Nickelodeon's *Backyardigans*, Disney's *That's So Raven*, and interstitials *Go Baby!*, *Shanna's Show*, and *Choo-Choo Soul with Genevieve*, and almost all of PBS's programming but especially long-standing *Sesame Street*, *Reading Rainbow*, and *Zoom*, provide alternative and progressive templates for viewing and understanding race, gender, humanity, and play. In addition to these programs for children, character-driven adult fare include Showtime's (and now BET's) *Soul Food*, HBO's *The Wire*, CW's *Everybody Hates Chris*, and over time *Girlfriends*, ABC's *Grey's Anatomy*, and Fox's former *The Bernie Mac Show*—programs that engagingly explore class, gender, sexuality, and race beyond the quick punch line and push to the next scene.[6]

In addition to what young people watch, media production programs exist in most major cities and increasingly, in smaller ones. Their purpose is to give hands-on experience with video, film, Internet, and radio production. For example, media-maker Ben Caldwell's KA'OS Network is a program geared for educational expression via media in Los Angeles. Funded through a variety of grants, the network gives young people a space to freely express themselves through music, dance, video, and the Internet. The creative force behind KA'OS, Caldwell brings more than thirty years of experience as a producer, director, editor, writer, and teacher in theatrical, documentary, and television arenas. The state-of-the-art facility serves nearly 150 young people weekly. Other programs include the work of feminist media scholar and documentary maker Rachel Raimist with girls, hip hop, and video in Minneapolis; the teaching of video production to Pasqua-Yaqui youth in Arizona by filmmaker Nicole Koschmann, and filmmaker Pablo Toledo's using media-making as a way to build workplace skills for at-risk youth in Tucson. Just Think (San Francisco), Street Level Youth for Media (Chicago), and Reel Works Teen Filmmaking (NYC) afford opportunities for both learning about and making media. Most colleges and universities offer communications and media studies as majors and minors (in addition to a deluge of courses now available online). And increasingly (albeit limitedly), media courses are being taught within high schools. These are just a few examples of the ways in which people are seeking to make media transparent.

Several media organizations around the world attempt to inform, teach, and challenge adults (parents, teachers, activists) to equip themselves for negotiation with, usage, and teaching of media effectively. In the U.S. and on the web, organizations include Media Education Foundation, the Center for Media Literacy, Media Literacy Clearinghouse, the Alliance for a Media Literate America

(AMLA), Listen Up! Youth Media Network, and the National Black Programming Coalition, which funds and promotes "quality, intelligent and compelling programming that celebrates the cultural heritage of African Americans and the African Diaspora" (nbpc.tv n.d.). Critical thinking is the preeminent goal of these programs—in the hope that adults and young people will make different choices, better-informed ones, about their viewing habits and their consumption patterns. And in terms of the media industries, a part of the focus must be on making the conglomerates matter to consumers. Furthermore, since this new media world leaves little room for those without extensive financial wherewithal—I turn to contemporary ideas of capital.

Makin' Paper

In "The Culture Industry: Enlightenment as Mass Deception," cultural critics Max Horkheimer and Theodor W. Adorno indicted the way that media businesses function. While their comments were directed at radio and film, the observations apply equally to television and cable. They argued that the "truth that they are just business is made into an ideology in order to justify the rubbish they deliberately produce. They call themselves industries; and when their directors' incomes are published, any doubt about the social utility of the finished products is removed" (Adorno and Horkheimer 2001: 71–72).

Prior to their assessment, reflections of scholar and activist W.E.B. Du Bois grounded this interpretation when he wrote: "Mass capitalistic control of books and periodicals, news gathering and distribution, radio, cinema, and television has made the throttling of democracy possible and the distortion of education and failure of justice widespread" (Du Bois April 1953). Returning to the Boogie Down Productions pimps epigraph of chapter 1, under capitalism the whores of their equation turned out to be the masses of black folks and other people of color who, under the guise of potential, property, and image, have made the big "pimps" like Robert L. Johnson wealthier, more powerful, more visible, and ultimately, detrimental to those who see no other option to visualize themselves.

Benign capitalism has not worked and faces extinction at each new Clear Channel, eBay, or NFL advertisement. Economist Daniel R. Fusfeld wrote that the progenitor to this notion, socialism, is rooted in communal ideals, defined as an "economic system based on social ownership of the means of production, in which the values of equality, brotherhood, and cooperation strongly influence social policy" (Fusfeld 1982: 605–606). While capitalists think of socialism as tyranny, socialists think of capitalism in the same way. Du Bois insisted that the caste system of capitalism would eventually crumble. He envisioned the masses, now working class, becoming socialists (Du Bois April 1953). Yet more than fifty years later, his prediction has not come to pass, and the capitalists' world reigns despite knowledge of its racist foundation and its problematic implementation and growth.

Capitalism flourishes in part because it keeps minds fixated on unnecessary goods, the perception of quality, and the assurance of acquiring more of these things. Yet the idea that African-Americans can be both quintessential capitalists and provide support to nuclear and extended family is a myth—the same kind of myth women bought into in the 1970s—the one that said they could do and have everything simultaneously, right now. While this version of capitalist thought marries capitalism with social consciousness, it requires sacrifice. In the case of Black Entertainment Television, the sacrifice has turned out to be its target audience.

Beyond the capitalist system itself, many black critical thinkers, including economist Andrew Brimmer, journalist Tony Brown, political theorist Manning Marable, and entrepreneur Yvonne Stafford, maintain that black capitalism is not black self-determination—the ideas upon which Johnson stood to forward the BET network. Wrote Stafford: "Entrepreneurs build community. Yet the programs that are created for our urban communities across the nation focus on jobs. The primary focus of these jobs is expanding the consumer class" (Stafford 16 October 2003). To get targeted potential consumers to come on board, they were addressed in a multiplicity of ways.

One approach, argued writer Amiri Baraka, is through what he called reactionary nationalism. "Reactionary nationalism is metaphysical, and like one variation of it, cultural nationalism, uses culture in a static, unchanging way. Reactionary nationalism is also the cover [by] which the bourgeoisie of a nation try to get over, so that we get black capitalism preached to us by certain Negroes as more positive than white capitalism. As if black exploitation was sweeter than white or black bullets … " (Baraka 1984 online). Similarly, sociologist E. Franklin Frazier wrote that the black bourgeoisie implied that it was the "sacred obligation" of blacks to patronize black business, and "they should not complain if they pay higher prices for goods and can not buy exactly what they want so long as they buy from Negroes" (Frazier 1957: 140). While both of their assertions have born fruit, black consumers still fight for and with the ideas of black capitalism—its current pay dirt evidenced as hip hop. The quintessential contemporary example of "living the good life" is the hip hop mogul (or in some cases, the video vixen). Recoupables, imaging, and the tax man are foreign and parodied pitfalls in this dance to riches.

And do not be naïve about what this wealth means for people of color. While it opens up greater opportunities to consume (and potentially explore and create opportunities for others), wealth taps into deep-seated and institutionalized problems as well. While many think otherwise, O.J. and Michael's acquittals, for example, (if you believe they committed their respective crimes) do not mean that their wealth protected them. In fact, their wealth, race, and their own stupidity put them in those courtrooms from the gitty up. In a different forum but with the same outcome, look to the Chocolate City; no, not D.C., the new chocolate city—the black Mecca, Hotlanta. Atlanta possesses one of the highest proportions of African-American government officials, educators, and professional people in the U.S. And in the new millennium, it promotes itself as the headquarters of the dirty south music empire. However not two miles west of downtown, you find abject poverty. And by abject I mean literally wood shacks, broken windows and crack vials, beer and wine bottles, and stray dog feces nestled between clothes lines, unemployed men and women, obesity, alcoholism, criminality, and filth. Hopelessness languishes and abounds in the shadow of the new south and King's legacy. Moreover, in 2006, Atlanta ranked number two in this nation's home foreclosures. If Hurricane Katrina's brother comes through Atlanta the way she did in New Orleans, calamity would reign. And this is the Promised Land?

Furthermore, the pervasive lack of knowledge regarding wealth acquisition in the U.S. is disquieting at best, if not downright conspiratorial. Every evening on the increasingly irrelevant nightly news, an anchor quotes figures of the Dow Jones; never mind that not one required class in most U.S. K–12s teach students about the market—how it works, what the numbers mean, or their significance. But this system of markets runs the U.S. And with ongoing discussions of privatizing Social Security (with Johnson's black face championing it), the growing prison-industrial complex, and the tenets of "No Child Left Behind," rational planning—one would think—should include the teaching of the economic underpinning of globalization. It doesn't, perhaps purposely.

Beyond knowledge of wealth, the focus on entertainment as a growth industry for black entrepreneurship and a panacea for sustained job loss is curious as well. Will Smith, Queen Latifah, L.L. Cool J, Ice-T, Ice Cube, MC Lyte, Ludacris, Mos Def, Master P, Snoop, Busta Rhymes, Eve, Lil' Romeo, and in 2006 T.I. in *ATL*, all migrated from the world of rap and hip hop to claim spaces as thespians. While Smith (both Will and L.L.) and Latifah have achieved success on Hollywood's big and small screens, others penetrate the marketplace sparingly. In other words, the hip hop entertainment business, like sports, extends wealth or even consistent employment only to a very few. Others develop music labels and hire additional personnel to accompany their stardom (public relations firms, management services, stylists, etc.). Yet the music and visual corporations retain the bulk of all cash revenues.

During a personal discussion, one Latino *Resurrection Boulevard* executive wondered why black entertainers fail to band together to fund films and create distribution venues. The voicing of this quandary convinced me that other groups outside of African-America ponder it, too. African-Americans still bear the standard for minority progress within capitalism and representation. This executive believed that television has the power to influence the gestalt in this country—the way people think—suggesting that it is the most crucial element for people of color to address. In this regard, coming directly from music video, the booming direct to DVD and syndication industries that hip hop helped facilitate both provide avenues for black business development and representation. Several rappers turned to this medium to expand their reach, including specifically Master P and Snoop Dog.

Most of these narratives, such as *I'm Bout It* (Moon Jones and Master P 1997), *Winner Takes All* (1999), *The Wash* (DJ Pooh 2001), and *Still Bout It* (Master P 2004) centered the difficulties and mythologies of black urban life (gangs, drugs, promiscuity, poverty, stupidity) and the desire for something else—in other words, coming-of-age stories. However as these tales continue to be produced, they never change. The same savage inequality plots regurgitate—performed even by those who no longer (if ever) inhabited those spaces—a significant fact inasmuch as their acting credibility comes in part from their presumably real-lived street cred. Moreover, several of the biggest distributors of these films possess limited (if any) black workers in their managerial ranks—such as Vision Films. The 1970s revisited twenty-first century representation through "ghetto theater"—as one online viewer called it—profiting primarily white distributors.

While billionaires such as philanthropist Warren Buffet prepared to donate the largesse of their capitalist acquired wealth to non-profits, African-Americans' (and most Americans) wealth credo remains "me me," "buy buy." Collectivity and "lifting as we climb" ethos that still exist within many African-American communities and in individuals (identity politics notwithstanding) are dying a slow, capital and assimilationist death. BET made the paradoxes of black business development and capitalism for African-Americans abundantly clear. In fact, Johnson always deployed race in very sophisticated ways—whether for BET or the Estate Tax—ultimately, to forward his personal wealth-building agenda. For example, in a late-2005 effort to accumulate wealth, he partnered with the Carlyle Group to launch a private-equity firm that planned to raise at least $500 million for a buyout firm. The firm would target corporate pension funds. Said Johnson: "State pension funds are often backed by minority workers: firemen and teachers ... This is an opportunity for a minority team to manage the wealth of the nation" (quoted in Dutt 2005). Yet I question what exactly his first statement has to do with the second, especially in terms of community empowerment, providing jobs, and transforming the racialized economic landscape? In looking at this quote initially, my mind inserted the word prison for pension, probably the more on-target assessment of Johnson's business maneuvers and his positioning of race to make it work.

Adults bear a responsibility, an obligation to those coming behind them. When African-Americans bemoan the fact that young people fail to recognize Angela Davis, Stokely Carmichael, and Thurgood Marshall; that they no longer appreciate their in-room DVD players, Ipods, Xboxes, laptops; that they no longer respect themselves (or them) enough to say "thank you," "please," "ma'am," or "may I" in the right tone, the blame rests right at the feet of those from whom the young came and a media and world proffered and promoted by these same folks. BET teaches African-Americans and others, in a way not seen before, that the bottom line to the representation game is profit—reinforcing *The Wire* epigraph. This is a needed and valuable lesson.

Many, such as journalists Sheldon Perry and Raoul Dennis, argue and fight for more representation, more ownership, more distribution—just more. They suggest that lost black opportunity, lost black employment, loss of editorial and visual control, and increased pressure on remaining black-owned media companies to provide these things, present challenges to and for black media businesses since the sale of BET (Perry and Dennis 23 November 2000). Yet they need to look long and hard at the Black Entertainment Television model, not only for what it illustrates about viewing black media ownership and financial success as the goal but also for what it suggests about the value of what is sought. In fact, one participant of the Clair Memorial UMC Church focus group summed it up best when talking about Robert L. Johnson's ownership:

Interviewer: The man is Robert Johnson.
Respondent 1: He owns the Bobcats.

Interviewer: He sold [BET] to Viacom for three billion dollars at the end of 2000.

Respondent 1: He was on the BET Awards, right?

Interviewer: Yes, he was the one talking 'bout "I want to thank all of you for coming …"

Respondent 1: Looking dumb with that hat on … (Laughter)

Interviewer: What else does he own?

Respondent 2: Bobcats.

Interviewer: What else?

Respondent 3: NBA and the WNBA.

Interviewer: Right.

Respondent 4: Three billion dollars?

Interviewer: Yes.

Respondent 4: I would've sold it too.

> (Clair Memorial United Methodist Church
> youth focus group, July 2004)

While the aforementioned concerns and call for critically characterize the circulating capitalists' business discourses, they fail to completely capture the cultural shifts operating in the wake of BET.

Cultural Transformations and BET Aesthetics

BET helped to make blackness a destination of choice for young people worldwide. While hip hop functioned as the engine, music video distribution drove the train. At predominately white universities, for example, the opportunity to encounter negotiations with and appropriations of racialized culture in general and blackness in particular occur regularly due in part to this worldwide dissemination. My favorite example of this sampling comes when walking on campus in Tucson and hearing (really, feeling) the percussion of a rap lyric from a passing car. The idea of cultural sampling, as media scholar Racquel J. Gates so eloquently theorized, is a technique straight from rap and taken up in different aspects of music, television, film, and lived culture. She suggested: "Sampling forces us to remember those things that we have forgotten. It makes us see what would otherwise be invisible. Sampling creates a living archive of both history and criticism, and is a process that is constantly exploring the relations between black popular culture and white mainstream culture, and offering up a critique of those relations" (Gates 2006: 9). However, the cultural sampling that occurs in this case belies the connections of history, time, and space and is hard-pressed to provide critique. Because more often than not when I turn to see where the sound is coming from, (whose music is pumpin' hard), I find a buxom blond girl in a luxury convertible of some kind, singing along with some version of how black women in the ghetto ain't shit. This scenario never fails to disorient and vex me. And unfortunately, this "white nigger" moment happens not just in Tucson but wherever the spaces of hip hop world music, hip hop aesthetics, and equal access collide.

In another example, *Nick Cannon's Wild 'N Out* (MTV 2005–) provides many opportunities for escapes to blackness. In fact, one recurring skit features four white comedians repeatedly contending "we love to act black." These instances, (along with continued blackface and pimps/hoes college parties across the nation), convince me that any sense of historic racism, institutionalized racism, and daily racist behavior fails to register contemporarily. Or as hip hop critic and former MTV *Real World* participant (and New York congressional candidate) Kevin Powell remarked, "Let's be honest … all this fascination with hip-hop is just a cultural safari for white people" (quoted in Samuels 5 May 2003)—and unfortunately, a considerable number of young black folks as well.

The ubiquity and omnipotence of black-faced hip hop as popular culture has brought many to a new conclusion about black Americans' status in the U.S. Researcher Howard Horowitz found: "There is the opinion that African-Americans are mainstream, and they respond to programming that we all share. So therefore, do we really need special channels" (quoted in Stilson)? While communications scholar and former journalist Arthur S. Hayes argued in his unpublished manuscript "Black Enough?" that "ethnic control of a media outlet may be just as important as ethnic *ownership* in promoting viewpoint diversity ..." (Hayes 3), CEO of BET Debra Lee lamented "... when you have successful African-American-targeted shows on other kinds of networks, it's a challenge [for us]" (quoted in Stilson). As I watch some of BET's original programming, I try to assess what about this network makes it less quintessentially black than programs on TV One that offers black-controlled programming and is at least partially owned by black folks.

The program content and interstitials from both BET and TV One seem to produce the same ethnic effect. BET features music video shows (with in-studio black youth audiences), black off-network situation comedies, a few dramas such as *Soul Food* from Showtime and *The Wire* from HBO, and news briefs. TV One features lifestyle programs, black off-network sitcoms, a few off-network dramas such as *New York Undercover* from Fox, and black entertainment specials. The difference seems to lie primarily with an age target rather than a racialized or ethnic authenticity split. What then is the significance of black ownership or black-led programming, since blackness has become a known and reproducible quantity by all? Has the confluence of black ownership, black representation, and in effect, black culture now reached a state of critical irrelevance? Or really the larger question is, are we now, in 2007, in a post-black era?

The performance of an essentialized blackness has not made the world a more understanding place. The space between engaging entertaining blackness and living it has become an increasingly more difficult one to traverse for black and brown members of the hip hop generation where the world seems to "know" you. Merging University of Houston focus group participant Fred Walker's idea about the loss of black covenant of BET with media scholar Ayanna Whitworth-Barner's notion that BET elevates whiteness (both discussed in chapter 2) gives evidence of and validation to the watershed impact of hip hop music and style on world culture. Yes, both BET and blackness are ubiquitous, but only as commodities.

Filmmaker Spike Lee's *Bamboozled* critiques one of the results of cultural transformation in an audition scene with a Luther Vandross/David Peaston wannabe (Figure 5.1). While the singer (Tuffy

Figure 5.1 *Bamboozled's* audition scene.

Questell) definitely possessed the vocal chops of an R & B ballad-eer, his lyrics created a totally different reality or moment for both diegetic and non-diegetic observers. He crooned:

> I … I be smackin' them hoes. I be smackin' my hoes. Everyone knows it goes. Kick em to the floor, step on 'em hard. Step on 'em hard, kick 'em to the floor. Cause I, I be smackin' my hoes. I be smackin' my hoes. I be smackin' my hoes. Thank you (*Bamboozled* 2000).

Immediately following, black female casting director (Liza Jessie Peterson) yells, "Next!" While this scene proved to be a quite humorous segment of the film, his perversion of the R & B impulse causes both painful allusions to and connections with music videos and the ways in which black relationships, gender respect, and musical acumen are reordered and contaminated by commercial imperatives.[3]

Networks such as BET and programming proliferating on them made entertainment the centerpiece of important knowledge content. In 2005, viewers knew more about the habits, lifestyle, growth, experiences, and thoughts of Michael Jackson and his trial than many did of their own family members and certainly any other national or international news of importance. Contemporary media culture made figures far away and unknown feel very close, and seemingly very personal. And commercialization pervaded everything—from advertisements to ancillary materials to product placement, the goal was to inundate consumers with the brand—recall Hudlin's comments from chapter 4 about his vision for BET—or as television program executives lamented, they needed to find a way to monetize content without cannabilizing it (NATPE 2007).

BET's branding incorporated the rise of hip hop as both music and as cultural arbiter, almost to the exclusion of anything else that black folks listen to or enjoy—even young ones. BET wants to claim, inhabit, usurp, and define all cultural territory seen or presumed to be about blackness and black authenticity as black essentialism. Corporations, the real stockholders for BET Holdings, want consumers and audiences to see and hear their product without competing interests. They need their product to stand out. Because corporations try to avoid clutter and noise, BET provides, must provide, a unified conception of black folks in order to sell it. So when BET markets "It's My Thing," the network means exactly that—"one" definition of blackness that simultaneously asserts individuality and racial ambiguity. Despite my belief that this new visuality closes down possibilities, black studies scholar Faith Smith suggested:

> The anonymity of Internet sites and cable networks offers consumers a chance to imagine themselves as part of any number of constituencies. And if they cannot yet afford the lifestyles that can be assembled with a dash of Martha Stewart here and a touch of Black Entertainment Television (BET) there, they can at least imagine it as theirs through these media. In this way, they can think of themselves as being like each other without the complication of otherwise troubling details ... The *experience* of these identities may be troubling and messy, but their narration provides the opportunity to set things straight (F. Smith 2001: 42–43).

While the world has changed tremendously since BET began in 1980, assertions of societal openness, one of the twenty-first century edicts, have not applied universally to African-American communities. For example, journalist Richard Turbo wrote: "As a society, we're more comfortable with homosexuality today. It's no longer taboo, it's portrayed on prime-time TV, and heterosexual men have become more comfortable with gay culture" (Turbo 28 July 2003: 1). His analysis may ring true in mainstream (white) communities, but a quick peek at BET (or many black churches) alerts you

to a consciousness circa 1950. On BET, heterosexual black masculinity maintains a ratcheted up personification. While allusions to
homosexuality surfaced periodically (i.e., the music video for Dru
Hill's "In My Bed" that suggested a lesbian affair, and MeShell
NdegéOcello's rendition of "Who Is He and What Is He to You?"
that flipped the genders of Bill Withers' 1972 classic), the notion and
discussion of homosexuality garnered very limited airtime on BET.
NdegéOcello remembered in fact her video for "Leviticus: Faggot"
never appeared on BET at all. She suspected that BET decided not
to air it because the song pointedly addresses homophobia. Said
NdegéOcello, "BET's not there to support artists … They're there
to support an image. They're not there to promote diversity. Black
people are known to be the most homophobic group ever, and I can
only hope and wish that BET would be open-minded and realistic"
(quoted in A. Jones 16 January 2001). However, hope is all you'll
find at this juncture in BET's history.[4]

As its overall programming thrust, BET centers thrift and mini-
malism—in other words, lowest common denominator selling. In
fact, before BET joined Viacom, black actors were reluctant to work
with the Network due to its air of low-budget-ness. Paraphrasing
one former employee: "the younger the entertainer, the more supportive. Older and more experienced industry players, however, are
concerned with professionalism issues. Many feel out of touch with
the channel and that it doesn't represent them." But since the sale,
well-regarded mainstream (those white people recognize) black
entertainers have appeared. Artists such as L.L. Cool J co-hosted
Rip the Runway in 2006; Steve Harvey hosted the *Celebration of
Gospel* extravaganza for six years running; and Will and Jada Pinkett
Smith hosted the BET Awards in 2005, with a seemingly inebriated
Damon Wayans helming it in 2006. Perhaps because BET became
part of Viacom, entertainers considered it less cheap and more
mainstream.

BET initiated its awards program in 2000. Recognizing the
challenge of getting a large African-American entertainer contin-
gency on the East Coast for the BET Awards program, the network
held the show in Los Angeles. Yet within the credits of the 2004,

Figure 5.2   *Hey Monie.*

2005, and 2006 BET Awards as well as its 2007 *Rip the Runway* annual special, a non-black production company emerged. Cossette Productions, known for producing the Grammys, among other programming specials, managed the programs. So what does it say about "Black Star Power" and black ability to produce quality productions when an outside company produces an "insider production"?[5]

Despite this seeming conundrum, BET found ways to produce and air innovative work. For example, its animated series *Hey Monie* originated with the Oxygen network yet partnered with BET in 2003 (Figure 5.2). Created and executive-produced by Dorothea Gillim, *Hey Monie* became the first animated series to feature African-American women and the first animated series on BET. The program was also the first to air on two different networks not owned by the same parent company. In line with BET's overall philosophy, Gillim said: "I've never thought about the show as a black show, actually. I just think of it as a funny show that happens to star two black women. And my mantra has always been, *race is not a plot point*. Because this is a comedy, and it's 22 minutes, and you can't really tackle big issues in that format without completely trivializing them" (quoted in Wieder 2003). *Hey Monie* illustrated the type of creative, original programming BET is capable of producing and airing. While the program earned a respectable audience for BET, (600,000 viewers on its Tuesday night spot), it never really caught on with audiences—at least not in the way music videos did.

Over time, the music videos on BET forwarded a very realist aesthetic, aside from work by directors such as Dave Myers (videos for Missy Elliott, Janet Jackson, Nas, and Jennifer Lopez). Meaning, they replicated rather directly the lyrics' narratives, whereas pop videos, for example, frequented toward abstraction. This difference in visual style is interpreted by young viewers in terms of race. Said one Tucson Urban League focus group participant, " … rock music is more about abstract art while hip hop is about gang stuff, shoot 'em up" (June 2004). In this realm, with no emphasis on intimacy, a trivialization of sexual intercourse, and an increasing tendency to make pornography a part of everyday iconography, black life (and black women especially) received validation as depravity in the world of black music videos.

Moreover, a report by the House Committee on Energy and Commerce found that between 1998 and 2002, the use of foul language on television increased by 94.8% during the family hour and by 109% during the 9:00 pm time slot (H.R. Rep. No 109-434 at 5). In the years since the 2004 Janet Jackson/Justin Timberlake "controversy," both houses of Congress have taken up the issue of television programming regulation and the possibility of regulating cable. And after extensive congressional wrangling, in June 2006 President George W. Bush signed into law an increase in broadcast fines from $32,500 to $325,000 per incident. While cable and satellite got a pass on the charges of indecency, of which this action falls, these legislative actions placed cable on notice. Congressional maneuvers make an entity like BET squirm, especially as it seeks to extend its brand to various platforms.

In the television industry, development in programming, platforms, and anticipated consumer demands continued to astound. Congress designated February 2009 as the final transition date for networks to move from analog to digital television. Mobile TV, online platforms, gaming, and ring tones have been forecasted as the futurist vehicles for delivering content. Interestingly, BET sits uniquely positioned for this new, changing world in some ways but primarily continues to follow its corporate mate, MTV, as the leader in innovation.

Lessons can be learned from the establishment, operation, and trajectory of the BET Network. The predicament of BET's relationship to black folks is analogous to that of people in automobile accidents. Called "comparative negligence," both parties in an accident are found to have contributed to its cause.

A part of reframing televisual parameters is to recognize and make provisions for the paradoxes inherent in calling for complete freedom for black folks while equating "proper" behavior with white middle-class values. In an article concerning the containment of African-Americans in public spaces, specifically those identified with rap, cultural critic Tricia Rose wrote about her experience attending a rap concert in the late 1980s. Poignantly, she reflected on the treatment of her fellow attendees by public officials and her inability to shift the paradigm based on her class status or generation. She lamented, "the language of entitlement couldn't erase my sense of alienation" (Rose 1995: 532). Her connections of entitlement to alienation reminded me of the relationship between disciplining black youth and Black Entertainment Television. In terms of public access in public spaces, the public rights of African-Americans have not been a priority for BET. As observed in my article on narrowcasting (Smith-Shomade 2004) for example, BET failed to intervene in the extremely slow cable wiring of black and brown neighborhoods nationwide, even in the multi-ethnic New York City, their target population. This belabored wiring process trampled on already tenuous rights of access for people of color.

Moreover, BET promotes jokes about the need to corral blacks in public spaces—even spaces constructed for and dominated by them. For example during the 2005 BET Awards, Will and Jada Pinkett-Smith opened the program with a list of rules: 1) a three-homeboy limit on the stage to accept any award, 2) no bright suits or gold goblets ("This is not the pimp of the year award"), and 3) do not thank God if you can't show or perform your work in church (BET Awards 2005). In all fairness, the impetus for this joke occurs within many awards programs (including the *Source* and *Vibe* Awards) that honor primarily young African-Americans. However, the tenor of it falls in line with Bill Cosby's now infamous remarks.

At a 2004, 50th commemoration of *Brown vs. Board of Education*, actor and comedian Bill Cosby's statements caused a significant uproar in black and outside communities. Essentially, he attacked lower socioeconomic black folks for "their" over population, inability to raise "their" children "properly," depravity of morals, materialism, criminality, style, inability to speak English well, and hedonism. While some argued for his bourgeois disconnection with common folks, others interpreted his comments as stating the truth. He attributed his position and material success to both a certain classist moral standing but also to the gains of the civil rights movement. But despite the brouhaha, isn't the legacy of the civil rights movement, at least in part, about black choice—the option to speak Ebonics in all situations, to be sexually free, and to acknowledge and air jacked-up familial connections as part of one's larger humanity? In other words, to be really free, the ties between uplift and middle-class white conformity must be loosened. This calls for respecting different ways of representing but also having diverse representations to examine. Audiences must make this a priority. Plus, these transformations not only impact culture and aesthetic practices but also larger political ones.

Political Activism and BET Constituents

The 2000 election of George W. Bush to the presidency was the closest in U.S. history, with black Floridians at the center of its novelty. So the 2004 election cycle found hip hop at the forefront of a grassroots movement. In Diddy's "Vote or Die" campaign, for example, he declared his mission to "make voting hot and relevant to a generation, 42 million young people 18 to 30, that hasn't reached full participation in the political process" (*The Black Collegian online* 2004). This effort partnered with Rock the Vote and MTV to get people to register to vote. Substantial numbers of 18-to-24-year-olds registered, yet with a surprisingly similar outcome to the 2000 election—both politically and intellectually. The depth of candidate and issue knowledge (or lack thereof) and transformation of Generation X "movement" sustainability quickly waned. Thus, McGruder's comic strip below exemplified the sort of radicalized results of efforts like this (Figure 5.3). This is not to say

Figure 5.3 The Boondocks. (The Boondocks) (2005) Aaron McGruder. Distributed by Universal Press Syndicate. Reprinted with permission. All rights reserved.

that Diddy et. al.'s accomplishments were insignificant or that they don't matter, because they were and they do. However, the flash of Diddy and Russell Simmons contributed virtually nothing to the substance of altering minds, motives, and actions.

In another vein, as much as I enjoy and pepper *Pimpin' Ain't Easy* with the comic political satire of Aaron McGruder, I recognize the writer's complicity with the entertainment business as well. For example, in an interview appearing the week before the release of the animated version of *The Boondocks* on the Cartoon Network's "Adult Swim" he flippantly stated: "I think we as black people spend way too much time worrying about what white people think of us. I don't give a f--- about what white people think" (quoted in Samuels 31 October 2005). This, however, contradicted his comments in an earlier interview where he said: "I sell angry Black kids to 2 million white people a day. 30 million on Sunday … Get your message out to people who would not ordinarily hear anything conscious. It's not easy but we have to be in the business of mainstreaming radicalism" (quoted in Datcher September/October 2003).

The Cartoon Network ordered a second season of McGruder's *The Boondocks* to begin in September 2007. Debuting on November 6, 2005 to 2.3 million viewers, the series proved to be a ratings bonanza for the Cartoon Network—the highest-rated series premiere in the network's five-year history (a series once rejected by BET). Many appreciated and defended the changes that young cultural workers like McGruder offer in contemporary culture. In fact, the chants against middle-class ways of being, aesthetics, and culture (more precisely, white culture identified as middle-class) brought forth viable insights and found a huge resonance within many circles. Yet some African-American cultural gatekeepers were not pleased with the shifts or *The Boondocks'* success. One in particular, the Rev. Al Sharpton, demanded an apology from the Cartoon Network after an episode depicted an animated Rev. Dr. Martin Luther King Jr. saying "niggas" repeatedly. He threatened: "If we don't receive an apology, we will picket the corporate head-quarters" (quoted in Crupi 25 January 2006). A Cartoon Network spokesperson issued the statement that the episode "in no way was meant to offend or desecrate the name of Dr. King" (quoted in Crupi 25 January 2006).

What remains absent, however, is clarity of the larger political goals of many in Generation X. If African-Americans become the individualist, capital-driven people that hip hop (and civil rights, in many respects) discourses encourage, what ultimately becomes of the group dynamic, or more importantly, the group itself, that systematically must stay at the bottom if the capitalist project is to work? It is not as if the new ways of being are designed to pro-duce an anti-racist society. It is not as if the question of "can't we all just get along" has become any more relevant with these changes than when Rodney King uttered this in 1992. The 2006 State of Black America report from the National Urban League stated once again that things were not bigger and better for African-Ameri-cans. Whether talking about the prison business, home ownership equity, educational gains (and losses), or even the most natural of things, childbirth—black folks had not caught up, gained, or moved ahead.

Yet intellectual and even comedic commentary has not flamed the fire of revolution or even just displeasure—either for a younger generation, or increasingly, with old schoolers. The fire is out. Veri-fication of this assertion came through BET's decision to not cable-cast civil rights leader Coretta Scott King's funeral, even though they streamed it on their website. In defense of this decision, senior vice president of corporate communications Michael Lewellen stated: "If BET erred, we erred on the side of giving viewers a different choice" (quoted in Shister 2006). Thus, BET ran music videos and offered the rhythm and shake of young black America as a tribute to a woman who helped make it possible for the network to exist.

Rose Catherine Pinkney, TV One executive vice president of programming and development, insisted: "When we control our own images, we no longer have the excuse of other people. And we can no longer complain. Once you have choice and options, it's harder to complain. As a consumer you simply have to act. You have to stop doing one thing and do another. Choose another network, choose a book. You have ... choice" (author interview 2006).

Beyond this choice, publishers of the website *The Black Commentator* argued that "failure to confront media means political impotence" (1 May 2003). They consider media the weakest link in the power structure of the U.S. and believe corporate media works as an active enemy of popular power in the U.S. They reasoned: "We must return to the basics—and this applies to activists of all ethnicities. The demand must be for *coverage* of community concerns and events. Nothing else matters. That means Black activists must measure media by the coverage it affords their activities, rather than the station's roster of Black employees or the race of the owners or managers. In a society such as ours, events do not exist unless media covers them" (*The Black Commentator* 1 May 2003). Thus directly addressing media businesses and secondarily, their advertisers, usually produces some type of affirmative result. Evidence that this mantra has at least some merit arrived in July 2006 when BET cancelled its six-year old video program *Uncut*—in part, it seems, due to the agitation of black women and recognition that this original soft porn program perhaps needed rethinking or just simply, cutting. In addition, the 2007 Don Imus firing refllected once again the power of actual protest.

Throughout *Pimpin' Ain't Easy*, I turn to the insights of cultural critics, political scientists, economists, and historians for support. I also incorporate the insights of lay scholars—students, family, and friends—whose visions may not be recognized on a broad or academic scale but add a necessary perspective and value. It is important to acknowledge voices that observe and call for a reconfiguration of dreams, imagination, and vision for all of us to manifest in this world. What these commentators do, or at least try to do, is jolt people into consciousness—and not even a necessarily deep one. This consciousness cries out for a simple recognition that the world's operating systems are askew—that somehow capitalism and representation are not the global panacea that they're being sold as. A cursory look at the Roman Empire (or even at the Mali and Songhai empires—ones not taught in school) should be sufficient to recognize that this economic and political system, too, shall pass away.

Conclusion

Increasingly as media scholars deconstruct images and assign meaning to discreet phenomena or programs, they move further away from interrogating and inciting activism against economic and media systems that disempower most individuals—including those within their own workplaces. In the twenty-first century cable universe, viewers see more people of color, hear more disparate voices, and experience more global places than at any moment previously. Yet the mechanics and backbone of representation have remained the same. The outward manifestation of this complex world produces young people who no longer witness the hard work that accompanies any success, including Robert L. Johnson's. What they do observe is ATM cards that magically produce money to buy things; credit cards that make any wish "priceless;" parents and teachers failing to give them tools to handle disappointment and the eventual "no thank you" that they will encounter; and weight condemnation that reigns in every televisual space, sandwiched between ads for Taco Bell, McDonalds, and KFC—all located abundantly in poor, colored communities as well as in the mall. Silence and "status" seem to go hand in hand to foster or allow for more drug use, suicide attempts, academic slovenliness, critical retardation, and homicide. The only way Generation Next knows to respond is "don't hate the playa, hate the game."

As part of the shift in advertisers' attacks on consumers, U.S. propaganda of "you can do anything" is ratcheted up, especially in the entertainment industry. Perhaps one of the last bastions of insularity and sanctioned discrimination, this expanded media world encourages all citizens to believe that they too can achieve their fifteen minutes of fame. The need for more and more programming demands it and the transformation in technology (Internet, digital cable, mobile) fosters it. The other aspect of this everyman superstar phenomenon, and more germane to this text, is the proliferation of hip hop. In fact, I maintain BET survives and thrives specifically because of the growth of this musical and cultural phenomenon. When the country shifts to another popular form of expression (as its reduced sales already indicate), BET's track record doesn't suggest a swift change to this new thing and certainly not innovation—but maybe its changed ownership will provide for a different response.

Beyond the representation game, the strategies of BET force its target (and non-targeted) black audiences to reconsider what matters. My focus group participants thought of BET as entertainment *and* business. And despite the duplicity that got it on the air, and in some ways has kept it there, these young people felt overwhelmingly ambivalent about BET's ownership. As one student from the Clair youth group said, " ... I don't think its BET's obligation to do nothin' for nobody. Because it's like, either you wanna do it or you don't wanna do it. You know? You wanna vote, you don't wanna vote. But it's not their obligation to tell you that you should go vote" (Clair Memorial UMC July 2004). The *Teen Summit* interviewee furthered: "BET takes a chance on people. People don't really understand the impact. You don't get that in the real world" (*Teen Summit* Interview 2006). Yet even with the existence of BET and forecasts of more program diversity with the expansion of cable and the Internet, the U.S. media landscape still looks overwhelmingly white and forces the question of what real alternatives exist in both genre and scope. Shouting for balance, in-depth knowledge, and sensitivity to subject matter continues, and must continue, alongside some movement in real-live problem solving.

In 2002, cable innovator Geraldine Laybourne was asked in an interview what she wanted the cable network Nickelodeon to be remembered for, a network of which she managed and prospered. She replied: "Taking its audience seriously ... We weren't looking for formulas, and we weren't looking to repeat what others had done. We were looking for something that was fresh, new, and worthy of kids" (quoted in Jenkins 2004: 151). When Robert L. Johnson answered a similar question, he responded: "I think BET is exactly where I hoped it would be—it's tied to a very dynamic media company, has terrific management and continued vision and focus on serving its core audience" (quoted in Umstead 2 June 2005).

He later stated: "Some prominent African-Americans have criticized BET for failing to generate more original intellectual and cultural programming. My goal was to create a company that would maximize value, that would have an impact on the culture of African-Americans, and that would be something I would be proud of having accomplished. The people who have criticized BET should have been, in effect, criticizing the fact that there weren't multiple BETs. They wanted BET to be everything to everybody. BET was a business to maximize value. But it also had a corner on the most influential cultural product of African-Americans. That's music. If you ask Mary J. Blige, if you ask Beyoncé, if you ask Ludacris or Jay-Z, they would say, 'BET made it possible for me to be the success I am today.' I make no apologies for what BET is, or for what it will be" (quoted in *Princeton Alumni Weekly* 22 March 2006). And tellingly, he confessed, "BET was never a legacy event for me … BET was something I started as an investment and I knew someday I would sell it. This [his basketball team] is a legacy event. This is something to keep around" (quoted in CBS 26 February 2006). Clearly, Johnson never quite recognized (or at least acknowledged) the value, magnitude, and possibilities of image making beyond profit potential—i.e., why he continues with a capitalist, self-centered focus even as he has moved to basketball ownership.[7]

Pimpin' Ain't Easy has attempted to trace the historical and cultural development of Black Entertainment Television within the larger conundrums it exemplifies. BET uniquely represents many of the paradoxes of living while black in twenty-first century U.S. culture. If African-Americans and other continually marginalized people want to move beyond the representational numbers game and employ media as part of that equation, they must get an agenda, take action on its tenets, support only those who forward that agenda, confront those who don't, and be willing to forego the television, the products it sells, and the shackles that excessive consumption lead to for the achievement of these goals. Black Entertainment Television helps viewers understand both the simultaneous criticality and insignificance of visual representation. As sociologist Herman Gray noted: "Though media representations do obviously signify at multiple levels in different times and places, they continue to bear the traces of their conditions of production and the historicity of their time and place" (Gray 2005 "Where Have" 323). Using the reflections explored within this text, I hope that people tele-visioning African-American life will begin to truly reassess what representation means against the rhetoric of capital progress. Ultimately, finding ways to undermine and move beyond a system that makes images the most fertile ground for people to challenge must be the goal.

Endnotes

Introduction

1. I am not, however, a communications' scholar and will not present statistical or quantifiable findings for the propositions made here.

Chapter 1

1. Italics are mine.
2. See Frantz Fanon's *Wretched of the Earth* (1963: 65), where he talked about the connections between colonialism, capitalism, and violence. Many African countries used the system of barter as a means of facilitating commerce—always aware of the value in their agriculture and crafts. Furthermore, let me be clear here. Africans from all parts of the continent possessed their own spiritual belief systems—well before the missionaries came.
3. Frazier 1957: 113. See also C.L.R. James, "The Atlantic Slave Trade and Slavery: Some Interpretations of Their Significance in the Development of the United States," *Amistad 1; Writings in Black History and Culture*, eds. John A. Williams and Charles F. Harris (New York: Vintage Books, 1970).
4. As found in Harris 1936: 26. See U.S. Senate, 46th Congress, 2nd session, Report 440—as found in Circular #1 issued by Douglass.
5. See John Hope Franklin, *From Slavery to Freedom: A History of Negro Americans*, 4th Edition, New York: Alfred A. Knopf, 1974, for a larger exploration of the black family.
6. It is important here to call attention to the emphasis of man-dome as the conduit by which progress is to be obtained for African-Americans. This mindset pervades all facets of society—politics, education, economics. Thus when discussions of "the Man" (the white man) surfaced in the 1970s, they were juxtaposed against an imagined parallel universe in the black community with "the man" there, meaning the black man. See Mark Anthony Neal's *New Black Man* (New York: Routledge, 2005) for a contemporary grappling with black masculinity. Furthermore, Wu-Tang Clan offered this version of the significance of money for young people with their rap C.R.E.A.M.—cash rules everything around me (1993).

7. See Todd Boyd's *The New H.N.I.C.* for a discussion on group identity and young black folks.

8. For a look at how capitalism infuses and directs black culture in film, see my "Rock-a-Bye, Baby!: Black Women Disrupting Gangs and Constructing Hip-Hop Gangsta Film" *Cinema Journal* 42: 2 (2003). Additionally, nearly all of Urban Entertainment's titles involve capitalists' conflicts.

9. I thank Deborah Elizabeth Whaley for reminding me of this reality.

10. In fact in his longer comments West said, "I hate the way they portray us in the media. You see a black family, it says, 'They're looting.' You see a white family, it says, 'They're looking for food.' And, you know, it's been five days because most of the people are black. And even for me to complain about it, I would be a hypocrite because I've tried to turn away from the TV because it's too hard to watch. I've even been shopping before even giving a donation, so now I'm calling my business manager right now to see what is the biggest amount I can give; and just to imagine if I was down there, and those are my people down there. So anybody out there that wants to do anything that we can help—with the way America is set up to help the poor, the black people, the less well-off, as slow as possible. I mean, the Red Cross is doing everything they can. We already realize a lot of people that could help are at war right now, fighting another way—and they've given them permission to go down and shoot us! [Back to Mike Myers, who after saying something stupid, tosses it back to West] George Bush doesn't care about black people!"

11. My father's family developed pretty much the same way in Smith County, Texas—only just outside of Lindale.

12. In fact, many argue for the U.S. military as being more progressive than society in general in its opening of opportunities for African-Americans, due in part to its rigid structure—see John Sibley Butler and Charles Moskos, *All That We Can Be: Black Leadership and Racial Integration the Army Way* (New York: Basic Books, 1997).

13. The *Tom Joyner Morning Show* features Myra Jay, "the poster child for single moms," who represents the single mother—but not in a way that questions the classist implication of what she offers up and her representation thereof.

14. Toni grows up dirt poor in a farming area of Fresno, California. She completely buys into the capitalist discourse of material success as a panacea to the taint of poverty.

15. While Maya dresses similar to all of the other characters, her attire periodically grounds issues of appropriateness and taste as shown most easily in the episode "Never a Bridesmaid" (UPN, initial airdate 27 November 2000).

16. Interestingly too, since 2003, *Girlfriends* is one of the acquired series running on Black Entertainment Television.

17. Unfortunately, this approach has led to the "rollercoaster" success of many black newspapers. See Walker 1999: 2.

18. John H. Johnson (now Linda Johnson Rice's) Johnson Publishing Company, Earl G. Graves Sr. who publishes *Black Enterprise*, Tom Joyner's Reach Media, Byron Allen's Entertainment Studios, Tavis Smiley's "The Smiley Group," Percy Sutton's Inner City Broadcasting, and Spike Lee's Forty Acres & a Mule Filmworks are all still family- or family majority-owned and helmed.

Chapter 2

1. Twenty-five years later, this same idealistic and self-serving business-technology speak resurfaced in the development of the Internet. Expectantly, the same type of minimalist consumer benefit has begun to manifest itself with this new technology as well.

2. As the FCC continues to toy with these ideas, Time Warner and Comcast "voluntarily" announced the creation of a "family" tier option for consumers in December 2005. For Comcast, this tier included all the broadcast networks and cablers Disney, Nickelodeon, and Discovery Kids along with a few of the Spanish-language networks and some religious programming as well. Cox Communications announced similar designations in January 2006. Cox simultaneously (or shortly thereafter) raised its subscriber rates. In the versions proposed thus far, BET appears not to be particularly "family friendly."

3. "Moving on Up" is the theme song for the television sitcom *The Jeffersons* (Norman Lear, creator, 1975–1985, CBS).

4. Furthermore, the term diversity has increasingly shifted. It is frequently implemented as a "range of experiences" while covertly maintaining its historic ties to race discourses.

5. This figure does not account for the 27% of U.S. television households that are satellite subscribers and receive cable networks as well.

6. I thank my colleague Gregory Crawford in the University of Arizona's Eller School of Management for sharing this insight.

7. Actually, Johnson and his former wife Sheila Crump Johnson achieved billionaire status simultaneously.

8. Certain aspects of Johnson's biography yield conflicting reports. He is cited as being born in East St. Louis, Illinois and Hickory, Mississippi. I use Hickory from Pulley's account.

9. Knowing this relationship fact puts a crimp in the bootstrap theory Johnson perpetuates inasmuch as it shows that Johnson is not, (based on his contemporary connections and his Princeton degree), "every man."

10. Beyond yielding the valued first mantra, this move made for very exciting times with African-Americans young and old beginning to dabble in the stock market—ala the Cosby model. Plus, tremendous growth had occurred in investment clubs and a euphoria of online trading that those college-educated African-Americans aimed to be a part of—a yuppie or buppie move to quick wealth.

11. Moving beyond its purported base, BET on Jazz has targeted the "affluent Latino" market with a weekly two-hour block of programming sponsored by the U.S. Navy. See Moses Frenck, "Latino Programming to Air on BET Jazz," *MediaWeek.com* 31 March 2005.

12. As of 2005, *Savoy* returned to circulation. However, it is published by Hermene Hartman of Jazzy Communications in Chicago, and in 2007, is published as an online magazine.

13. The most popular site for African-Americans was blackplanet.com.

14. I distinguish "key personnel" from regular staff as it seemed that the riches did not trickle down to below the line players. This will be explored later in the chapter.

15. Quote from Johnson discussing what he was most proud of regarding the growth and sale of BET as found in George Winslow, "The Birth of BET: John Malone and Robert Johnson Recall the Long, Winding Road to Viacom," *Broadcasting & Cable*, 11 April 2005, Infotrac Online.

16. See Dan Herman's "Al Ries might be dangerous to your brand," Themanager. org, accessed 18 April 2005, where he took Ries to task for outmoded thinking.

17. Nonetheless, the network is generally located on cable systems around music channels. In Tucson, Arizona, for example, BET appears on channel 49, MTV channel 50, VH-1 51, CMT 52, and MTV2 is channel 53. BET is positioned on most cable systems in some configuration of this order, this clustering. Thus it seems in the collective minds of cable systems, BET is more about offering up music videos than anything else.

18. I thank Crystal Quintero for her work on Jennifer Lopez in helping me to think about this.

19. As noted in Scot Brown, *Fighting for US: Maulana Karenga, the US Organiza-tion, and Black Cultural Nationalism* (New York: New York University Press, 2003) 51.

20. Upstarts such as ImaginAsian TV ("America's First 24/7 Asian American Net-work") and SíTV ("Speak English. Live Latin.) use BET's model as a blueprint for targeting Asian-American and Latino audiences, respectively.

21. I thank Barbara Selznick for making me think about this aspect as well.

22. Johnson's wish came true in 2005 when Essence Communications is sold to Time Inc.

23. An earlier example on the network shows that in 1993, during the network's original series *Comic View*, a Schlitz Malt Liquor logo ran in the lower third of the screen for several minutes after each commercial break. This "logomania" continues as a popular trend (*Brandweek* 6 December 1993).

24. This Johnson even met with President Jimmy Carter to commemorate the opening of KBLE. ("The Daily Diary of President Jimmy Carter," 23 Septem-ber 1978).

25. Following in the footsteps of Black Family Channel that hired director/actor/ writer/ producer Robert Townsend as President of Production, BET selected filmmaker Reginald Hudlin to fill the created position of network entertain-ment president in July 2005. Said CEO Debra L. Lee: "This signals to the world that we're looking toward the future and we're serious about doing origi-nal programming" (*Multichannel News* 18 July 2005: 18).

26. See Karen M. Rowley and David D. Kurpius, "Separate and Still Unequal: A Comparative Study of Blacks in Business Magazines," *The Howard Journal of Communications* 14 (2003): 245–255.

27. Said former *Source* co-owner Raymond "Benzino" Scott about Black Enter-prise: "They have tried to cover up their hostile takeover attempt by falsely attacking the character and business acumen of the two people who have been the driving force of *The Source's* success for the last 18 years and who have positioned *The Source* brand to capitalize on multiple revenue streams going forward … It is clear to me that *Black Enterprise* has little regard for the mil-lions of loyal Hip-Hop fans who read The Source each month when the first thing they do after their fraudulent 'takeover' last month is publicly denounce the strong stance the magazine has taken in the past few years against the corporate-driven monopolization, corruption, payola and violence plaguing the Hip-Hop music industry" (quoted in rapindustry.com February 2006).

Co-founder Dave Mays added: "Their scheme to steal our magazine is probably fueled by their desire to add it to their own struggling publishing operation (*Black Enterprise* magazine), that I believe has not been nearly as profitable for them in recent years as it once was" (quoted in rapindustry.com, February 2006). By May 2006, Black Enterprise controlled *The Source* and terminated both Mays and Benzino.

28. Like Washington of Mitgo, rumors circulated that Robert L. Johnson was just the face of BET and actually possessed no ultimate authority. However through my findings, much of that talk can be seemingly attributed to player hatin!

29. I address this audience/press/BET relationship more in chapter 3.

30. I thank scholar and friend Denise Davis-Maye for drawing me a very vivid visual image of that time and place.

31. In Houston A. Baker Jr.'s *Black Studies, Rap, and the Academy*, Michael Eric Dyson's *Between God and Gangsta Rap*, Cornel West's hip hop CD *Sketches of My Culture*, Todd Boyd's *The New H.N.I.C.: The Death of Civil Rights and the Reign of Hip Hop*, Cora Daniels's *Black Power Inc.: The New Voice of Success*, and many others, the relevance of hip hop finds support. However, others such as writers and scholars Armond White, Norman Kelley, Martin Kilson, and Louis A. Thomas take these supporters and their elevation of hip hop to task for either their stance or their lack of movement beyond the obvious.

32. I address these ideas further in chapter 4.

33. Yet Walker added that despite substantial gains, changes in the recording industry still leave black artists exploited. Sublabeling, a designation given when independent black producers allow their companies to become subsidiaries of major record labels, makes these folks executives—but no longer owners. They generally retain no control of their budgets or release dates for records. Mike Ellis, president of Source Entertainment, remarked: "It's the most brilliant mind game I've seen" (Walker 1998: 329–330).

34. See Todd Boyd's *Young, Black, Rich, and Famous: The Rise of the NBA, the Hip Hop Invasion, and the Transformation of American Culture*, Aaron Baker's *Out of Bounds: Sports, Media, and the Politics of Identity*, Gena Dagel Caponi, *Signifyin(g), Sanctifyin' & Slam Dunking: A Reader in African American Expressive Culture*, and Museum of Television and Radio satellite seminar *Bebopping, Hip-Hopping, & Slam-Dunking: The Influence of African-American Endeavors in Music and Sports on Mainstream Culture*.

Chapter 3

1. These quotes by Robert L. Johnson were found in both Pulley's *Billion* text pages 109 and 59 and in an additional magazine article.

2. See Dan Rubey, "Voguing at the Carnival: Desire and Pleasure on MTV," *South Atlantic Quarterly* 90.4 (Fall 1991): 871–906, Andrew Ross, "Back on the Box," *Artforum* (May1995), and Tricia Rose, "Never Trust a Big Butt and a Smile," *Camera Obscura* 23 (1991): 108–31 and *Black Noise: Rap Music and Black Culture in Contemporary America* (Hanover: Wesleyan University Press, 1994).

3. Damon Wayans's character calls the hired television consultant Myrna Gold-farb (Dina Pearlman) "the great niggerologist" in *Bamboozled*; songwriter/art-ist Bill Withers terms the white executives who populate the music industry "blacksperts" in a 2003 interview; and *The Dave Chappelle Show* presents a laugh out loud skit of a game show called "I Know Black People."

4. I thank Catherine Squires for helping me understand the foci of communications.

5. UPN maintained a black Monday night from its inception through the begin-ning of 2006. After its merger with WB, they dropped all but three of their African-American dominated programs.

6. See my "Narrowcasting in the New World Information Order: A Space for the Audience?" *Television & New Media* 5.1 (February 2004): 69–81.

7. BET launched the BET Comedy Awards in 2004.

8. Subsequent versions of the awards program continued to increase viewer-ship—if not consistently maintaining quality.

9. To be fair, I guess, his remarks referenced an earlier performance of Desti-ny's Child where they sang and performed faux-lap dances for three audience members—former basketball player Magic Johnson, rapper Nelly, and actor Terrance Howard.

10. The peculiar acceptance of James's behavior within black communities at the time, (his misogyny in particular), went along with his seeming connection to both r & b and disco and his celebrity. Unfortunately, his behavior and the acceptance thereof laid some of the ground work for the pervasive misogyny within hip hop.

11. I thank William Broussard for pointing out this connection and making me think about the one above.

12. Many hip hop artists talk about high-end products even as some of the manu-facturerers deride said patronage. A recent example of this (June 2006) came with the champagne Cristal and comments made by its president Frederic Rouzaud. His nonchalant reception of the impact of rappers on Cristal's brand lead rapper and music executive Jay-Z to boycott the beverage both in his busi-ness and personal life.

13. It should be remembered, however, BET discontinued both of these magazines.

14. I thank my student Jennifer Cady for her insight into this arena.

15. The actress Iesha was a terror on the set due to her unhappiness dealing with fame and the pressure of supporting her family, working twenty hours per day, and having no friends. Ralph Farquhar executive produced *The Proud Family* and also co-created *Moesha*.

16. I thank my student Katie Moran for helping me to consider this angle.

Chapter 4

1. I thank Dana E. Mastro for her insight into this communication studies move toward a different kind of specificity.

2. These studies include: Felicia G. Jones, "The Black Audience and the BET Channel," Alice A. Tait and John T. Barber, "Black Entertainment Televi-sion: Breaking New Ground and Accepting New Responsibilities?" and "The New Model of Black Media Entrepreneurship: BET Holdings Inc.", and my own "Narrowcasting on the New World Information Order: A Space for the Audience?" Other articles employ BET as part of an overall examination of a subject—particularly music videos. For example, current scholarship includes:

L. Monique Ward et al. "Contributions of Music Video Exposure to Black Ado-
lescents' Gender and Sexual Schemes," Michael T. Elliott, "Differences in the
Portrayal of Blacks: A Content Analysis of General Media Versus Culturally-
Targeted Commercials," and Stacy L. Smith and Aaron R. Boyson, "Violence in
Music Videos: Examining the Prevalence and Context of Physical Aggression."

3. See Smith-Shomade, *Shaded Lives: African-American Women and Television*
chapter three and Sut Jhally's documentaries *DreamWorlds* I, II, and III.

4. For example, see studies like Dana E. Mastro and Susannah R. Stern, "Representations of Race in Television Commercials: A Content Analysis of Prime-
Time Advertising," *JOBEM* (December 2003).

5. Lee has on many occasions critiqued BET's programming. However in the
film, it is "the Man" and his minions laying out the brothas.

6. This video interpretation is found on the online rap dictionary.

7. Since his departure, Smiley started his own radio and television talk shows on
PBS, published five books, convened eight conferences on the state of black
America which aired on C-SPAN, and in 2006, co-authored the text *The Covenant with Black America* that aimed to serve as a "blueprint" for transforming "black America as usual."

8. These corporations included: the Magic Johnson Foundation, National Medi-
cal Association, One Voice Gospel Music, Respond to AIDS, African-American
AIDS Policy and Training Institute, Kaiser Family Foundation, Cable Positive,
AIDS, and Life/Beat.

9. I thank Deborah Elizabeth Whaley for smacking me in the head with this
nugget!

10. For years, film studios et al. argued that African-American stories and faces
failed to translate commercially abroad—a lucrative and desired revenue
stream. This assumption seems to hold sway when discussing white European
markets. However, others show that this is, at least in part, a fiction (as discussed in chapter three and within the works of Jesse Algernon and Timothy
Havens). The truth of viable markets, however, has not transformed the making of more programs centering African-American stories in U.S. media.

Chapter 5

1. His daughter's absence is significant inasmuch as it continues to show black succes-
sion of capital power where women tend to not be envisioned as heir apparent.

2. *The Omaha Star* is a black-owned newspaper in Omaha Nebraska, and Paschal's is a historic black-owned restaurant in Atlanta where civil rights leaders
gathered to strategize in the 1960s.

3. For more on this connection, revisit chapter 4 and see my "I Be Smackin' My
Hoes: Paradox and Authenticity in *Bamboozled*" in *The Spike Lee Reader*, ed.
Paula Massood, (Philadelphia: Temple University Press, forthcoming 2008).

4. Interestingly, one of the house members of BET's 2005–2006 season of *College Hill* was Ray, a gay co-ed. His sexuality, however, served as a point of
accessory rather than as a reflection of an alternative life. Yet that same season,
BET began airing Fox's *In Living Color* series. Its popular "Men on Film" segments relied on a homophobic conception of black male homosexuality.

5. Revisit Herman Gray's idea of insider production in *Watching Race: Television
and the Struggle for "Blackness"* (1995).

6. Although media scholar and producer/writer Felicia Henderson made a convincing argument against *Chris*'s program in particular as doing little more than reifying race as the major plot point—subordinating class to function as black poverty (*SCMS*, March 2007).

7. His lack of understanding and desire to make more money explains why Johnson announced in July 2006 a partnership with film industry executives Bob and Harvey Weinstein to create movies exclusively targeted at African-American audiences. He stated that Our Stories Films will make two low-budget comedies per year initially and increase that number to four or five films annually. This focus on capital beyond everything else really is his legacy—not a transformation of the televisual landscape.

Bibliography

Adorno, Theodor W. *The Culture Industry: Selected Essays on Mass Culture.* London: Routledge, 1991.

Adorno, Theodor, and Max Horkheimer. "The Culture Industry: Enlightenment as Mass Deception." In *Media and Cultural Studies: KeyWorks*, edited by Meenakshi Gigi Durham and Douglas M. Kellner. UK: Blackwell, 2001.

Advertising Age. "Special Advertising Section of *Advertising Age*—BET 25." *Advertising Age*, April 11, 2005.

Aikat, Debashis. "Violent Content in Online Music Videos: Characteristics of Violence in Online Videos on BET.com, Country.com, MTV.com, and VH1.com." Paper presented at the Annual Conference for the International Communication Association, New Orleans, LA, May 27–31, 2004.

Ainslie, Ricardo C. "Cultural Mourning, Immigration, and Engagement: Vignettes from The Mexican Experience." In *Crossing: Immigration and the Socio-Cultural Remaking of the North American Space*, edited by Marcelo Suarez-Orozco. Cambridge, MA: Harvard University Press, 1998: 284–305.

Akbar, Na'im. *Chains and Images of Psychological Slavery.* Jersey City, NJ: New Mind, 1984.

Alexander, Keith L. "BET Chief Debra Lee Aims to Make a Difference—On the Air and in the World." *Black MBA Magazine*, Fall conference issue, 2005.

Axtman, Kris. "After Years in the Suburbs, Many Blacks Return to City Life," *The Christian Science Monitor* 29 April 2004.

Baldwin, Davarian L. "Black Empires, White Desires: The Spatial Politics of Identity in the Age of Hip Hop." *Black Renaissance/ Renaissance Noire* 2.2 (Summer 1999): 138–159.

Baraka, Imamu Amiri. (1984) "Black Liberation/Socialist Revolution." In *Daggers and Javelins: Essays, 1974–1979*, New York: William Morrow and Company, 1984. Online (19 June 2004).

Barber, John T. and Alice A. Tait, Eds. *The Information Society and the Black Community.* Westport, CT: Praeger, 2001.

Bender, Stephen. "Oh God, You Devil: Black Entertainment Television Has Put Sleazy Televangelist Robert Tilton Back on the Air. Is BET Giving People What They Want, or Taking Advantage of the Faithful?" *salon.com* November 21, 2000.

Bennett, Lerone Jr. *The Challenge of Blackness*. Chicago: Johnson, 1972.

BET Editors et al. *Celebrating 20 Years: BET Black Star Power*. Washington, DC: BET Books, 2000.

"BET Pictures II Continues Arabesque Momentum with Three New Made-For-TV Films for 2001 Debut." *PR Newswire*. 19 October 2000.

Black Commentator, The. http://blackcommentator.com. 40 (May 1, 2003), accessed 25 March 2004.

"Black Power." *Economist* 10 April 1999.

Blake, John. "Bishop's Charity Generous to Bishop: New Birth's Eddie Long Got $3 Million." *Atlanta Journal-Constitution*, 28 August 2005.

Booker, Will and Deborah Jermyn, Eds. *The Audience Studies Reader*. London: Routledge, 2003.

Booker T. Washington Foundation. *How Blacks Use Television for Entertainment and Information*. Washington, DC: National Science Foundation, 1978.

Boyd, Todd. *The New H.N.I.C.: The Death of Civil Rights and the Reign of Hip Hop*. New York: New York University Press, 2003.

Brimmer, Andrew F. "Long-term Trends and Prospects for Black-Owned Businesses." *The Review of Black Political Economy* 26:1 (Summer 1998): 19–36.

Brownfield, Paul. "BET's Fees for Comics Less of a Joke," *Milwaukee Journal-Sentinel* 10 August 2000.

Butler, John Sibley. "Myrdal Revisited: the Negro in Business." *Daedalus* (Winter 1995): 199–221.

CBS. "Second Act for Robert Johnson." *cbsnews.com* 26 February 2006. (11 July 2006).

Center for Digital Democracy, "Minorities and the Media: Little Ownership and Even Less Control" 16 December 2002, www.democraticmedia.org/news/marketwatch/minoritymedia.htm, accessed 23 August 2006.

Chait, Jonathan. "Painted Black." *The New Republic*, 27 August–3 September 2001, 30–33.

Clarke, John Henrik. *Africans at the Crossroads: Notes for an African World Revolution*. Trenton, NJ: Africa World Press, 1991.

Coclanis, Peter A. "What Made Booker Wash(ington)? The Wizard of Tuskegee in Economic Context." In *Booker T. Washington and Black Progress: Up From Slavery 100 Years Later*, edited by W. Fitzhugh Brundage. Gainesville: University Press of Florida, 2003: 81–106.

Comaroff, Jean and John L. Comaroff. *Millennial Capitalism and the Culture of Neoliberalism*. Durham, NC: Duke University Press, 2001.

Cox, Harvey. "The Market as God: Living in the New Dispensation." *The Atlantic Monthly*, March 1999, 18–23.

Crowdus, Gary, and Dan Georgakas. "Thinking about the Power of Images: An Interview with Spike Lee." *Cineaste* 26.2 (2001): online.

Crupi, Anthony. "Adult Swim Orders More Boondocks for '06." *Mediaweek*, 25 January 2006.

Daniels, Cora. *Black Power Inc.: The New Voice of Success*. New York: John Wiley & Sons 2004.

Daniels, Ron. "The Demise of *Emerge* and the Ethics of Black Capitalism," *The Black World Today*, 29 June 2000, www.hartford-hwp.com/archives/45a/341.html (21 November 2002).

Datcher, Michael. "Free Huey: Aaron McGruder's Outer Child Is Taking on America." *The Crisis* (September-October 2003): online.

Dávila, Arlene. *Latinos, Inc.: The Marketing and Making of a People*. Berkeley: University of California Press, 2001.

"The Death of Black-Owned Media or the Birth of New Opportunities?" workshop, National Urban League 2005 National convention.

deCastro, Ronald T. Interview by author, 8 February 2006.

DeJong, Allard Sicco and Benjamin Bates. "Channel Diversity in Cable Television." *Journal of Broadcasting & Electronic Media* 35.2 (1991): 154–166.

Du Bois, W.E.B. "Negroes and Socialism." *National Guardian* 29 (April 1957): online.

———. "Negroes and the Crisis of Capitalism in the United States." *Monthly Review* 4 (April 1953): 478–485. In *W.E.B. Du Bois: A Reader*, edited by David Levering Lewis. New York: Henry Holt and Company, 1995: 624.

———. "The Talented Tenth: Memorial Address." *Boulé Journal* 15 (October 1948): 3–13.

Dutt, Rimin. "Carlyle, Johnson Team Up For Private-Equity Firm." *Wall Street Journal*, 14 December 2005.

Edwards, Richard C., Michael Reich, and Thomas E. Weisskopf. *The Capitalist System: A Radical Analysis of American Society*, 2nd Edition. Englewood Cliffs, NJ: Prentice-Hall, 1978.

Einstein, Mara. *Media Diversity: Economics, Ownership, and the FCC*. Mahwah: NJ: Lawrence Erlbaum Associates, 2004.

Elasmar, Michael G. "Can U.S. Entertainment TV Programs Influence the Culture of Young Adults Overseas?" Paper presented at the annual conference of the International Communication Association, New Orleans, LA, May 27–31, 2004.

Elliott, Michael T. "Differences in the Portrayal of Blacks: A Content Analysis of General Media Versus Culturally-targeted Commercials." *Journal of Current Issues and Research in Advertising* 17.1 (Spring 1995): 75–86.

Entman, Robert M. and Andrew Rojecki. *The Black Image in the White Mind*. Chicago: University of Chicago Press, 2000.

Fanon, Frantz. *Wretched of the Earth*. New York: Grove Weidenfeld, 1963.

Fiske, John. *Media Matters: Everyday Culture and Political Change*. Minneapolis: University of Minnesota, 1994.

Frankel, Daniel. "BET Wagers on Original Fare: New Programming Topper Reginald Hudlin Energizes Cabler's Development Slate." *Daily Variety*, 24 February 2006, B4.

Frazier, E. Franklin. *Black Bourgeoisie*. New York: Free Press, 1957 first printing. edition cited, London: Collier Books, 1969.

Friedman, Wayne. "The Elusive Ad Target," *Broadcasting & Cable*, 5 February 2007.

Fulcher, James. *Capitalism: A Very Short Introduction*. New York: Oxford University Press, 2004.

Fusfeld, Daniel R. *Economics: Principles of Political Economy*. Illinois, Scott, Foresman and Company, 1982.

Gates, Racquel J. "Sampling: A New Metaphor for Understanding Black Visual Culture." Paper presented at the annual conference of Society for Cinema and Media Studies conference, Vancouver, BC, Canada, March 2–5, 2006.

George, Nelson. *Hip Hop America*. New York: Penguin Books, 1998.

Goodman, Steven. *Teaching Youth Media: A Critical Guide to Literacy, Video Production, and Social Change*. New York: Teachers College Press, 2003.

Gordon, Ed. "Effect of 'Essence' Sale on Black-Owned Media," *News & Notes with Ed Gordon*, National Public Radio, 1 March 2005.

Gordon, Ed. "Bobby Jones: Gospel Music on the Rise," *News & Notes with Ed Gordon*, National Public Radio, November 2005.

Graser, Marc. "McDonald's Buying Way into Hip-Hop Song Lyrics." *Advertising Age*, March 23, 2005.

Gray, Herman S. *Cultural Moves: African Americans and the Politics of Representation*. Berkeley: University of California Press, 2005.

_____"The Politics of Representation in Network Television." In *Television: The Critical View*, 6th ed., edited by Horace Newcomb. New York: Oxford University Press, 2000.

_____*Watching Race: Television and the Struggle for "Blackness"*. Minneapolis: University of Minnesota Press, 1995.

_____"Where Have All the Black Shows Gone?" In *Black Cultural Traffic: Crossroads in Global Performance and Popular Culture*, edited by Harry J. Elam, Jr. and Kennell Jackson. Ann Arbor: University of Michigan Press, 2005.

Greenberg, Bradley S. and Larry Collette. "The Changing Faces in TV Guide: An Analysis of Television's New Season Demography, 1966–1992." Paper presented at the annual conference of the Association for Education in Journalism and Mass Communications, New Orleans, LA, August 1999.

Grimaldi, Vincent. "The Fundamentals of Branding." *Brandchannel.com* November 3, 2003. (10 April 2005).

Gupta, Udayan. "Cable TV: Electronic Redlining." *Black Enterprise*, October 1981, 87–94.

Hall, Stuart, Ed. *Representation: Cultural Representations and Signifying Practices*. London: Sage, 1997.

Halter, Marilyn. *Shopping for Identity: The Marketing of Ethnicity*. New York: Schocken Books, 2000.

Harris, Abram L. *The Negro as Capitalist: A Study of Banking and Business Among American Negroes*. College Park, MD: McGrath, 1936.

Havens, Timothy. "'It's Still a White World Out There': The Interplay of Culture and Economics in International Television Trade." *Critical Studies in Media Communication* 19.4 (December 2002): 377–397.

Hayes, Arthur S. "Black Enough?" unpublished manuscript, 2005.

Hayes III, Floyd W., Ed. *A Turbulent Voyage: Readings in African American Studies*, 2nd Edition. San Diego: Collegiate Press, 1997.

Haygood, Daniel. "Globalization through Global Brands: Purely an American-Made Phenomenon?" Paper presented at the annual conference of the International Communication Association, New Orleans, LA, May 27–31, 2004.

Higgins, John M. "Breakthrough for Black Network." *Broadcasting & Cable*, 7 May 2001, 12.

Hinckley, David. "From the Golden Age of Radio … Amos 'n Andy Chapter 67." *Daily News*, 14 May 2002.

Hoffer, William. "Black Entrepreneurship in America." *Nation's Business*, June 1987, online, (18 November 2002).

Hogan, Monica. "BET Plans $5M Image, Branding Campaign." *Multichannel News*, 20 December 1999: online. (17 March 2003).

hooks, bell. *Where We Stand: Class Matters*. New York: Routledge, 2000.

hooks, bell. "Thinking about Capitalism: A Conversation with Cultural Critic Paul Gilroy," *Z Magazine* April 1996 (accessed 21 November 2002).

Howard, Glenda. *Cita's World*. Washington, DC: BET Publications, 2001.

Hunt, Darnell M., Ed. *Channeling Blackness: Studies on Television and Race in America*. New York: Oxford University Press, 2005.

Ice T. *The Ice Opinion: Who Gives a Fuck?* New York: St. Martin's Press, 1994.

Jackson, John L. Jr. *Real Black: Adventures in Racial Sincerity*. Chicago: University of Chicago Press, 2005.

Jaramillo, Deborah. "Opening Up the Representation Discussion: Pay Cable, Minority Programming & the Capitalist Paradigm." unpublished manuscript, May 2, 2002.

Jaynes, Gerald David and Robin M. Williams, Jr., Eds. *A Common Destiny: Blacks and American Society*. Washington, DC: National Academy Press, 1989.

Jenkins, Henry. "Interview with Geraldine Laybourne." In *Nickelodeon Nation: The History, Politics, and Economics of America's Only TV Channel for Kids*, edited by Heather Hendershot. New York: New York University Press, 2004: 134–152.

John-Hill, Annette. "Despite Its Critics, BET Stays the Course." *The Philadelphia Inquirer*, 17 March 2002.

Johnson, E. Patrick. *Appropriating Blackness: Performance and the Politics of Authenticity*. Durham, NC: Duke University Press, 2003.

Johnson, John H. *Succeeding Against the Odds*. New York: Warner Books, 1989.

Johnson, Robert L. *BET Promotional*. 1980. Videocassette.

Jones, Anderson. "Invisible Lover." *The Advocate*, 16 January 2001, online.

Jones, Felicia G. "The Black Audience and the BET Channel." *Journal of Broadcasting and Electronic Media* 34.4 (Fall 1990): 477–486.

Jones, Vernon Clement. "Not Black Like Me." *The Globe and Mail* 19 February 2001, online (22 January 2003).

Karim, Karim H. "From Ethnic Media to Global Media: Transnational Communication Networks Among Diasporic Communities." International Comparative Research Group, Strategic Research and Analysis, Department of Canadian Heritage, June 1998.

Katz, Richard. "Johnson Bets Vertical Niche on Black Pix." *Variety*, 3–9 August 1998.

Kelley, Norman. "Rhythm Nation: The Political Economy of Black Music." *Black Renaissance/Renaissance Noire* 2.2 (Summer 1999): 8–21.

Kelley, Robin D.G. *Race Rebels: Culture, Politics, and the Black Working Class*. New York: Free Press, 1994.

Klein, Naomi. *No Logo: Taking Aim at the Brand Bullies*. New York: Picador, 1999.

Krantz, Michael. "Marketing on the Superhighway; The Question Isn't If but When, Where, What and How Brand Building Will Surface in the New Technologies." *Mediaweek* 18 October 1993, S29.

Kubey, Robert, Mark Shifflet, Niranjala Weerakkody, and Stephen Ukeiley. "Demographic Diversity on Cable: Have the New Cable Channels Made a Difference in the Representation of Gender, Race, and Age?" *Journal of Broadcasting and Electronic Media* 39.4 (Fall 1995): 459–471.

Landau, Saul. *The Business of America: How Consumers Have Replaced Citizens and How We Can Reverse the Trend*. New York: Routledge, 2004.

Larson, Megan. "One More Choice." *Brandweek*, 4 April 2005, online.

Lasica, J.D. "Interview with Ben Bagdikian." *USC Annenberg Online Journalism Review*, May 23, 2002. <www.ojr.org> (3 January 2006).

Lee, Spike. *Bamboozled*. Film 2000.

_____*Do the Right Thing*. Film 1989.

Leigh, Allan. "All BET's Are On." *Billboard* online, April 22, 2000. (25 September 2004).

Light Alan, Ed. *The Vibe History of Hip Hop.* New York: Three Rivers Press, 1999.

Lloyd, Blake Te'Neil, and Julia L. Mendez. "Batswana Adolescents' Interpretation of American Music Videos: So That's What That Means!" *Journal of Black Psychology* 27.4 (November 2001): 464–476.

Lowry, Mark. "'Chitlin Circuit' Continues to Tap Into Need for a Theater of Our Own," *Black Voices.com*, 24 July 2004, http://new.blackvoices.com/travel/destinations/dallas/bv (14 September 2004).

Lubiano, Wahneema. "But Compared to What? Realism, Essentialism, and Representation in Spike Lee's *School Daze, Do the Right Thing*, and the Spike Lee Discourse." *Black American Literature Forum* 25.2 (Summer 1991): 253–282.

MacDonald, J. Fred. *Blacks and White TV: African Americans in Television Since 1948* 2nd Edition. Chicago: Nelson-Hall Publishers, 1992.

Malveaux, Julianne. "Wall Street, Main Street, and the Side Street." In *Black Genius: African American Solutions to African American Problems*, edited by Walter Mosley, Manthia Diawara, Clyde Taylor, and Regina Austin. New York: W.W. Norton & Company, 1999.

Marable, Manning. "History, Liberalism, and the Black Radical Tradition." *Radical History Review*, 71 (Spring 1998). http://chnm.gmu.edu/rhr/marable.htm (28 April 2004).

_____*How Capitalism Underdeveloped Black America*. Boston: South End Press, 2000.

Mason, Laurie, Christine M. Bachen, and Stephanie L. Craft, "Support For FCC Minority Ownership Policy: How Broadcast Station Owner Race or Ethnicity Affects News and Public Affairs Programming Diversity," *Communication Law and Policy* 6.1 (2001): 37–73.

McConnell, Bill. "BET's Johnson Hits Proposed Tax Break." *Broadcasting & Cable*, 22 November 1999, 19.

McDonald, Daniel G. and Shu-Fang Lin. "The Effect of New Networks on U.S. Television Diversity." *Journal of Media Economics* 17.2 (2004): 105–121.

Melewar, T.C. and Christopher M. Walker. "Global Corporate Brand Building: Guidelines and Case Studies." *Journal of Brand Management* (November 2003): 157–170.

Mitchell, Gail. "Q & A: Debra L. Lee." *Billboard*, 2 July 2005, 21.

Moody, Nekesa Mumbi. "BET Provides More 'Exposure' for Music Videos." *Associated Press* online, 5 April 2004. (27 August 2004).

Moskowitz, Dara. "Stopping Northern Time." *City Pages*, 18 April 2001. www.citypages.com.

Muhammad, Elijah. Ed. "The Nation of Islam Economic Blueprint." *Message to the Blackman*. Newport News, VA: United Brothers Communications Systems 1965.

Muhammad, Tariq K. "The Branding of BET." *Black Enterprise*, June 1997, 156–158.

Mullen, Megan. *The Rise of Cable Programming in the United States: Revolution or Evolution?* Austin: University of Texas Press, 2003.

Mundy, Alicia. "Does Bob Johnson Stand Alone?" *Mediaweek.com*, 31 March 1997, online. <14 October 2005>.

Murray, Susan and Laurie Ouellette. *Reality TV: Remaking Television Culture*. New York: New York University Press, 2004.

Myrdal, Gunnar. *An American Dilemma: The Negro Problem and Modern Democracy.* New York: Harper & Bros., 1944.

National Editorial Board, News & Letters, www.newsandletters.org, October 2003.

Neal, Mark Anthony. "Critical Noir: Bigger and Better?" *PopMatters.com,* July 15, 2004. http:/africana.com/articles/daily/mu20040715bet.asp (23 July 2004).

_____ "Critical Noire: "Big Pimpin' Bourgeois Style: the Demise of Tavis Smiley's *BET Tonight.*" *Popmatters.com,* March 29, 2001. <http://www.popmatters.com/columns/criticalnoire/010329.shtml> (2 June 2006).

_____ *Songs in the Key of Black Life: A Rhythm and Blues Nation.* New York: Routledge, 2003.

_____ *Soul Babies: Black Popular Culture and the Post-Soul Aesthetic.* New York: Routledge, 2002.

Ngwainmbi, Emmanuel K. "The Black Media Entrepreneur and Economic Implications for the 21st Century." *Journal of Black Studies* 36.1 (September 2005): 3–33.

Nichols, Bill. *Representing Reality: Issues and Concepts in Documentary.* Bloomington, IN: Indiana University Press, 1991.

Noguera, Pedro A. "Anything but Black: Bringing Politics Back to the Study of Race." In *Problematizing Blackness: Self-Ethnographies by Black Immigrants to the United States,* edited by Percy C. Hintzen and Jean Muteba Rahier. New York: Routledge, 2003: 193–200.

O.J. Simpson: Beyond the Verdict, BET, 1996, television program.

Ouellette, Laurie. *Viewers Like You: How Public TV Failed the People.* New York: Columbia University Press, 2002.

Parsons, Patrick R. and Robert M. Frieden. *The Cable and Satellite Television Industries.* Boston: Allyn and Bacon, 1998.

Pennock, Pam. "Televising Sin: Efforts to Restrict the Televised Advertisement of Cigarettes and Alcohol in the United States, 1950s to 1980s." *Historical Journal of Film, Radio and Television* 25.4 (October 2005): 619–636.

Perry, Sheldon and Raoul Dennis. "Selling of Black-Owned Companies: Cash Gains, Culture Loss?" *New York Amsterdam News* 23 November 2000, online.

Phillips, Jennie L. "Unpacking the Transparency of Social Class." Paper presented at the annual conference of the International Communication Association, New Orleans, LA, May 27–31, 2004.

Princeton Alumni Weekly. "A Moment with Robert L. Johnson '72." Online, 22 March 2006.

Proud Family, The. Creator Bruce Smith, 2001–2005, Disney, television program.

Pulley, Brett. The Billion Dollar BET: Robert Johnson and the Inside Story of Black Entertainment Television. New York: John Wiley & Sons, 2004.

_____ ."The Cable Capitalist." *Forbes,* October 8, 2001. online.

Raimist, Rachel. Author Interview. November 2005.

Randolph, Asa Philip. "Truth about Lynching" in *Truth about Lynching: Its Causes and Effects.* New York: Cosmo-Advocate, 1917.

Riggs, Karen E. *Mature Audiences: Television in the Lives of Elders.* New Brunswick, NJ: Rutgers University Press, 1998.

Ries, Al and Jack Trout. *Positioning: The Battle for Your Mind.* New York: McGraw-Hill 1986.

Ries, Al and Laura Ries. *The Origin of Brands.* New York: Harper Business, 2004.

Romano, Allison. "A Rival for BET: New TV One Is Targeting African-American Adults." *Broadcasting & Cable* 15 September 2003: 10–12.

Rose, Tricia. "'Fear of a Black Planet:' Rap Music and Black Cultural Politics in the 1990s." In *Gender, Race and Class in Media*, edited by Gail Dines and Jean M. Humez. Thousand Oaks, CA: Sage, 1995: 531–544.

Rosin, Hanna. "White TV Evangelists Courting Blacks," *Chicago Sun-Times* 20 September 1998.

Ross, Michael E. "Black TV Networks Slowly Rising." *MSNBC.com*, February 27, 2003.

Rummel, R.J. *Understanding Conflict and War, Vol. 2: The Conflict Helix*. Beverly Hills, CA: Sage, 1976.

Samuels, Allison. "Boyz in the 'Burbs." *Newsweek*, 31 October 2005: online.

_____. "Minstrels in Baggy Jeans?" *Newsweek*, 5 May 2003: online.

Sandler, Kevin S. "Synergy Nirvana: Brand Equity, Television Animation, and Cartoon Network." In *Prime Time Animation*, edited by Carol A. Stebile and Mark Harrison. London: Routledge, 2003: 89–109.

Scott, Megan. "Hangin' with the Girls." *St. Petersburg Times*, July 3, 2003, online. (4 July 2006).

Segato, Rita Laura. "Two Ethno-Racial Paradigms: Brazil and the U.S." *Série Antropologia*, 233 (1998) Brasília.

Seiter, Ellen. *Television and New Media Audiences*. London: Oxford University Press, 1999.

Selznick, Barbara. "Programming the World: Television Programming in the Global Media Environment." Paper presented at the Console-ing Passions International Conference, Bristol, UK, July 2001.

Shister, Gail. "BET Passes on Televising Coretta Scott King's Funeral." *Philadelphia Inquirer*, 8 February 2006.

Shohat, Ella and Robert Stam. *Unthinking Eurocentrism: Multiculturalism and the Media*. New York: Routledge, 1994.

Shomade, Salmon A. Author Interview. October 2005.

Smikle, Ken. "Johnson Publishing Company: An Empire Built on Valuing Black Consumers." *Chicago Defender*, 9 August 2005.

Smith, Christopher Holmes. "'I Don't Like to Dream about Getting Paid': Representations of Social Mobility and the Emergence of the Hip-Hop Mogul." *Social Text 77* 21.4 (Winter 2003): 69–97.

Smith, Faith. "'You Know You're West Indian if …': Codes of Authenticity in Colin Channer's *Waiting in Vain*." *Small Axe* 5.2 (2001): 41–59.

Smith-Shomade, Beretta E. "Narrowcasting in the New World Information Order: A Space for the Audience?" *Television & New Media* 5.1 (February 2004): 69–81.

_____. *Shaded Lives: African-American Women and Television*. New Brunswick, NJ: Rutgers University Press, 2002.

Sowell, Thomas. *Race and Culture: A World View*. New York: Basic Books, 1994.

Squires, Catherine R. "Black Talk Radio: Defining Community Needs and Identity." *The Harvard International Journal of Press Politics* 5.2 (2000): 73–95.

Stafford, Yvonne. "Learning to Fish: Economic Empowerment and the African-American Community," *New York Amsterdam News*, 16 October 2003, online (16 June 2004).

Steadman, Jana. "African-American Audience," *Nielsen Media Research* (Summer 2005): 1–41.

Stilson, Janet. "Mainstream Dreams: African-Americans Watch More TV Than Most, So Why Are So Few African-American-themed Channels Carried on Cable?" *CableWorld* 5 February 2007.

Stoltenberg, John. "How Men Have (A) Sex." In *Reconstructing Gender: A Multicultural Anthology*, 4th Edition, edited by Estelle Disch. Boston: McGraw-Hill, 2006.

Straubhaar, Joseph. "Choosing National TV: Cultural Capital, Language, and Cultural Proximity in Brazil." *The Impact of International Television: A Paradigm Shift*, edited by Michael G. Elasmar. Mahwah: NJ: Lawrence Erlbaum Associations Publishers, 2003.

Streeter, Thomas. "Blue Skies and Strange Bedfellows: The Discourse of Cable Television." In *The Revolution Wasn't Televised: Sixties Television and Social Conflict*, edited by Lynn Spigel and Michael Curtin. New York: Routledge, 1997: 221–242.

_____"The Cable Fable Revisited: Discourse, Policy, and the Making of Cable Television." *Critical Studies in Mass Communication* (1987): 174–200.

_____*Selling the Air: A Critique of the Policy of Commercial Broadcasting in the United States*. Chicago: University of Chicago Press, 1996.

"Study: Black Wealth Growing But Still a Ways to Go." *USA Today*, 2005.

Sylvie, George. "Technology and African American newspapers: Implications for Survival & Change." In *The Information Society and the Black Community*, edited by John T. Barber and Alice A. Tait. Westport, CT: Greenwood, 2001 :77–93.

Tait, Alice A. and John T. Barber. "Black Entertainment Television: Breaking New Ground and Accepting New Responsibilities?" In *Mediated Messages and African-American Culture*, edited by Venise T. Berry and Carmen L. Manning-Miller. Thousand Oaks, CA: Sage, 1996: 184–197.

Tate, Greg. "Hiphop Turns 30: Whatcha Celebratin' For?" *Village Voice*, 4 January 2005. Online (26 August 2005).

Turbo, Richard. "Metrosexuals: It's a Gay Thing." *medicinenet.com*, July 28, 2003.

Umstead, R. Thomas. "BET Builds Conglomerate Amid Criticism." *Multichannel News*, April 29, 1996, 62.

_____"BET's Founder and CEO, Bob Johnson Leaves Network, Hands Control to Debra Lee." *Multichannel News*, June 2, 2005.

Walker, Juliet E. K., Ed. *Encyclopedia of African American Business History*. Westport, CT: Greenwood Press, 1999.

_____*The History of Black Business in America: Capitalism, Race, Entrepreneurship*. New York: Macmillan Library Reference, 1998.

Wallenstein, Andrew. "BET Putting Original Series on Schedule." *Reuters*, 4 April 2005.

Ward, L. Monique, Edwina Hansbrough, and Eboni Walker. "Contributions of Music Video Exposure to Black Adolescents' Gender and Sexual Schemes." *Journal of Adolescent Research* (March 2005): 143–166.

Washington, Booker Taliaferro. "Atlanta Exposition Speech." 18 September 1895, Library of Congress. <http://memory.loc.gov/ammem/aaohtml/exhibit/aopart6.html> (27 April 2004).

_____*Black-Belt Diamonds: Gems from the Speeches, Addresses, and Talks to Students of Booker T. Washington*, edited by Victoria E. Matthews. New York: Fortune and Scott, 1898.

Watkins, S. Craig. *Hip Hop Matters: Politics, Pop Culture, and Struggle for the Soul of a Movement*. Boston: Beacon Press, 2005.

Waxler, Caroline. "Bob Johnson's Brainchild." *Forbes*, 22 April 1996.

Weems, Robert E. Jr. and Lewis A. Randolph. "The National Response to Richard M. Nixon's Black Capitalism Initiative: The Success of Domestic Détente." *Journal of Black Studies* 32.1 (September 2001): 66–83.

Whitworth-Barner, Ayanna Bobbi. "The BET Super-text: An Analysis of Economics, Imagination and Identity of BET." University of Arizona, 29 April 2004. unpublished master's report.

Wible, Scott. "Media Advocates, Latino Citizens, and Niche Cable: The Limits of 'No Limits TV' 27 March 2003." *Cultural Studies* 18.1 (January 2004): 34–66.

Wieder, Tamara. "Show Her the Monie." *ThePhoenix.com*. www.bostonphoenix.com (4 July 2006).

Wilkerson, Isabel and Cora Daniels, "A Dollar & a Dream," *Essence* December 2005.

Williams, Chancellor. *The Destruction of Black Civilization: Great Issues of a Race from 4500 B.C. to 2000 A.D.* Dubuque, IA: Kendall/Hunt, 1971.

Williams, Rene. "Interview with Dr Bobby Jones." *www.gospelcity.com*, December 24, 2004.

Williams, Saul. "Coded Language" on *Coded Language*, artist DJ Krust, 1999.

Wilson, William Julius. *The Declining Significance of Race: Blacks and Changing American Institutions.* Chicago: University of Chicago Press, 1978.

Woodford, John. "Bill Cosby, Education, and the Lumpenizing of the Contemporary Black World." *The Black Scholar* 34:4 (Winter 2004): online.

Woodson, Carter Godwin. *The Mis-Education of the Negro.* Washington, DC: Associated Publishers, 1933.

X, Malcolm. "Black Revolution." In *I Am Because We Are: Readings in Black Philosophy*, edited by Fred Lee Hord (Mzee Lasana Okpara) and Jonathan Scott Lee. Amherst: University of Massachusetts Press, 1995: 272–273.

Yang, Catherine. "BET, Say Hello to the Competition." *Business Week*, January 15, 2004, online.

Young, Jeffrey R. "Does 'Digital Divide' Rhetoric Do More Harm Than Good?" *Chronicle of Higher Education*, November 9, 2001, online.

Zook, Kristal Brent. "All Hype, No Action." *The Crisis*, March/April 2002, 21–23.

_____ "Don't Bet on BET to Illuminate Anything." *Newsday* 23 December 2002: A26.

Index

A

Action Pay-Per-View, 44
Activism, black audience, 132
Actors, rap and hip hop artists as, 160
Adams, Yolanda, 105
African-American(s), *see also* Black(s)
    audiences, advertiser undervaluing of, 38
    authenticity, 98
    business, magazine featuring, 61
    Christian experiences, 140
    class conundrum, 14
    communities, class divisions in, 12
    cultural gatekeepers, 174
    daily confrontation with racism, 14
    depiction of in online world, 147
    feelings about BET programming, 131
    implementation of capitalism for, 2
    interviews, high-profile, 86
    ministers, 142
    net worth, 139
    pride of, 111
    public rights of, 171
    representations, need to revise, 150
    slave mentality of, 7
    tortured relationship with white
        Americans, 42
    viewing choices of, 121
    wealth credo of, 161
African American Images, 28
African Diaspora, programming celebrating,
    157
After All, 108
Ala carte scenario, 35

Alliance for a Media Literate America
    (AMLA), 156–157
All of Us, 134
American Dilemma, An, 24
American Dream, mythology of, 4
American Federation of Television and
    Radio Artists, 55
American Saver, 138
AMLA, *see* Alliance for a Media Literate
    America
Amos n' Andy, 127
Animation, self-branding by, 100
AOL Black Voices, 60
Apprentice, The, 78
Arabesque Books, 44
Arabesque Films, original, 107
*Archives of Pediatric and Adolescent
    Medicine*, 120
Associated Press, 86
Athletes, connection between entertainers
    and, 70
Atlanta, ranking of home foreclosures in,
    159–160
Atlanta Cotton States' International
    Exposition, 21
Atlantic slave trade, 4
Audience
    complaints, 132
    loyalty, building of, 52
Authenticity
    discourses of, 99
    hallmark of, 86
    seeking, 97, 98
    sincerity and, 99

B

Backyardigans, 155
Bakker, Jim 144
Bamboozled, 9, 127, 150, 165
Bank of America Foundation, 138
Barbershop, 10, 11
Barry, Marion, 123
BE, see Black Enterprise magazine
Beloved community, King's vision of, 133
Bernie Mac Show, The, 156
Best-interest notion, 35
BET (Black Entertainment Television)
    acronym, harsh characterizations for, 151
    air innovative work produced by, 169
    animated character, 96–97, 98
    Black Star Power of, 3
    bleaching of artists on, 49–50
    boycotting of, 130
    branding
        mantra, 69
        strategy, 47
    brand name, 46
    campaign against, 109
    CEO, 96
    charter sponsors, 42
    commercials on, 119, 120
    conundrums facilitated by, 117
    corporate social responsibility, 82
    criticism of, 178
    development, oxymoron of, 16
    employees, 135
    first foray into music videos, 90
    first legitimate competition to, 59–60
    founding of, 32
    goal as brand, 111
    greatest impact of, 148
    image consultant, 47
    It's My Thing logo, 145
    jokes promoted on, 171
    logo, 43
    low-income viewers, 126
    masculinist vision of, 87
    model, 162
    movie, 108
    number of households viewing, 113
    original series on, 79
    overall philosophy of, 169
    pandering of to mainstream
        expectations, 127
    paradox(es), 19, 96, 152, 178
    as parasitic animal system, 56
    pervasive criticism of, 76

pimp metaphor of, 65
problematic business pursuits, 54
profitability of, 43, 114
programming translation, 146
psychic impact of, 118
quantity of female employees, 96
reputation for low wages, 56
rumored illegitimacy, 62
schedule, 76
social welfare drive, 137
Speak Now campaign, 136
strategies of, 177
success factors, 32
as super text, 67
target audience, 120, 121
underpayment by, 85
vocal media critic of, 109
BET Awards program, 92, 93, 113, 116, 168
BET Holdings, 72, 109
BET Inspiration, 141
BET International, 44
BET on Jazz: The Cable Jazz Channel, 44,
    90
BET Movies/Starz3, 44
BET Network
    lessons learned from trajectory of, 171
    sharecropping accusations, 66
BET News, 86
BET Pictures
    films made to date, 108
    successful formula at, 107
BET Sound Stage Restaurant, 44
BET Tonight with Tavis Smiley, 110
Beyoncé, 101
Biblical teaching, distortion of, critics citing,
    141
Billboard, 92
Billion Dollar BET, The, 32
Bi-racialness, 17
Black(s), *see also* African-American(s)
    assimilation into status quo, 73
    Atlantic diaspora, 148
    authenticity, 98
    business(es), 19, *see also* Business, BET
        as defensive enterprises, 20
        development, goals of, 19
        existence of in Colonial America, 20
        growth, Harlem's, 92
        motivation of, 21
        paradoxical, 32
        post-emancipation development of,
        20
        prospects for, 151

shield for, 25
success, primary barrier to, 14
capitalism, rejection of, 8
communities, comedy covering territory
    familiar to, 83
consumer thought process, slavery
    dominating, 122
culture, personification of, 67
economy, BET claim to boost, 133
erotic literature, 138
essentialism, 165, 167
family gatherings, clichéd example of, 92
film narratives, motivation in, 10
identity, development of, 31
inability of mass marketers to
    distinguish, 51
innovation, imitatable, 73
media, agenda for, 153
ownership, myth about significance of,
    23
progress
    commodification of human beings as
        sign of, 70
    key components of, 74
representations, global appeal of, 148
sacred obligation of, 159
self-determination, 28
success, symbol of, 148
tele-visioning
    artists contributing to, 76
    meaning of representation in, 179
wealth, 137
Black Agenda of the Seventies, 153
Black America Saves, 138
Black Bourgeoisie, 50
Black Commentator, The, 175
Black Enterprise magazine (*BE*), 24, 39,
    46, 61
    captain of capitalism, 62
    cover story of, 150
    shifted focus of, 62
    target market, 61
Black Entertainment Television, *see* BET
Black Family Channel, 58
    advertisement, 52, 53
    logo, 59
    target of, 59
Black Mecca, 159
Blackness
    competing deployments of, 47
    contemporary, embodiment of, 67
    conundrum of, 117
    definition of, 167

on demand, 111
escape to, 164
essentialized, 165, 167
selling, 28
on sitcoms, 126
Black Noise, 63
Black Panthers, 6
Black Star Power, 3, 47, 48, 50, 104
Blacks and White TV, 124
Black Wealth Initiative, 138
Black World Today, The, 52
Blowin' Up: Fatty Koo, 79
Blue Sky discourse, cable industry, 32
Bobby Jones Gospel, 75, 79, 80, 81, 134, 140
Boogie Down Productions, 1, 3, 9, 64
Boomerang, 43, 112
Boondocks, 29, 63, 109, 110, 134, 173
Boyz n the Hood, 68
Brand
    BET goal as, 111
    endorsement, 69
    inundation, 166
Branding
    definition of, 45
    mantras, 144
Bring the Noise, 63
Broadcast television station, first black
    owner of, 57
Bro-ing, 69
Brown, Tony, 31
Brown vs. Board of Education, 172
Brown Sugar, 68
Buffet, Warren, 161
Buffy the Vampire Slayer, 83
Bush, George W.
    appearance after Hurricane Katrina, 13,
        14
    broadcast fines signed into law by, 170
Business
    education, poor student access to, 24
    know-how, cultural connection vs., 148
Business, BET, 31–70
    black progress, 69
    black star power, 47–56
    branding blackness, 45–47
    cable business, 32–38
    competition, 56–61
    coverage of BET, 61–62
    resonance of hip hop, 63–69
    Robert L. Johnson and BET, 38–45
Business of America, The, 51
Buy Black, 46

C

Cablecast syndication, 78
Cable industry
    case for governmental deregulation of, 32
    emergence of, 32
Cable networks
    black-themed, 153
    dissimilarity of BET to other, 49
Cable operators, sample letter for, 54
Cable programmers, stance against liquor
        advertising, 55
Cable systems, growth in number of, 36
Cable Television Advertising Bureau, 36, 38
Capital, acquisition of, films revolving
        around, 10
Capital: A Critique of Political Economy, 5
Capitalism
    appending of, 6
    benign, 158
    black, rejection of, 8
    community, 16
    conservatism and, 42
    conundrum of, 1
    demands of, class and, 14
    global, 5
    ideological currency of, 2
    implementation of for African-
        Americans, 2
    intellectual father of, 2
    linkage to other isms, 8
    missionary impulse and, 4
    monopoly, 4
    natural, 3
    organization committed to abolition of,
        11
    perverted meaning of, 9
    post-Civil Rights generation view of, 8–9
    racist nature of, 7
    racist system of, 5
    reason for success of, 158
    as religion, 140
    socialist view of, 158
    underground, 11
    violence of, 6
Capitalism, class, and promise of black
        media, 1–29
    black business, 19–25
    capitalism manifest, 4–12
    promise, 25–29
    wages of class, 12–19
Capitalist

production, 2
    representation, paradoxes in, 92
    state, ideological apparatuses of, 73
Capitalist System, The, 2
Carlyle Group, 161
Carmichael, Stokely, 25, 162
Carsey-Werner, now defunct, 134
Carter, Sherry, 95, 96
*Celebrating Twenty Years: BET Black Star
        Power*, 64
Celebration of Gospel, 168
Center for Digital Democracy, 38
Center for Media Literacy, 156
Chamberlin, Lee, 16
Changing Your World, 141
Chapman, Tracy, 9
Chappelle, Dave, 94, 95
Chappelle Show, 94
Chicago Defender, 26
Chick-Fil-A Bowl, 61
Children's programming, 155
Chitlin Circuit, 84, 107
Choreography, erratic, 92
Christian music videos, 140
Christian Science Monitor, 15
Cinema, transformation offered by, 27
Cita's World, 78, 97, 99
Class, *see also* Capitalism, class, and
                promise of black media
    analysis, development of, 13
    conflict, appearance of in television
            episode, 16
    dilemma, 15
    distinction, contemporary iteration of, 12
    divisions, 12
    me-me, 12
    property ownership and, 13
    significance of, 18
Clockers, 10
CNN, 86, 119
Coded Language, 99
College Hill, 78, 112, 134
Colonialism, new, 144
Colored Museum, 17
Comcast, 59
Comedies, 83, 84, 154
Comic strips, 109
Comic View, 79, 83, 84, 134
Commercialism, cultural purity and, 98
Commercials
    African-Americans in, 119
    risk of facing obsolescence, 61

Commitments, 108
Communalism, 15
Communications
  businesses, 25
  -entertainment industries,
    transformation offered by, 27
  industry, black capitalists attracted to, 25
Communism, 8
Community
  beloved, 133
  capitalism, 16
  events, coverage of, 175
Comparative negligence, 171
Competition, BET's lack of, 56
Concert industry, music videos vs., 129
Consciousness-raising programs, 137
Conservatism, capitalism and, 42
Consumer Federation of America, 138
Consumers, cultural transformation of
    citizens to, 51
Consumption, politics prioritizing, 50
Content diversity, 37
Corporate social responsibility, BET's
    attempt to show, 82
Cosby, Bill, 16
Cosby Show, The, 88
Cousin Jeff Chronicles, The, 79
Cultural capital, imported media as, 145
Cultural expressions, capitalizing on for
    economic reward, 68
Cultural imperialism, media-induced, 144
Cultural integrity, lack of, 146
Cultural Moves, 47
Cultural sampling, 164
Cultural transformations, 163, 165
Cultural validity, 111
Culture
  appreciation vs. appropriation of, 128
  industry, 149
  mythic, music video and, 64
Customer loyalty, 46
Cuts, 134
Cyber-creation, 97

D

*Dancing in the Distraction Factory: Music
    Television and Popular Culture*,
    129
Dancing in September, 150
Das Kapital, 5
Davis, Angela, 6, 162

Dead Presidents, 10
*Declining Significance of Race: Blacks and
    Changing American Institutions,
    The*, 19
Def Comedy Jam, 83, 85
Defensive enterprises, 20
Deregulation, 34
Desegregation, 6
Diary of a Mad Black Woman, 107
Digital television, move from analog to, 170
Dirty south, 101
Discovery Networks, 55
Disney, 88, 109, 155
Docudramas, 112
Dollar, Creflo, 106, 141
Do the Right Thing, 19, 20, 23, 68, 69
Double consciousness, 100
Double parody, 111
Douglass, Frederick, 4–5, 23
DreamWorlds II, 155
Droppin' Science, 63
Du Bois, W.E.B., 6, 21, 149, 157
  black elite of, 23
  double consciousness identified by, 100
  Talented Tenth dubbed by, 22

E

Ebonics, 172
Ebony, 24, 26
Economic Blueprint plan, 27
Economic viability, mistaken assumption
    about, 117
Education, as way out of no way, 14
Education Coalition, The (TEC), 82
8 Mile, 68
Eikerenkoetter, Frederick "Rev. Ike", 144
EMI Group, 66
End of an era, 52
Engels, Friedrich, 13
Entertainers
  connection between athletes and, 70
  consumer bling, 50
Entertainment
  industry, transformation of, 36–37
  news, 86
  web potentialities, 147
Entitlement, language of, 171
Erotics of capitalistic ethos, 138
Escapism, comedy shows offering, 84
ESPN, 55
Essence Magazine, 24, 27

Estate Tax, 139, 161
Ethnic broadcasting, cultural programming
　　in, 146
Ethnicities, fake construction of, 49
Ethnic targeting cues, 120
Eurocentric ideology, 127
Eve, 88, 134
Everybody Hates Chris, 156
Everything But the Burden: What White
　　People Are Taking from Black
　　Culture, 125
Experiencing Music Videos: Aesthetics and
　　Cultural Context, 129

F

Family, communities organized around, 6
Fan letters, 106
Fanon, Frantz, 6
Fantasy creation, music videos and, 89
Fat Albert and the Cosby Kids, 12
FCC, see Federal Communications
　　Commission
Federal Communications Commission
　　(FCC), 33, 143, 153
Female millionaire, first self-made, 21
Film actors, categories of, 108
Fire & Ice, 108
Firsts, as symbols of progress, 38
Focus group, BET assessment by, 108, 115,
　　123
Fourth Atlanta University Conference, 22
Freedman's Savings Bank, 4–5
Freedom's Journal, 26
Fresh Prince of Bel-Air, The, 88
Friends, 85
Future of BET, 149–179
　　cultural transformations, 163–172
　　making money, 157–163
　　media movement, 152–157
　　political activism, 172–176

G

Garvey, Marcus, 6
Gaye, Marvin, 104
Gay and Lesbian Alliance Against
　　Defamation, 134
Generation Next, 176
Generations, 128
Generation X
　　movement, transformation of,
　　172

political goals of, 174
　　reality programs for, 112
Get Ready with T.D. Jakes, 142
Ghetto fabulousness, 100, 101
Ghetto theater, 161
Girlfriends, 17, 18, 88, 134, 156
Glover, Danny, 92
Gordon, Ed, 123
Gordy, Berry, 26
Gospel music, 80
Graham, Billy, 141
Graphic lyrics, 104
Grey's Anatomy, 156
Group economy, need for, 22

H

Half and Half, 88, 134
Harlem civic leaders, 92
HBO (Home Box Office), 33, 58, 83, 108,
　　156
Healthy BET campaign, 136, 137
Heart and Soul, 108
Hey Monie, 169
Hickey, Marilyn, 142
Hidden Blessings, 108
Hinn, Benny, 142
Hip hop
　　black entrepreneurial spirit advocated
　　　by, 18
　　brand endorsement, 69
　　commodification of, 73
　　corporate spreading of, 69
　　culture, BET and, 65
　　early history, 63–64
　　fascination with, 164
　　feminist scholar, 65
　　gangsta films, 10
　　history of on wax, 113
　　hoop dreams, 9
　　industry
　　　BET's partnership with, 62, 63
　　　entrepreneurs of, 68
　　"keepin' it real" bravado, 68
　　moguls, 12, 66, 159
　　narratives, social mobility in, 50
　　web site, 48
Hip Hop America, 63–64
Hip Hop Matters, 64, 66
Home Box Office, see HBO
Homosexuality
　　allusions to, 168
　　society's attitude about, 167

hooks, bell, 6, 12, 28
Hotlanta, 159
House Committee on Energy and
    Commerce, 170
Housing projects, 15
*How Capitalism Underdeveloped Black
    America*, 7, 72–73
Hurricane Katrina, displaced evacuees of,
    13
Hustle and Flow, 68
Hyperreality, 74, 99
Hypocrisy, money–Christianity system and,
    140

I

Iconic brand, BET as, 45
I'm Bout It, 161
Immigrant status, 125
Impact, BET, 115–148
    audiences, 120–126
    black church, 140–143
    black wealth, 137–139
    buffoonery and booty shake, 126–131
    community impact, 133–137
    firing of Tavis Smiley, 132–133
    globalization, 143–148
    influence and, 118
    research, 119
    studies, 118–120
Imported media, 145
Imus, Don, firing of, 175
Incognito, 108
Individualism, 9
Infomercials, 106
Information industry, transformation of,
    36–37
In Living Color, 11, 128
*Inquiry into the Nature and Causes of the
    Wealth of Nations, An*, 2
Insider creation, 113
Internet sites, anonymity of, 167
Intimate Betrayal, 108
In-womb branding, 45
It's Showtime at the Apollo, 83

J

Jakes, T.D., 142
James, Rick, 92, 94
Jay-Z, 103, 116
Jeffersons, The, 128
Jesus, 4, 80

Jet, 24, 26
Jive-talk images, 146
Job loss, panacea for, 160
Johnson, Robert L., 41
    business venture in athletics, 70
    as captain of capitalism, 62
    case for necessity of BET, 22
    championing of Social Security
        privatization, 139
    color blindness by profit potential, 125
    contentious relationship with Tavis
        Smiley, 132
    entrepreneurship of, 28
    firsts of, 38
    focus on building business, 52
    goal of, 178
    named Humanitarian of the Year, 139
    NBA franchise acquisition of, 39
    primary mission of BET, 71
    promotional tape of, 42
    purchase of NBA franchise, 150
    relationship with TCI, 40
    self-serving protest of, 34
Jones, Bobby, 80
Jones, Quincy, 27, 59
Just Think, 156

K

Kaiser Family Foundation, 136
KA'OS Network, 156
Kelley, Robin D.G., 19
King, Coretta Scott, funeral of, 174
King, Martin Luther, Jr., 133
King, Rodney, 174
King of the Hill, 85
Knowledge
    content, entertainment as centerpiece of,
        166
    transfer, 151
Kravitz, Lenny, 103

L

Laissez-faire, contradiction to principles
    of, 4
Latina market, 69
Latinos, Inc., 50
Lawrence, Martin, 85
Lead Story, 79
Lee, Debra, 96, 97, 136, 145
Lee, Spike, 9, 19, 68, 127, 165
Let's Do It Again, 10

Lewis, Amanda, 96
Liberal individualism, 15
Lifetime Television, 55, 88
Lift Every Voice, 80
Lil' Kim: Countdown to Lockdown, 112, 134
Liquor advertisements, 54
Listen Up! Youth Media Network, 157
Literature, erotic, 138
Live in L.A., 79
Long, Eddie, L., 142
Los Angeles Riots/Rebellion, 11
Lowest common denominator selling, 168

M

Made-for-television productions, 107
Mainstream culture, hip hop in, 63
Mainstream media, lack of alternative voices
    in, 117
Major Broadcasting Cable (MBC) Network,
    58
Malcolm X, 8, 122
Male success, women as examples of, 95
Malone, John, 40, 41
Manifest Destiny, mantra of, 4
Marable, Manning, 6, 7, 21, 72–73
Marshall, Thurgood, 162
Martin, Kevin, 34
Marx, Karl, 5, 13
Marxists/Humanists organization, 11
Masquerade, 108
Mass communications, power of, 25
Materialphilia, 138
Material success, literature focusing on,
    138
MBC Network, *see* Major Broadcasting
    Cable Network
Meaning, dissolution of, 74
Media
    black, agenda for, 153
    businesses, indictment of, 157
    commentary, 109
    content, inappropriate, 155
    failure to confront, 175
    moguls, forward thinking of, 27
    non-profit, 150
    organizations, teaching by, 156
    outlet, ethnic control of, 164–165
*Media Diversity: Economics, Ownership,
    and the FCC*, 35
Media Education Foundation, 156
Media Literacy Clearinghouse, 156
Meet the Faith, 81

Mega-church leaders, 12
Me-me class, 12
Michael Jackson clones, 67
Micheaux, Oscar, 27
Microsoft, BET partnership with, 44
Midnight Blue, 108
Mini-documentaries, topics of, 79
Minister(s)
    fan letters to, 106
    spiritual legitimacy of, 142
Ministrywatch.com, 141
Minorities-on-television discussion, 111
Minority
    enterprises, growth in, 27
    euphemism of, 35
Mis-Education of the Negro, The, 23
Mitgo Corporation, 33
Moesha, 110
Money, as motivation in film narratives, 10
MóNique, 92, 101, 102
Monopoly, 57
Monopoly capitalism, 4
Motown, 26
MTV, 78, 91
Muhammad, 4
Muhammad, Elijah, 6, 25, 27
Muhammad Speaks, 28
Multichoice, 147
Murphy, Charlie, 94, 95
Music business, plantation-like structuring
    of, 66
Music distribution, U.S., conglomerates
    controlling, 66
Music video(s), 88
    Christian, 140
    competition among, 91
    culture mythic and, 64
    depravity in, 170
    fantasy creation and, 89
    influences of, 129
    interrogation of, 89
    lyrics and images within, 10
    soft pornography of, 103
    violence in, 89

N

NAACP
    Image Awards, 82
    threatened network boycott, 136
Narrowcasting, 37, 51, 116
National Association of Black Owned
    Broadcasters, 52

National Black MBA Conference, 52
National Black Programming Coalition,
       157
National Cable & Telecommunications
       Association (NCTA), 36, 40
National Editorial Board of the News &
       Letters Committees, 11
National Pan-Hellenic Council, 130
National Urban League, 174
Nation of Islam, 25
Natural capitalism, 3
NCTA, *see* National Cable &
       Telecommunications Association
Negro(es), *see also* African-American(s);
       Black(s)
    as article of commerce, 4
    capitalist employer class, 21
    lumpenproletariat, 21
    pathological situation of, 24
Negro Digest, 26
Network television, cable vs., 33
New Jack City, 10, 68
Newspaper, first black, 26
Newsweek Interactive, 61
New Urban Entertainment (NUE-TV), 59
New York Stock Exchange, 39, 44
New York Undercover, 165
Niagara Movement, 22
Niche programming, 37
Nick Cannon's Wild 'N Out, 164
Nickelodeon, 88, 119, 155, 177
Nielsen Ratings Company, 46, 81, 120
Niggerologist, 100
Nightly News, 96
No Child Left Behind, rational planning,
       160
Noggin, 88
Non-profit media, 150
Non-reformist reform, 7
NUE-TV, *see* New Urban Entertainment

O

Observational cinema, 112
O.C., The, 83
Oddcast, 101
Off-network programs, 128
Oh Drama!, 79
O'Jays, 9
*O.J. Simpson: Beyond the Verdict with Ed
       Gordon*, 123
Once Upon a Time When We Were Colored,
       107

106 & Park, 78, 91, 92
One on One, 134
One Special Moment, 108
Online news services, 62
Online world, depiction of African-
       Americans in, 147
Originality, profit vs., 77
Original programming, benefits of, 76
Our Voices with Bev Smith, 79, 95
Ownership knowledge, lack of, 122
Oxymoronic programming, 81

P

Paid in Full, 10
Parents Resource Council, crackdown on
       television sexuality, 72
Parkers, The, 128
Partners in Crime, 83
Paula White Ministries, 142
PBS, 155
Pimp
    evolution of, 65
    metaphor, 1, 3, 65, 66, 157
Pimptionary/Glossary, 65
Playing with Fire, 108
Poitier, Sidney, 16
Political impotence, 175
Political interviews, high-profile, 123
Political satire, 173
Positioning, 46
Poverty, 9
Premium channels, 58
Presidential Task Force on Communication
       Policy, 35
Print media, mass capitalistic control of, 157
Private Affair, A, 108
Product positioning, 46
Professional lifestyles, magazines
       highlighting, 24
Profit
    potential, color blindness by, 125
    principle of, 55
Programming, 71–114
    African-American feelings about, 131
    blackness on demand, 111–114
    children's, 155
    collectivist function of, 118
    costs, exorbitant, 36
    criticism of, 152
    diverse, 36
    framing of parameters, 72–75
    media commentary of BET, 109–111

metaphor, 92–109
   case study one, 93–101
   case study two, 101–104
   case study three, 105–109
   music videos on BET, 88–92
   original, benefits of, 76
   overview, 75–88
   oxymoronic, 81
   satire of, 110
   skepticism about, 75
Programs, syndicated, 144
Prosperity gospel teachings, 141–142
Protest, power of, 175
Proud Family, The, 88, 109, 110
Psychological border crossings, 125
Public trust, public interest vs., 35

R

Race Rebels: Culture, Politics, and the Black Working Class, 19
Racial sincerity, 99
Racism
   African-Americans' daily confrontation with, 14
   as barrier to black business success, 14
   black success vs., 15
   structural, 9
Racist animosity, 14
Radicalization, collective, 6
Radio, music television and, 129
Radio One, 59
Rap, 61
Rap City, 78
Rap-It-Up campaign, 136
Reactionary nationalism, 158, 159
Reading Rainbow, 155
Reagan, Roland, 42
Reality television
   definition of, 135
   for Generation Xers, 112
   MTV, 91
Real World, The, 78
Record companies, music videos supplied by, 88
Recording industry, black management positions in, 68
Reel Works Teen Filmmaking, 156
Reid, Jacque, 86, 96, 97
Remixed, 134
Rendezvous, 108
Representation(s)

audiences' desire for, 124
   capital progress and, 179
   definition of, 74
   global appeal of, 148
   impact scholarship, 74
   mainstream, paradoxes in, 92
   profit and, 162
   progressive, need to revise, 150
   significance of, 74
Resurrection Boulevard, 160
Rhapsody, 108
Right On magazine, 90
Rip the Runway, 168
Robertson, Pat, 141

S

Sampling, 163–164
Sanford and Son, 128
Satellite technology, expansion of cable capabilities with, 32
Save the Last Dance, 68
Season of the Tiger, 112, 135
Secondary television markets, 77
Second Time Around, 134
Segregation
   product of, 21
   as protective tariff to black-owned businesses, 25
Segregationist Senator, 124
Seinfeld, 85
Self-branding, 100
Self-determination, 28, 48, 158
Self-visioning, 117
Sesame Street, 155
Set It Off, 10
Sex and the City, 16, 17
Sexism, capitalism and, 10
Shaded Lives, 128
Sharecropping accusations, 66
Sherman Anti-Trust Act, violation of, 61
Silence, status and, 176
Simpson, Donnie, 76
Sincerity, authenticity and, 99
Sitcoms
   notion of blackness on, 126
   off-network, 128
Slave(s)
   emancipated, mantra of, 5
   mentality, capitalism and, 7
   trade, commercial imperatives of, 4
Slavery, 70
Smiley, Tavis, 86, 132

Smiley Report, The, 86
Smith, Adam, 2, 5
Smith, Bev, 95
Smith, Will, 116
Snoop Dogg, 103
Social actors, 112
Socialism, capitalist view of, 158
Social Security system, privatization of, 139
Soft pornography, of music videos, 103
SOHH.com, 48
Sony BMG Music Entertainment, 66
Soul Food, 88, 156
Soul Train, 42
Source, The, 88
Southern Word of Faith minister, 106
Spanish language channels, 37
Special interest group, blacks as, 132
Spelman College students, protest by, 130
Spiritual corporation, legality of, 106
Stanley, Charles, 144
Status quo
    black assimilation into, 73
    depressing reminder of, 155
    U.S., 75
Steve Harvey Show, The, 154
Stewart, Martha, 167
Street Level Youth for Media, 156
Subscription channels, 58
Succeeding Against the Odds, 57
Success, hard work accompanying, 176
Sugar Hill, 10
Super freak, Rick James as, 94
Swaggert, Jimmy, 144
Sweet Sweetback's Baadasssss Song, 27
Sylvie, George, 26
Syndicated programs, 144

T

Taft Broadcasting Company, 40
Talented Tenth, 22, 23
Talk show, teen, 81
Tax credit program, abuse of, 33
TCI, *see* Telecommunications Inc
TEC, *see* Education Coalition, The
Teena Marie, 92
Teen Summit, 79, 81, 82, 96, 112, 177
Telecommunications Act (1996), 34
Telecommunications Inc. (TCI), 40, 133
Tele-evangelism, 104, 105
Televangelists
    fiscal malfeasance of, 142
    gospel followed by, 141

Television
    advertising-supported norms, BET
        conforming to, 152
    blacks over-represented on, 72
    digital, 170
    diversity in, 37, 154
    evangelism, growth of, 140
    markets, secondary, 77
    networks, diversity of, 37–38
    programming
        regulation, 170
        social class entrenched in, 17
    sexuality on, 72, 96
    shows, classic, 128
    stations, minority ownership of, 33
    use of foul language on, 170
That's So Raven, 88, 155
Thea, 128
Theme network, 37
Thurmond, Strom, 124
Tired ol' reruns, 128
TNT, 88
Today with Marilyn Hickey, 142
Toil and save mantra, 5
Token gesture, 34
Tom Joyner Morning Show, The, 86, 132, 154
Tony Brown's Journal, 42
Topics Education, 136
Transformation, black college radical to
        corporate suit, 23
TRL-Total Request Live, 78
Tupac, 116
Turner, Tina, 9
TV One, 59, 60, 154, 175

U

UA-Columbia Cablevision satellite, 40
Ultimate Hustler, 78, 112
Uncut, 101, 102, 103, 131, 147, 175
Underclass identity, 19
Underground capitalism, 11
United States
    black imagery, leading provider of, 28
    mandate of overt racism, 84
    music distribution, conglomerates
        controlling, 66
    propaganda, 176
Unity Broadcasting Network, 57
Universal Music Group, 66
Univision (UVN), 60
UPN, 88, 110, 134, 154
Uptown Saturday Night, 16

Urban League, 46
Urban life, narratives centering difficulties of, 161
Urbanworld Film Festival, 56
UVN, *see* Univision

V

Vast Wasteland speech, FCC, 143
V-chip, 155
Viacom, 33–34, 38, 78, 134
    press statements, 45
    sale of BET to, 44, 51
Vibe, 24, 27
Vibe History of Hip Hop, 64
Video Gospel, 78, 80
Video Soul, 76, 78, 86, 90
Video Soul Gold, 90
Viewers Like You?, 35
Violence, in music videos, 89
Virtual America, 9
Visual lack factor, 46
Vote or Die campaign, 172

W

Walker, Juliet E.K., 4, 13, 20, 68
Walker, Madam C.J., 21
Wall Street, psychology of, 23
Wall Street Journal, 62
WAN, *see* World African Network
Warner Music Group, 66
Wash, The, 161
Washington, Booker T., 21, 23
    admonition of, 22
    economic plan of, 21
    philosophy of, 40
Washington, Denzel, 64–65
Watching Race, 47
Wayans, Damon, 9
Way out of no way, education as, 14
Wealth credo, African-American, 161
Web, entertainment potentialities of, 147
West, Kanye, 105
White(s)
    insertion, iteration of, 73
    institutionalized actions of, 14
    philanthropists, capitalism and, 5
Whiteness, pervasive rhetoric of, 77
Whoopi Goldberg Show, The, 154
Winner Takes All, 161
Women
    BET programming by, 95
    black, value of bigger-bodied, 102
    devaluation of on cable, 94
Woodson, Carter G., 23
Word-of-Faith supporters, 141
World African Network (WAN), 58
World Bank, 5, 7

Y

"You can do anything" propaganda, 176
Youth social concerns, programming addressing, 83

Z

Zoom, 155